ISBN 0-8373-3228-1

C-3228   CAREER EXAMINATION SERIES

This is your
PASSBOOK® for...

Transit Management Analyst Trainee

Test Preparation Study Guide

Questions & Answers

NATIONAL LEARNING CORPORATION®

Copyright © 2017 by

National Learning Corporation

212 Michael Drive, Syosset, New York 11791

(516) 921-8888
(800) 632-8888
(800) 645-6337
FAX: (516) 921-8743
www.passbooks.com
info @ passbooks.com

PRINTED IN THE UNITED STATES OF AMERICA

PASSBOOK®

NOTICE

This book is SOLELY intended for, is sold ONLY to, and its use is RESTRICTED to *individual*, bona fide applicants or candidates who qualify by virtue of having seriously filed applications for appropriate license, certificate, professional and/or promotional advancement, higher school matriculation, scholarship, or other legitimate requirements of educational and/or governmental authorities.

This book is NOT intended for use, class instruction, tutoring, training, duplication, copying, reprinting, excerption, or adaptation, etc., by:

(1) Other publishers

(2) Proprietors and/or Instructors of "Coaching" and/or Preparatory Courses

(3) Personnel and/or Training Divisions of commercial, industrial, and governmental organizations

(4) Schools, colleges, or universities and/or their departments and staffs, including teachers and other personnel

(5) Testing Agencies or Bureaus

(6) Study groups which seek by the purchase of a single volume to copy and/or duplicate and/or adapt this material for use by the group as a whole without having purchased individual volumes for each of the members of the group

(7) Et al.

Such persons would be in violation of appropriate Federal and State statutes.

PROVISION OF LICENSING AGREEMENTS. — Recognized educational commercial, industrial, and governmental institutions and organizations, and others legitimately engaged in educational pursuits, including training, testing, and measurement activities, may address a request for a licensing agreement to the copyright owners, who will determine whether, and under what conditions, including fees and charges, the materials in this book may be used by them. In other words, a licensing facility exists for the legitimate use of the material in this book on other than an individual basis. However, it is asseverated and affirmed here that the material in this book *CANNOT* be used without the receipt of the express permission of such a licensing agreement from the Publishers.

NATIONAL LEARNING CORPORATION
212 Michael Drive
Syosset, New York 11791

Inquiries re licensing agreements should be addressed to:
The President
National Learning Corporation
212 Michael Drive
Syosset, New York 11791

PASSBOOK® SERIES

THE *PASSBOOK® SERIES* has been created to prepare applicants and candidates for the ultimate academic battlefield – the examination room.

At some time in our lives, each and every one of us may be required to take an examination – for validation, matriculation, admission, qualification, registration, certification, or licensure.

Based on the assumption that every applicant or candidate has met the basic formal educational standards, has taken the required number of courses, and read the necessary texts, the *PASSBOOK® SERIES* furnishes the one special preparation which may assure passing with confidence, instead of failing with insecurity. Examination questions – together with answers – are furnished as the basic vehicle for study so that the mysteries of the examination and its compounding difficulties may be eliminated or diminished by a sure method.

This book is meant to help you pass your examination provided that you qualify and are serious in your objective.

The entire field is reviewed through the huge store of content information which is succinctly presented through a provocative and challenging approach – the question-and-answer method.

A climate of success is established by furnishing the correct answers at the end of each test.

You soon learn to recognize types of questions, forms of questions, and patterns of questioning. You may even begin to anticipate expected outcomes.

You perceive that many questions are repeated or adapted so that you can gain acute insights, which may enable you to score many sure points.

You learn how to confront new questions, or types of questions, and to attack them confidently and work out the correct answers.

You note objectives and emphases, and recognize pitfalls and dangers, so that you may make positive educational adjustments.

Moreover, you are kept fully informed in relation to new concepts, methods, practices, and directions in the field.

You discover that you are actually taking the examination all the time: you are preparing for the examination by "taking" an examination, not by reading extraneous and/or supererogatory textbooks.

In short, this PASSBOOK®, used directedly, should be an important factor in helping you to pass your test.

TRANSIT MANAGEMENT ANALYST TRAINEE

DUTIES

Under close supervision, is trained in and performs beginning-level work for the purpose of acquiring knowledge, skill and competence in the application of industrial and/or management engineering, and cost analysis techniques to studies and analyses of departmental operations and administrative procedures; performs related work.

EXAMPLES OF TYPICAL TASKS

Is trained in and assists in the collection of data concerning operating department procedures, administrative systems, machine and equipment utilization, manpower requirements, and space layouts; is trained in and assists in the analyses of data for the preparation of reports of findings; is trained in and assists in the preparation of charts, graphs, drawings and other related material.

TESTS

The written test will be designed to evaluate candidate's ability to solve management problems in a mass transit setting. It will be of the multiple-choice type and may include questions on: collecting, interpreting and analyzing data; computer data storage and retrieval capabilities; administrative and operating systems and procedures; machine, equipment and space utilization; personnel requirements and utilization; management principles and techniques; management analysis, cost accounting and budget techniques; preparing and interpreting charts, graphs and drawings; and other related areas including: written comprehension, written expression, number facility, mathematical reasoning, deductive reasoning, information ordering, problem solving, customer service, and clerical ability.

PROMOTION OPPORTUNITIES

At the end of one year of satisfactory training and service, employees in this class of positions will receive appointment in the title of Assistant Transit Management Analyst. Employees in the title of Assistant Transit Management Analyst are accorded promotion opportunities, when eligible, to the title of Transit Management Analyst.

HOW TO TAKE A TEST

I. YOU MUST PASS AN EXAMINATION

A. WHAT EVERY CANDIDATE SHOULD KNOW

Examination applicants often ask us for help in preparing for the written test. What can I study in advance? What kinds of questions will be asked? How will the test be given? How will the papers be graded?

As an applicant for a civil service examination, you may be wondering about some of these things. Our purpose here is to suggest effective methods of advance study and to describe civil service examinations.

Your chances for success on this examination can be increased if you know how to prepare. Those "pre-examination jitters" can be reduced if you know what to expect. You can even experience an adventure in good citizenship if you know why civil service exams are given.

B. WHY ARE CIVIL SERVICE EXAMINATIONS GIVEN?

Civil service examinations are important to you in two ways. As a citizen, you want public jobs filled by employees who know how to do their work. As a job seeker, you want a fair chance to compete for that job on an equal footing with other candidates. The best-known means of accomplishing this two-fold goal is the competitive examination.

Exams are widely publicized throughout the nation. They may be administered for jobs in federal, state, city, municipal, town or village governments or agencies.

Any citizen may apply, with some limitations, such as the age or residence of applicants. Your experience and education may be reviewed to see whether you meet the requirements for the particular examination. When these requirements exist, they are reasonable and applied consistently to all applicants. Thus, a competitive examination may cause you some uneasiness now, but it is your privilege and safeguard.

C. HOW ARE CIVIL SERVICE EXAMS DEVELOPED?

Examinations are carefully written by trained technicians who are specialists in the field known as "psychological measurement," in consultation with recognized authorities in the field of work that the test will cover. These experts recommend the subject matter areas or skills to be tested; only those knowledges or skills important to your success on the job are included. The most reliable books and source materials available are used as references. Together, the experts and technicians judge the difficulty level of the questions.

Test technicians know how to phrase questions so that the problem is clearly stated. Their ethics do not permit "trick" or "catch" questions. Questions may have been tried out on sample groups, or subjected to statistical analysis, to determine their usefulness.

Written tests are often used in combination with performance tests, ratings of training and experience, and oral interviews. All of these measures combine to form the best-known means of finding the right person for the right job.

II. HOW TO PASS THE WRITTEN TEST

A. *NATURE OF THE EXAMINATION*

To prepare intelligently for civil service examinations, you should know how they differ from school examinations you have taken. In school you were assigned certain definite pages to read or subjects to cover. The examination questions were quite detailed and usually emphasized memory. Civil service exams, on the other hand, try to discover your present ability to perform the duties of a position, plus your potentiality to learn these duties. In other words, a civil service exam attempts to predict how successful you will be. Questions cover such a broad area that they cannot be as minute and detailed as school exam questions.

In the public service similar kinds of work, or positions, are grouped together in one "class." This process is known as *position-classification*. All the positions in a class are paid according to the salary range for that class. One class title covers all of these positions, and they are all tested by the same examination.

B. *FOUR BASIC STEPS*

1) Study the announcement

How, then, can you know what subjects to study? Our best answer is: "Learn as much as possible about the class of positions for which you've applied." The exam will test the knowledge, skills and abilities needed to do the work.

Your most valuable source of information about the position you want is the official exam announcement. This announcement lists the training and experience qualifications. Check these standards and apply only if you come reasonably close to meeting them.

The brief description of the position in the examination announcement offers some clues to the subjects which will be tested. Think about the job itself. Review the duties in your mind. Can you perform them, or are there some in which you are rusty? Fill in the blank spots in your preparation.

Many jurisdictions preview the written test in the exam announcement by including a section called "Knowledge and Abilities Required," "Scope of the Examination," or some similar heading. Here you will find out specifically what fields will be tested.

2) Review your own background

Once you learn in general what the position is all about, and what you need to know to do the work, ask yourself which subjects you already know fairly well and which need improvement. You may wonder whether to concentrate on improving your strong areas or on building some background in your fields of weakness. When the announcement has specified "some knowledge" or "considerable knowledge," or has used adjectives like "beginning principles of…" or "advanced … methods," you can get a clue as to the number and difficulty of questions to be asked in any given field. More questions, and hence broader coverage, would be included for those subjects which are more important in the work. Now weigh your strengths and weaknesses against the job requirements and prepare accordingly.

3) Determine the level of the position

Another way to tell how intensively you should prepare is to understand the level of the job for which you are applying. Is it the entering level? In other words, is this the position in which beginners in a field of work are hired? Or is it an intermediate or advanced level? Sometimes this is indicated by such words as "Junior" or "Senior" in the class title. Other jurisdictions use Roman numerals to designate the level – Clerk I, Clerk II, for example. The word "Supervisor" sometimes appears in the title. If the level is not indicated by the title, check the description of duties. Will you be working under very close supervision, or will you have responsibility for independent decisions in this work?

4) Choose appropriate study materials

Now that you know the subjects to be examined and the relative amount of each subject to be covered, you can choose suitable study materials. For beginning level jobs, or even advanced ones, if you have a pronounced weakness in some aspect of your training, read a modern, standard textbook in that field. Be sure it is up to date and has general coverage. Such books are normally available at your library, and the librarian will be glad to help you locate one. For entry-level positions, questions of appropriate difficulty are chosen – neither highly advanced questions, nor those too simple. Such questions require careful thought but not advanced training.

If the position for which you are applying is technical or advanced, you will read more advanced, specialized material. If you are already familiar with the basic principles of your field, elementary textbooks would waste your time. Concentrate on advanced textbooks and technical periodicals. Think through the concepts and review difficult problems in your field.

These are all general sources. You can get more ideas on your own initiative, following these leads. For example, training manuals and publications of the government agency which employs workers in your field can be useful, particularly for technical and professional positions. A letter or visit to the government department involved may result in more specific study suggestions, and certainly will provide you with a more definite idea of the exact nature of the position you are seeking.

III. KINDS OF TESTS

Tests are used for purposes other than measuring knowledge and ability to perform specified duties. For some positions, it is equally important to test ability to make adjustments to new situations or to profit from training. In others, basic mental abilities not dependent on information are essential. Questions which test these things may not appear as pertinent to the duties of the position as those which test for knowledge and information. Yet they are often highly important parts of a fair examination. For very general questions, it is almost impossible to help you direct your study efforts. What we can do is to point out some of the more common of these general abilities needed in public service positions and describe some typical questions.

1) General information

Broad, general information has been found useful for predicting job success in some kinds of work. This is tested in a variety of ways, from vocabulary lists to questions about current events. Basic background in some field of work, such as sociology or economics, may be sampled in a group of questions. Often these are principles which have become familiar to most persons through exposure rather than through formal training. It is difficult to advise you how to study for these questions; being alert to the world around you is our best suggestion.

2) Verbal ability

An example of an ability needed in many positions is verbal or language ability. Verbal ability is, in brief, the ability to use and understand words. Vocabulary and grammar tests are typical measures of this ability. Reading comprehension or paragraph interpretation questions are common in many kinds of civil service tests. You are given a paragraph of written material and asked to find its central meaning.

3) Numerical ability

Number skills can be tested by the familiar arithmetic problem, by checking paired lists of numbers to see which are alike and which are different, or by interpreting charts and graphs. In the latter test, a graph may be printed in the test booklet which you are asked to use as the basis for answering questions.

4) Observation

A popular test for law-enforcement positions is the observation test. A picture is shown to you for several minutes, then taken away. Questions about the picture test your ability to observe both details and larger elements.

5) Following directions

In many positions in the public service, the employee must be able to carry out written instructions dependably and accurately. You may be given a chart with several columns, each column listing a variety of information. The questions require you to carry out directions involving the information given in the chart.

6) Skills and aptitudes

Performance tests effectively measure some manual skills and aptitudes. When the skill is one in which you are trained, such as typing or shorthand, you can practice. These tests are often very much like those given in business school or high school courses. For many of the other skills and aptitudes, however, no short-time preparation can be made. Skills and abilities natural to you or that you have developed throughout your lifetime are being tested.

Many of the general questions just described provide all the data needed to answer the questions and ask you to use your reasoning ability to find the answers. Your best preparation for these tests, as well as for tests of facts and ideas, is to be at your physical and mental best. You, no doubt, have your own methods of getting into an exam-taking mood and keeping "in shape." The next section lists some ideas on this subject.

IV. KINDS OF QUESTIONS

Only rarely is the "essay" question, which you answer in narrative form, used in civil service tests. Civil service tests are usually of the short-answer type. Full instructions for answering these questions will be given to you at the examination. But in case this is your first experience with short-answer questions and separate answer sheets, here is what you need to know:

1) Multiple-choice Questions

Most popular of the short-answer questions is the "multiple choice" or "best answer" question. It can be used, for example, to test for factual knowledge, ability to solve problems or judgment in meeting situations found at work.

A multiple-choice question is normally one of three types—
- It can begin with an incomplete statement followed by several possible endings. You are to find the one ending which *best* completes the statement, although some of the others may not be entirely wrong.
- It can also be a complete statement in the form of a question which is answered by choosing one of the statements listed.

- It can be in the form of a problem – again you select the best answer.

Here is an example of a multiple-choice question with a discussion which should give you some clues as to the method for choosing the right answer:

When an employee has a complaint about his assignment, the action which will *best* help him overcome his difficulty is to
- A. discuss his difficulty with his coworkers
- B. take the problem to the head of the organization
- C. take the problem to the person who gave him the assignment
- D. say nothing to anyone about his complaint

In answering this question, you should study each of the choices to find which is best. Consider choice "A" – Certainly an employee may discuss his complaint with fellow employees, but no change or improvement can result, and the complaint remains unresolved. Choice "B" is a poor choice since the head of the organization probably does not know what assignment you have been given, and taking your problem to him is known as "going over the head" of the supervisor. The supervisor, or person who made the assignment, is the person who can clarify it or correct any injustice. Choice "C" is, therefore, correct. To say nothing, as in choice "D," is unwise. Supervisors have and interest in knowing the problems employees are facing, and the employee is seeking a solution to his problem.

2) True/False Questions

The "true/false" or "right/wrong" form of question is sometimes used. Here a complete statement is given. Your job is to decide whether the statement is right or wrong.

SAMPLE: A roaming cell-phone call to a nearby city costs less than a non-roaming call to a distant city.

This statement is wrong, or false, since roaming calls are more expensive.

This is not a complete list of all possible question forms, although most of the others are variations of these common types. You will always get complete directions for answering questions. Be sure you understand *how* to mark your answers – ask questions until you do.

V. RECORDING YOUR ANSWERS

Computer terminals are used more and more today for many different kinds of exams.

For an examination with very few applicants, you may be told to record your answers in the test booklet itself. Separate answer sheets are much more common. If this separate answer sheet is to be scored by machine – and this is often the case – it is highly important that you mark your answers correctly in order to get credit.

An electronic scoring machine is often used in civil service offices because of the speed with which papers can be scored. Machine-scored answer sheets must be marked with a pencil, which will be given to you. This pencil has a high graphite content which responds to the electronic scoring machine. As a matter of fact, stray dots may register as answers, so do not let your pencil rest on the answer sheet while you are pondering the correct answer. Also, if your pencil lead breaks or is otherwise defective, ask for another.

Since the answer sheet will be dropped in a slot in the scoring machine, be careful not to bend the corners or get the paper crumpled.

The answer sheet normally has five vertical columns of numbers, with 30 numbers to a column. These numbers correspond to the question numbers in your test booklet. After each number, going across the page are four or five pairs of dotted lines. These short dotted lines have small letters or numbers above them. The first two pairs may also have a "T" or "F" above the letters. This indicates that the first two pairs only are to be used if the questions are of the true-false type. If the questions are multiple choice, disregard the "T" and "F" and pay attention only to the small letters or numbers.

Answer your questions in the manner of the sample that follows:

32. The largest city in the United States is
   A. Washington, D.C.
   B. New York City
   C. Chicago
   D. Detroit
   E. San Francisco

1) Choose the answer you think is best. (New York City is the largest, so "B" is correct.)
2) Find the row of dotted lines numbered the same as the question you are answering. (Find row number 32)
3) Find the pair of dotted lines corresponding to the answer. (Find the pair of lines under the mark "B.")
4) Make a solid black mark between the dotted lines.

VI. BEFORE THE TEST

Common sense will help you find procedures to follow to get ready for an examination. Too many of us, however, overlook these sensible measures. Indeed, nervousness and fatigue have been found to be the most serious reasons why applicants fail to do their best on civil service tests. Here is a list of reminders:

- Begin your preparation early – Don't wait until the last minute to go scurrying around for books and materials or to find out what the position is all about.
- Prepare continuously – An hour a night for a week is better than an all-night cram session. This has been definitely established. What is more, a night a week for a month will return better dividends than crowding your study into a shorter period of time.
- Locate the place of the exam – You have been sent a notice telling you when and where to report for the examination. If the location is in a different town or otherwise unfamiliar to you, it would be well to inquire the best route and learn something about the building.
- Relax the night before the test – Allow your mind to rest. Do not study at all that night. Plan some mild recreation or diversion; then go to bed early and get a good night's sleep.
- Get up early enough to make a leisurely trip to the place for the test – This way unforeseen events, traffic snarls, unfamiliar buildings, etc. will not upset you.
- Dress comfortably – A written test is not a fashion show. You will be known by number and not by name, so wear something comfortable.

- Leave excess paraphernalia at home – Shopping bags and odd bundles will get in your way. You need bring only the items mentioned in the official notice you received; usually everything you need is provided. Do not bring reference books to the exam. They will only confuse those last minutes and be taken away from you when in the test room.
- Arrive somewhat ahead of time – If because of transportation schedules you must get there very early, bring a newspaper or magazine to take your mind off yourself while waiting.
- Locate the examination room – When you have found the proper room, you will be directed to the seat or part of the room where you will sit. Sometimes you are given a sheet of instructions to read while you are waiting. Do not fill out any forms until you are told to do so; just read them and be prepared.
- Relax and prepare to listen to the instructions
- If you have any physical problem that may keep you from doing your best, be sure to tell the test administrator. If you are sick or in poor health, you really cannot do your best on the exam. You can come back and take the test some other time.

VII. AT THE TEST

The day of the test is here and you have the test booklet in your hand. The temptation to get going is very strong. Caution! There is more to success than knowing the right answers. You must know how to identify your papers and understand variations in the type of short-answer question used in this particular examination. Follow these suggestions for maximum results from your efforts:

1) Cooperate with the monitor
The test administrator has a duty to create a situation in which you can be as much at ease as possible. He will give instructions, tell you when to begin, check to see that you are marking your answer sheet correctly, and so on. He is not there to guard you, although he will see that your competitors do not take unfair advantage. He wants to help you do your best.

2) Listen to all instructions
Don't jump the gun! Wait until you understand all directions. In most civil service tests you get more time than you need to answer the questions. So don't be in a hurry. Read each word of instructions until you clearly understand the meaning. Study the examples, listen to all announcements and follow directions. Ask questions if you do not understand what to do.

3) Identify your papers
Civil service exams are usually identified by number only. You will be assigned a number; you must not put your name on your test papers. Be sure to copy your number correctly. Since more than one exam may be given, copy your exact examination title.

4) Plan your time
Unless you are told that a test is a "speed" or "rate of work" test, speed itself is usually not important. Time enough to answer all the questions will be provided, but this does not mean that you have all day. An overall time limit has been set. Divide the total time (in minutes) by the number of questions to determine the approximate time you have for each question.

5) Do not linger over difficult questions

If you come across a difficult question, mark it with a paper clip (useful to have along) and come back to it when you have been through the booklet. One caution if you do this – be sure to skip a number on your answer sheet as well. Check often to be sure that you have not lost your place and that you are marking in the row numbered the same as the question you are answering.

6) Read the questions

Be sure you know what the question asks! Many capable people are unsuccessful because they failed to *read* the questions correctly.

7) Answer all questions

Unless you have been instructed that a penalty will be deducted for incorrect answers, it is better to guess than to omit a question.

8) Speed tests

It is often better NOT to guess on speed tests. It has been found that on timed tests people are tempted to spend the last few seconds before time is called in marking answers at random – without even reading them – in the hope of picking up a few extra points. To discourage this practice, the instructions may warn you that your score will be "corrected" for guessing. That is, a penalty will be applied. The incorrect answers will be deducted from the correct ones, or some other penalty formula will be used.

9) Review your answers

If you finish before time is called, go back to the questions you guessed or omitted to give them further thought. Review other answers if you have time.

10) Return your test materials

If you are ready to leave before others have finished or time is called, take ALL your materials to the monitor and leave quietly. Never take any test material with you. The monitor can discover whose papers are not complete, and taking a test booklet may be grounds for disqualification.

VIII. EXAMINATION TECHNIQUES

1) Read the general instructions carefully. These are usually printed on the first page of the exam booklet. As a rule, these instructions refer to the timing of the examination; the fact that you should not start work until the signal and must stop work at a signal, etc. If there are any *special* instructions, such as a choice of questions to be answered, make sure that you note this instruction carefully.

2) When you are ready to start work on the examination, that is as soon as the signal has been given, read the instructions to each question booklet, underline any key words or phrases, such as *least, best, outline, describe* and the like. In this way you will tend to answer as requested rather than discover on reviewing your paper that you *listed without describing*, that you selected the *worst* choice rather than the *best* choice, etc.

8

3) If the examination is of the objective or multiple-choice type – that is, each question will also give a series of possible answers: A, B, C or D, and you are called upon to select the best answer and write the letter next to that answer on your answer paper – it is advisable to start answering each question in turn. There may be anywhere from 50 to 100 such questions in the three or four hours allotted and you can see how much time would be taken if you read through all the questions before beginning to answer any. Furthermore, if you come across a question or group of questions which you know would be difficult to answer, it would undoubtedly affect your handling of all the other questions.

4) If the examination is of the essay type and contains but a few questions, it is a moot point as to whether you should read all the questions before starting to answer any one. Of course, if you are given a choice – say five out of seven and the like – then it is essential to read all the questions so you can eliminate the two that are most difficult. If, however, you are asked to answer all the questions, there may be danger in trying to answer the easiest one first because you may find that you will spend too much time on it. The best technique is to answer the first question, then proceed to the second, etc.

5) Time your answers. Before the exam begins, write down the time it started, then add the time allowed for the examination and write down the time it must be completed, then divide the time available somewhat as follows:
   - If 3-1/2 hours are allowed, that would be 210 minutes. If you have 80 objective-type questions, that would be an average of 2-1/2 minutes per question. Allow yourself no more than 2 minutes per question, or a total of 160 minutes, which will permit about 50 minutes to review.
   - If for the time allotment of 210 minutes there are 7 essay questions to answer, that would average about 30 minutes a question. Give yourself only 25 minutes per question so that you have about 35 minutes to review.

6) The most important instruction is to *read each question* and make sure you know what is wanted. The second most important instruction is to *time yourself properly* so that you answer every question. The third most important instruction is to *answer every question.* Guess if you have to but include something for each question. Remember that you will receive no credit for a blank and will probably receive some credit if you write something in answer to an essay question. If you guess a letter – say "B" for a multiple-choice question – you may have guessed right. If you leave a blank as an answer to a multiple-choice question, the examiners may respect your feelings but it will not add a point to your score. Some exams may penalize you for wrong answers, so in such cases *only,* you may not want to guess unless you have some basis for your answer.

7) Suggestions
   a. Objective-type questions
      1. Examine the question booklet for proper sequence of pages and questions
      2. Read all instructions carefully
      3. Skip any question which seems too difficult; return to it after all other questions have been answered
      4. Apportion your time properly; do not spend too much time on any single question or group of questions

5. Note and underline key words – *all, most, fewest, least, best, worst, same, opposite,* etc.
6. Pay particular attention to negatives
7. Note unusual option, e.g., unduly long, short, complex, different or similar in content to the body of the question
8. Observe the use of "hedging" words – *probably, may, most likely,* etc.
9. Make sure that your answer is put next to the same number as the question
10. Do not second-guess unless you have good reason to believe the second answer is definitely more correct
11. Cross out original answer if you decide another answer is more accurate; do not erase until you are ready to hand your paper in
12. Answer all questions; guess unless instructed otherwise
13. Leave time for review

b. Essay questions
1. Read each question carefully
2. Determine exactly what is wanted. Underline key words or phrases.
3. Decide on outline or paragraph answer
4. Include many different points and elements unless asked to develop any one or two points or elements
5. Show impartiality by giving pros and cons unless directed to select one side only
6. Make and write down any assumptions you find necessary to answer the questions
7. Watch your English, grammar, punctuation and choice of words
8. Time your answers; don't crowd material

8) Answering the essay question

Most essay questions can be answered by framing the specific response around several key words or ideas. Here are a few such key words or ideas:

M's: manpower, materials, methods, money, management
P's: purpose, program, policy, plan, procedure, practice, problems, pitfalls, personnel, public relations

a. Six basic steps in handling problems:
1. Preliminary plan and background development
2. Collect information, data and facts
3. Analyze and interpret information, data and facts
4. Analyze and develop solutions as well as make recommendations
5. Prepare report and sell recommendations
6. Install recommendations and follow up effectiveness

b. Pitfalls to avoid
1. *Taking things for granted* – A statement of the situation does not necessarily imply that each of the elements is necessarily true; for example, a complaint may be invalid and biased so that all that can be taken for granted is that a complaint has been registered

2. *Considering only one side of a situation* – Wherever possible, indicate several alternatives and then point out the reasons you selected the best one
3. *Failing to indicate follow up* – Whenever your answer indicates action on your part, make certain that you will take proper follow-up action to see how successful your recommendations, procedures or actions turn out to be
4. *Taking too long in answering any single question* – Remember to time your answers properly

IX. AFTER THE TEST

Scoring procedures differ in detail among civil service jurisdictions although the general principles are the same. Whether the papers are hand-scored or graded by machine we have described, they are nearly always graded by number. That is, the person who marks the paper knows only the number – never the name – of the applicant. Not until all the papers have been graded will they be matched with names. If other tests, such as training and experience or oral interview ratings have been given, scores will be combined. Different parts of the examination usually have different weights. For example, the written test might count 60 percent of the final grade, and a rating of training and experience 40 percent. In many jurisdictions, veterans will have a certain number of points added to their grades.

After the final grade has been determined, the names are placed in grade order and an eligible list is established. There are various methods for resolving ties between those who get the same final grade – probably the most common is to place first the name of the person whose application was received first. Job offers are made from the eligible list in the order the names appear on it. You will be notified of your grade and your rank as soon as all these computations have been made. This will be done as rapidly as possible.

People who are found to meet the requirements in the announcement are called "eligibles." Their names are put on a list of eligible candidates. An eligible's chances of getting a job depend on how high he stands on this list and how fast agencies are filling jobs from the list.

When a job is to be filled from a list of eligibles, the agency asks for the names of people on the list of eligibles for that job. When the civil service commission receives this request, it sends to the agency the names of the three people highest on this list. Or, if the job to be filled has specialized requirements, the office sends the agency the names of the top three persons who meet these requirements from the general list.

The appointing officer makes a choice from among the three people whose names were sent to him. If the selected person accepts the appointment, the names of the others are put back on the list to be considered for future openings.

That is the rule in hiring from all kinds of eligible lists, whether they are for typist, carpenter, chemist, or something else. For every vacancy, the appointing officer has his choice of any one of the top three eligibles on the list. This explains why the person whose name is on top of the list sometimes does not get an appointment when some of the persons lower on the list do. If the appointing officer chooses the second or third eligible, the No. 1 eligible does not get a job at once, but stays on the list until he is appointed or the list is terminated.

X. HOW TO PASS THE INTERVIEW TEST

The examination for which you applied requires an oral interview test. You have already taken the written test and you are now being called for the interview test – the final part of the formal examination.

You may think that it is not possible to prepare for an interview test and that there are no procedures to follow during an interview. Our purpose is to point out some things you can do in advance that will help you and some good rules to follow and pitfalls to avoid while you are being interviewed.

What is an interview supposed to test?

The written examination is designed to test the technical knowledge and competence of the candidate; the oral is designed to evaluate intangible qualities, not readily measured otherwise, and to establish a list showing the relative fitness of each candidate – as measured against his competitors – for the position sought. Scoring is not on the basis of "right" and "wrong," but on a sliding scale of values ranging from "not passable" to "outstanding." As a matter of fact, it is possible to achieve a relatively low score without a single "incorrect" answer because of evident weakness in the qualities being measured.

Occasionally, an examination may consist entirely of an oral test – either an individual or a group oral. In such cases, information is sought concerning the technical knowledges and abilities of the candidate, since there has been no written examination for this purpose. More commonly, however, an oral test is used to supplement a written examination.

Who conducts interviews?

The composition of oral boards varies among different jurisdictions. In nearly all, a representative of the personnel department serves as chairman. One of the members of the board may be a representative of the department in which the candidate would work. In some cases, "outside experts" are used, and, frequently, a businessman or some other representative of the general public is asked to serve. Labor and management or other special groups may be represented. The aim is to secure the services of experts in the appropriate field.

However the board is composed, it is a good idea (and not at all improper or unethical) to ascertain in advance of the interview who the members are and what groups they represent. When you are introduced to them, you will have some idea of their backgrounds and interests, and at least you will not stutter and stammer over their names.

What should be done before the interview?

While knowledge about the board members is useful and takes some of the surprise element out of the interview, there is other preparation which is more substantive. It *is* possible to prepare for an oral interview – in several ways:

1) Keep a copy of your application and review it carefully before the interview

This may be the only document before the oral board, and the starting point of the interview. Know what education and experience you have listed there, and the sequence and dates of all of it. Sometimes the board will ask you to review the highlights of your experience for them; you should not have to hem and haw doing it.

2) Study the class specification and the examination announcement

Usually, the oral board has one or both of these to guide them. The qualities, characteristics or knowledges required by the position sought are stated in these documents. They offer valuable clues as to the nature of the oral interview. For example, if the job involves supervisory responsibilities, the announcement will usually indicate that knowledge of modern supervisory methods and the qualifications of the candidate as a supervisor will be tested. If so, you can expect such questions, frequently in the form of a hypothetical situation which you are expected to solve. NEVER go into an oral without knowledge of the duties and responsibilities of the job you seek.

3) Think through each qualification required

Try to visualize the kind of questions you would ask if you were a board member. How well could you answer them? Try especially to appraise your own knowledge and background in each area, *measured against the job sought*, and identify any areas in which you are weak. Be critical and realistic – do not flatter yourself.

4) Do some general reading in areas in which you feel you may be weak

For example, if the job involves supervision and your past experience has NOT, some general reading in supervisory methods and practices, particularly in the field of human relations, might be useful. Do NOT study agency procedures or detailed manuals. The oral board will be testing your understanding and capacity, not your memory.

5) Get a good night's sleep and watch your general health and mental attitude

You will want a clear head at the interview. Take care of a cold or any other minor ailment, and of course, no hangovers.

What should be done on the day of the interview?

Now comes the day of the interview itself. Give yourself plenty of time to get there. Plan to arrive somewhat ahead of the scheduled time, particularly if your appointment is in the fore part of the day. If a previous candidate fails to appear, the board might be ready for you a bit early. By early afternoon an oral board is almost invariably behind schedule if there are many candidates, and you may have to wait. Take along a book or magazine to read, or your application to review, but leave any extraneous material in the waiting room when you go in for your interview. In any event, relax and compose yourself.

The matter of dress is important. The board is forming impressions about you – from your experience, your manners, your attitude, and your appearance. Give your personal appearance careful attention. Dress your best, but not your flashiest. Choose conservative, appropriate clothing, and be sure it is immaculate. This is a business interview, and your appearance should indicate that you regard it as such. Besides, being well groomed and properly dressed will help boost your confidence.

Sooner or later, someone will call your name and escort you into the interview room. *This is it.* From here on you are on your own. It is too late for any more preparation. But remember, you asked for this opportunity to prove your fitness, and you are here because your request was granted.

What happens when you go in?

The usual sequence of events will be as follows: The clerk (who is often the board stenographer) will introduce you to the chairman of the oral board, who will introduce you to the other members of the board. Acknowledge the introductions before you sit down. Do not be surprised if you find a microphone facing you or a stenotypist sitting by. Oral interviews are usually recorded in the event of an appeal or other review.

Usually the chairman of the board will open the interview by reviewing the highlights of your education and work experience from your application – primarily for the benefit of the other members of the board, as well as to get the material into the record. Do not interrupt or comment unless there is an error or significant misinterpretation; if that is the case, do not hesitate. But do not quibble about insignificant matters. Also, he will usually ask you some question about your education, experience or your present job – partly to get you to start talking and to establish the interviewing "rapport." He may start the actual questioning, or turn it over to one of the other members. Frequently, each member undertakes the questioning on a particular area, one in which he is perhaps most competent, so you can expect each member to participate in the examination. Because time is limited, you may also expect some rather abrupt switches in the direction the questioning takes, so do not be upset by it. Normally, a board member will not pursue a single line of questioning unless he discovers a particular strength or weakness.

After each member has participated, the chairman will usually ask whether any member has any further questions, then will ask you if you have anything you wish to add. Unless you are expecting this question, it may floor you. Worse, it may start you off on an extended, extemporaneous speech. The board is not usually seeking more information. The question is principally to offer you a last opportunity to present further qualifications or to indicate that you have nothing to add. So, if you feel that a significant qualification or characteristic has been overlooked, it is proper to point it out in a sentence or so. Do not compliment the board on the thoroughness of their examination – they have been sketchy, and you know it. If you wish, merely say, "No thank you, I have nothing further to add." This is a point where you can "talk yourself out" of a good impression or fail to present an important bit of information. Remember, *you close the interview yourself.*

The chairman will then say, "That is all, Mr. _____, thank you." Do not be startled; the interview is over, and quicker than you think. Thank him, gather your belongings and take your leave. Save your sigh of relief for the other side of the door.

How to put your best foot forward

Throughout this entire process, you may feel that the board individually and collectively is trying to pierce your defenses, seek out your hidden weaknesses and embarrass and confuse you. Actually, this is not true. They are obliged to make an appraisal of your qualifications for the job you are seeking, and they want to see you in your best light. Remember, they must interview all candidates and a non-cooperative candidate may become a failure in spite of their best efforts to bring out his qualifications. Here are 15 suggestions that will help you:

1) Be natural – Keep your attitude confident, not cocky

If you are not confident that you can do the job, do not expect the board to be. Do not apologize for your weaknesses, try to bring out your strong points. The board is interested in a positive, not negative, presentation. Cockiness will antagonize any board member and make him wonder if you are covering up a weakness by a false show of strength.

2) Get comfortable, but don't lounge or sprawl

Sit erectly but not stiffly. A careless posture may lead the board to conclude that you are careless in other things, or at least that you are not impressed by the importance of the occasion. Either conclusion is natural, even if incorrect. Do not fuss with your clothing, a pencil or an ashtray. Your hands may occasionally be useful to emphasize a point; do not let them become a point of distraction.

3) Do not wisecrack or make small talk

This is a serious situation, and your attitude should show that you consider it as such. Further, the time of the board is limited – they do not want to waste it, and neither should you.

4) Do not exaggerate your experience or abilities

In the first place, from information in the application or other interviews and sources, the board may know more about you than you think. Secondly, you probably will not get away with it. An experienced board is rather adept at spotting such a situation, so do not take the chance.

5) If you know a board member, do not make a point of it, yet do not hide it

Certainly you are not fooling him, and probably not the other members of the board. Do not try to take advantage of your acquaintanceship – it will probably do you little good.

6) Do not dominate the interview

Let the board do that. They will give you the clues – do not assume that you have to do all the talking. Realize that the board has a number of questions to ask you, and do not try to take up all the interview time by showing off your extensive knowledge of the answer to the first one.

7) Be attentive

You only have 20 minutes or so, and you should keep your attention at its sharpest throughout. When a member is addressing a problem or question to you, give him your undivided attention. Address your reply principally to him, but do not exclude the other board members.

8) Do not interrupt

A board member may be stating a problem for you to analyze. He will ask you a question when the time comes. Let him state the problem, and wait for the question.

9) Make sure you understand the question

Do not try to answer until you are sure what the question is. If it is not clear, restate it in your own words or ask the board member to clarify it for you. However, do not haggle about minor elements.

10) Reply promptly but not hastily

A common entry on oral board rating sheets is "candidate responded readily," or "candidate hesitated in replies." Respond as promptly and quickly as you can, but do not jump to a hasty, ill-considered answer.

11) Do not be peremptory in your answers

A brief answer is proper – but do not fire your answer back. That is a losing game from your point of view. The board member can probably ask questions much faster than you can answer them.

12) Do not try to create the answer you think the board member wants

He is interested in what kind of mind you have and how it works – not in playing games. Furthermore, he can usually spot this practice and will actually grade you down on it.

13) Do not switch sides in your reply merely to agree with a board member

Frequently, a member will take a contrary position merely to draw you out and to see if you are willing and able to defend your point of view. Do not start a debate, yet do not surrender a good position. If a position is worth taking, it is worth defending.

14) Do not be afraid to admit an error in judgment if you are shown to be wrong

The board knows that you are forced to reply without any opportunity for careful consideration. Your answer may be demonstrably wrong. If so, admit it and get on with the interview.

15) Do not dwell at length on your present job .

The opening question may relate to your present assignment. Answer the question but do not go into an extended discussion. You are being examined for a *new* job, not your present one. As a matter of fact, try to phrase ALL your answers in terms of the job for which you are being examined.

Basis of Rating

Probably you will forget most of these "do's" and "don'ts" when you walk into the oral interview room. Even remembering them all will not ensure you a passing grade. Perhaps you did not have the qualifications in the first place. But remembering them will help you to put your best foot forward, without treading on the toes of the board members.

Rumor and popular opinion to the contrary notwithstanding, an oral board wants you to make the best appearance possible. They know you are under pressure – but they also want to see how you respond to it as a guide to what your reaction would be under the pressures of the job you seek. They will be influenced by the degree of poise you display, the personal traits you show and the manner in which you respond.

ABOUT THIS BOOK

This book contains tests divided into Examination Sections. Go through each test, answering every question in the margin. We have also attached a sample answer sheet at the back of the book that can be removed and used. At the end of each test look at the answer key and check your answers. On the ones you got wrong, look at the right answer choice and learn. Do not fill in the answers first. Do not memorize the questions and answers, but understand the answer and principles involved. On your test, the questions will likely be different from the samples. Questions are changed and new ones added. If you understand these past questions you should have success with any changes that arise. Tests may consist of several types of questions. We have additional books on each subject should more study be advisable or necessary for you. Finally, the more you study, the better prepared you will be. This book is intended to be the last thing you study before you walk into the examination room. Prior study of relevant texts is also recommended. NLC publishes some of these in our Fundamental Series. Knowledge and good sense are important factors in passing your exam. Good luck also helps. So now study this Passbook, absorb the material contained within and take that knowledge into the examination. Then do your best to pass that exam.

———

EXAMINATION SECTION

EXAMINATION SECTION
TEST 1

DIRECTIONS: Each question or incomplete statement is followed by several suggested answers or completions. Select the one that BEST answers the question or completes the statement. *PRINT THE LETTER OF THE CORRECT ANSWER IN THE SPACE AT THE RIGHT.*

1. An executive assigns A, the head of a staff unit, to devise plans for reducing the delay in submittal of reports by a local agency headed by C. The reports are under the supervision of C's subordinate line official B with whom A is to deal directly. In his investigation, A finds: (1) the reasons for the delay; and (2) poor practices which have either been overlooked or condoned by line official B.
   Of the following courses of action A could take, the BEST one would be to

    1.____

   A. develop recommendations with line official B with regard to reducing the delay and correcting the poor practices and then report fully to his own executive
   B. discuss the findings with C in an attempt to correct the situation before making any formal report on the poor practices
   C. report both findings to his executive, attaching the explanation offered by C
   D. report to his executive on the first finding and discuss the second in a friendly way with line official B
   E. report the first finding to his executive, ignoring the second until his opinion is requested

2. Drafts of a proposed policy, prepared by a staff committee, are circulated to ten members of the field staff of the organization by route slips with a request for comments within two weeks. Two members of the field staff make extensive comments, four offer editorial suggestions and the remainder make minor favorable comments. Shortly after, it found that the statement needs considerable revision by the field staff.
   Of the following possible reasons for the original failure of the field staff to identify difficulties, the MOST likely is that the

    2.____

   A. field staff did not take sufficient time to review the material
   B. field staff had not been advised of the type of contribution expected
   C. low morale of the field staff prevented their showing interest
   D. policy statement was too advanced for the staff
   E. staff committee was not sufficiently representative

3. Operator participation in management improvement work is LEAST likely to

    3.____

   A. assure the use of best available management technique
   B. overcome the stigma of the outside expert
   C. place responsibility for improvement in the person who knows the job best
   D. simplify installation
   E. take advantage of the desire of most operators to seek self-improvement

4. In general, the morale of workers in an agency is MOST frequently and MOST significantly affected by the

    4.____

A. agency policies of organizational structure and operational procedures
B. distance of the employee's job from his home community
C. fringe benefits
D. number of opportunities for advancement
E. relationship with supervisors

5. Of the following, the PRIMARY function of a work distribution chart is to   5.____

A. analyze the soundness of existing divisions of labor
B. eliminate unnecessary clerical detail
C. establish better supervisory techniques
D. simplify work methods
E. weed out core functions

6. In analyzing a process chart, which one of the following should be asked FIRST?   6.____

    A. How   B. When   C. Where   D. Who   E. Why

7. Which one of the following is NOT an advantage of the interview method of collecting   7.____
data?
It

A. enables interviewer to judge the person interviewed on such matters as general
attitude, knowledge, etc.
B. helps build up personal relations for later installation of changes
C. is a flexible method that can be adjusted to changing circumstances
D. permits the obtaining of *off the record* information
E. produces more accurate information than other methods

8. Which one of the following may be defined as *a regularly recurring appraisal of the man-*   8.____
ner in which all elements of agency management are being carried out?

A. Functional survey   B. Operations audit
C. Organization survey   D. Over-all survey
E. Reconnaissance survey

9. An analysis of the flow of work in a department should begin with the _____ work.   9.____

A. major routine   B. minor routine
C. supervisory   D. technical
E. unusual

10. Which method would MOST likely be used to get first-hand information on complaints   10.____
from the public?

A. Study of correspondence
B. Study of work volume
C. Tracing specific transactions through a series of steps
D. Tracing use of forms
E. Worker desk audit

11. People will generally produce the MOST if   11.____

A. management exercises close supervision over the work
B. there is strict discipline in the group

C. they are happy in their work
D. they feel involved in their work
E. they follow *the one best way*

12. The normal analysis of which chart listed below is MOST closely related to organiza-   12._____
tional analysis?
_____ chart.

   A. Layout   B. Operation
   C. Process   D. Work count
   E. Work distribution

13. The work count would be LEAST helpful in accomplishing which one of the following?   13._____

   A. Demonstrating personnel needs
   B. Improving the sequence of steps
   C. Measuring the value of a step
   D. Spotting bottlenecks
   E. Stimulating interest in work

14. Which of the following seems LEAST useful as a guide in interviewing an employee in a   14._____
procedure and methods survey?

   A. Explaining who you are and the purpose of your visit
   B. Having a general plan of what you intend to get from the interview
   C. Listening carefully and not interrupting
   D. Trying out his reactions to your ideas for improvements
   E. Trying to analyze his reasons for saying what he says

15. Which one of the following is an advantage of the questionnaire method of gathering   15._____
facts as compared with the interview method?

   A. Different people may interpret the questions differently.
   B. Less *off the record* information is given.
   C. More time may be taken in order to give exact answers.
   D. Personal relationships with the people involved are not established.
   E. There is less need for follow-up.

16. Which one of the following is generally NOT an advantage of the personal observation   16._____
method of gathering facts?
It

   A. enables staff to use *off the record* information if personally observed
   B. helps in developing valid recommendations
   C. helps the person making the observation acquire *know how* valuable for later
      installation and follow-up
   D. is economical in time and money
   E. may turn up other problems in need of solution

17. Which of the following would MOST often be the best way to minimize resistance to   17._____
change?

   A. Break the news about the change gently to the people affected.
   B. Increase the salary of the people affected by the change.

C. Let the people concerned participate in arriving at the decision to change.
D. Notify all people concerned with the change, both orally and in writing.
E. Stress the advantages of the new system.

18. The functional organization chart   18.____

    A. does not require periodic revision
    B. includes a description of the duties of each organization segment
    C. includes positions and titles for each organization segment
    D. is the simplest type of organization chart
    E. is used primarily by newly established agencies

19. The principle of span of control has frequently been said to be in conflict with the   19.____

    A. principle of unity of command
    B. principle that authority should be commensurate with responsibility
    C. principle that like functions should be grouped into one unit
    D. principle that the number of levels between the top of an organization and the bottom should be small
    E. scalar principle

20. If an executive delegates to his subordinates authority to handle problems of a routine nature for which standard solutions have been established, he may expect that   20.____

    A. fewer complaints will be received
    B. he has made it more difficult for his subordinates to solve these problems
    C. he has opened the way for confusion in his organization
    D. there will be a lack of consistency in the methods applied to the solution of these problems
    E. these routine problems will be handled efficiently and he will have more time for other non-routine work

21. Which of the following would MOST likely be achieved by a change in the basic organization structure from the *process* or *functional* type to the *purpose* or *product* type?   21.____

    A. Easier recruitment of personnel in a tight labor market
    B. Fixing responsibility at a lower level in the organization
    C. Greater centralization
    D. Greater economy
    E. Greater professional development

22. Usually the MOST difficult problem in connection with a major reorganization is   22.____

    A. adopting a pay plan to fit the new structure
    B. bringing the organization manual up-to-date
    C. determining the new organization structure
    D. gaining acceptance of the new plan by the higher level employees
    E. gaining acceptance of the new plan by the lower level employees

23. Which of the following statements MOST accurately describes the work of the chiefs of MOST staff divisions in departments?   23.____
Chiefs

A. focus more on getting the job done than on how it is done
B. are mostly interested in short-range results
C. nearly always advise but rarely if ever command or control
D. usually command or control but rarely advise
E. provide service to the rest of the organization and/or assist the chief executive in planning and controlling operations

24. In determining the type of organization structure of an enterprise, the one factor that might be given relatively greater weight in a small organization than in a larger organization of the same nature is the

24.____

A. geographical location of the enterprise
B. individual capabilities of incumbents
C. method of financing to be employed
D. size of the area served
E. type of activity engaged in

25. Functional foremanship differs MOST markedly from generally accepted principles of administration in that it advocates

25.____

A. an unlimited span of control
B. less delegation of responsibility
C. more than one supervisor for an employee
D. nonfunctional organization
E. substitution of execution for planning

KEY (CORRECT ANSWERS)

1.	A	11.	D
2.	B	12.	E
3.	A	13.	B
4.	E	14.	D
5.	A	15.	C
6.	E	16.	D
7.	E	17.	C
8.	B	18.	B
9.	A	19.	D
10.	A	20.	E

21.	B
22.	D
23.	E
24.	B
25.	C

TEST 2

DIRECTIONS: Each question or incomplete statement is followed by several suggested answers or completions. Select the one that BEST answers the question or completes the statement. *PRINT THE LETTER OF THE CORRECT ANSWER IN THE SPACE AT THE RIGHT*

1. Decentralization of the authority to make decisions is a necessary result of increased complexity in an organization, but for the sake of efficiency and coordination of operations, such decentralization must be planned carefully.
   A good general rule is that

   A. any decision should be made at the lowest possible point in the organization where all the information and competence necessary for a sound decision are available
   B. any decision should be made at the highest possible point in the organization, thus guaranteeing the best decision
   C. any decision should be made at the lowest possible point in the organization, but always approved by management
   D. any decision should be made by management and referred to the proper subordinate for comment
   E. no decision should be made by any individual in the organization without approval by a superior

   1.____

2. One drawback of converting a conventional consecutive filing system to a terminal digit filing system for a large installation is that

   A. conversion would be expensive in time and manpower
   B. conversion would prevent the proper use of recognized numeric classification systems, such as the Dewey decimal, in classifying files material
   C. responsibility for proper filing cannot be pinpointed in the terminal digit system
   D. the terminal digit system requires considerably more space than a normal filing system
   E. the terminal digit system requires long, specialized training on the part of files personnel

   2.____

3. The basic filing system that would ordinarily be employed in a large administrative headquarters unit is the _____ file system.

   A. alphabetic   B. chronological
   C. mnemonic   D. retention
   E. subject classification

   3.____

4. A records center is of benefit in a records management program primarily because

   A. all the records of the organization are kept in one place
   B. inactive records can be stored economically in less expensive storage areas
   C. it provides a place where useless records can be housed at little or no cost to the organization
   D. obsolete filing and storage equipment can be utilized out of view of the public
   E. records analysts can examine an organization's files without affecting the unit's operation or upsetting the supervisors

   4.____

5. In examining a number of different forms to see whether any could be combined or eliminated, which of the following would one be MOST likely to use?

   A. Forms analysis sheet of recurring data
   B. Forms control log
   C. Forms design and approval request
   D. Forms design and guide sheet
   E. Numerical file

6. The MOST important reason for control of *bootleg* forms is that

   A. they are more expensive than authorized forms
   B. they are usually poorly designed
   C. they can lead to unnecessary procedures
   D. they cannot be reordered as easily as authorized forms
   E. violation of rules and regulations should not be allowed

7. With a box design of a form, the caption title or question to be answered should be located in the _____ of the box.

   A. center at the bottom   B. center at the top
   C. lower left corner   D. lower right corner
   E. upper left corner

8. A two-part snapout form would be MOST properly justified if

   A. it is a cleaner operation
   B. it is prepared ten times a week
   C. it saves time in preparation
   D. it is to be filled out by hand rather than by typewriter
   E. proper registration is critical

9. When deciding whether or not to approve a request for a new form, which reference is normally MOST pertinent?

   A. Alphabetical Forms File
   B. Functional Forms File
   C. Numerical Forms File
   D. Project completion report
   E. Records retention data

10. Which of the following statements BEST explains the significance of the famed Hawthorne Plant experiments? They showed that

   A. a large span of control leads to more production than a small span of control
   B. morale has no relationship to production
   C. personnel counseling is of relatively little importance in a going organization
   D. the special attention received by a group in an experimental situation has a greater impact on production than changes in working conditions
   E. there is a direct relationship between the amount of illumination and production

11. Which of the following would most often NOT result from a highly efficient management control system?

A. Facilitation of delegation
B. Highlighting of problem areas
C. Increase in willingness of people to experiment or to take calculated risks
D. Provision of an objective test of new ideas or new methods and procedures
E. Provision of information useful for revising objectives, programs, and operations

12. The PERT system is a   12.____

    A. method for laying out office space on a modular basis utilizing prefabricated partitions
    B. method of motivating personnel to be continuously alert and to improve their appearance
    C. method of program planning and control using a network or flow plan
    D. plan for expanding reporting techniques
    E. simplified method of cost accounting

13. The term *management control* is MOST frequently used to mean   13.____

    A. an objective and unemotional approach by management
    B. coordinating the efforts of all parts of the organization
    C. evaluation of results in relation to plan
    D. giving clear, precise orders to subordinates
    E. keeping unions from making managerial decisions

14. Which one of the following factors has the MOST bearing on the frequency with which a control report should be made?   14.____

    A. Degree of specialization of the work
    B. Degree of variability in activities
    C. Expense of the report
    D. Number of levels of supervision
    E. Number of personnel involved

15. The value of statistical records is MAINLY dependent upon the   15.____

    A. method of presenting the material
    B. number of items used
    C. range of cases sampled
    D. reliability of the information used
    E. time devoted to compiling the material

16. When a supervisor delegates an assignment, he should   16.____

    A. delegate his responsibility for the assignment
    B. make certain that the assignment is properly performed
    C. participate in the beginning and final stages of the assignment
    D. retain all authority needed to complete the assignment
    E. oversee all stages of the assignment

17. Assume that the department in which you are employed has never given official sanction to a mid-afternoon coffee break. Some bureaus have it and others do not. In the latter case, some individuals merely absent themselves for about 15 minutes at 3 P.M. while others remain on the job despite the fatigue which seems to be common among all employees in this department at that time.
The course of action which you should recommend, if possible, is to

    A. arrange a schedule of mid-afternoon coffee breaks for all employees
    B. forbid all employees to take a mid-afternoon coffee break
    C. permit each bureau to decide for itself whether or not it will have a coffee break
    D. require all employees who wish a coffee break to take a shorter lunch period
    E. arrange a poll to discover the consensus of the department

17.____

18. The one of the following which is LEAST important in the management of a suggestion program is

    A. giving awards which are of sufficient value to encourage competition
    B. securing full support from the department's officers and executives
    C. publicizing the program and the awards given
    D. holding special conferences to analyze and evaluate some of the suggestions needed
    E. providing suggestion boxes in numerous locations

18.____

19. The one of the following which is MOST likely to decrease morale is

    A. insistence on strict adherence to safety rules
    B. making each employee responsible for the tidiness of his work area
    C. overlooking evidence of hostility between groups of employees
    D. strong, aggressive leadership
    E. allocating work on the basis of personal knowledge of the abilities and interests of the members of the department

19.____

20. Assume that a certain office procedure has been standard practice for many years. When a new employee asks why this particular procedure is followed, the supervisor should FIRST

    A. explain that everyone does it that way
    B. explain the reason for the procedure
    C. inform him that it has always been done that way in that particular office
    D. tell him to try it for a while before asking questions
    E. tell him he has never thought about it that way

20.____

21. Several employees complain informally to their supervisor regarding some new procedures which have been instituted. The supervisor should IMMEDIATELY

    A. explain that management is responsible
    B. state frankly that he had nothing to do with it
    C. refer the matter to the methods analyst
    D. tell the employees to submit their complaint as a formal grievance
    E. investigate the complaint

21.____

22. A new employee asks his supervisor *how he is doing*. Actually, he is not doing well in some phases of the job, but it is felt that he will learn in time.
The BEST response for the supervisor to make is: 22.____

    A. Some things you are doing well, and in others I am sure you will improve
    B. Wait until the end of your probationary period when we will discuss this matter
    C. You are not doing too well
    D. You are doing very well
    E. I'll be able to tell you when I go over your record

23. The PRINCIPAL aim of a supervisor is to   23.____

    A. act as liaison between employee and management
    B. get the work done
    C. keep up morale
    D. train his subordinates
    E. become chief of the department

24. When the work of two bureaus must be coordinated, direct contact between the subordinates in each bureau who are working on the problem is   24.____

    A. *bad,* because it violates the chain of command
    B. *bad,* because they do not have authority to make decisions
    C. *good,* because it enables quicker results
    D. *good,* because it relieves their superiors of any responsibility
    E. *bad,* because they may work at cross purposes

25. Of the following, the organization defect which can be ascertained MOST readily merely by analyzing an accurate and well-drawn organization chart is   25.____

    A. ineffectiveness of an activity
    B. improper span of control
    C. inappropriate assignment of functions
    D. poor supervision
    E. unlawful delegation of authority

KEY (CORRECT ANSWERS)

1.	A		11.	C
2.	A		12.	C
3.	E		13.	C
4.	B		14.	B
5.	A		15.	D
6.	C		16.	B
7.	E		17.	A
8.	E		18.	E
9.	B		19.	C
10.	D		20.	B

21.	E
22.	A
23.	B
24.	C
25.	B

EXAMINATION SECTION
TEST 1

DIRECTIONS: Each question or incomplete statement is followed by several suggested answers or completions. Select the one that BEST answers the question or completes the statement. *PRINT THE LETTER OF THE CORRECT ANSWER IN THE SPACE AT THE RIGHT.*

1. In almost every organization, there is a nucleus of highly important functions commonly designated as *management.* Which of the following statements BEST characterizes *management?*

    A. Getting things done through others
    B. The highest level of intelligence in any organization
    C. The process whereby democratic and participative activities are maximized
    D. The *first among equals*

1.____

2. Strategies in problem-solving are important to anyone aspiring to advancement in the field of administration. Which of the following is BEST classified as the first step in the process of problem-solving?

    A. Collection and organization of data
    B. The formulation of a plan
    C. The definition of the problem
    D. The development of a method and methodology

2.____

3. One of the objectives of preparing a budget is to

    A. create optimistic goals which each department can attempt to meet
    B. create an overall company goal by combining the budgets of the various departments
    C. be able to compare planned expenditures against actual expenditures
    D. be able to identify accounting errors

3.____

4. The rise in demand for *systems* personnel in industrial and governmental organizations over the past five years has been extraordinary.
In which of the following areas would a *systems* specialist assigned to an agency be LEAST likely to be of assistance?

    A. Developing, recommending, and establishing an effective cost and inventory system
    B. Development and maintenance of training manuals
    C. Reviewing existing work procedures and recommending improvements
    D. Development of aptitude tests for new employees

4.____

5. Management experts have come to the conclusion that the traditional forms of motivation used in industry and government, which emphasize authority over and economic rewards for the employee, are no longer appropriate.
To which of the following factors do such experts attribute the GREATEST importance in producing this change?

    A. The desire of employees to satisfy material needs has become greater and more complex.

5.____

B. The desire for social satisfaction has become the most important aspect of the job for the average worker.

C. With greater standardization of work processes, there has been an increase in the willingness of workers to accept discipline.

D. In general, employee organizations have made it more difficult for management to fire an employee.

6. In preparing a budget, it is usually considered advisable to start the initial phases of preparation at the operational level of management.
Of the following, the justification that management experts usually advance as MOST reasonable for this practice is that operating managers, as a consequence of their involvement, will

    6._____

    A. develop a background in finance or accounting
    B. have an understanding of the organizational structure
    C. tend to feel responsible for carrying out budget objectives
    D. have the ability to see the overall financial picture

7. An administrative officer has been asked by his superior to write a concise, factual report with objective conclusions and recommendations based on facts assembled by other researchers.
Of the following factors, the administrative officer should give LEAST consideration to

    7._____

    A. the educational level of the person or persons for whom the report is being prepared
    B. the use to be made of the report
    C. the complexity of the problem
    D. his own feelings about the importance of the problem

8. In an agency, upon which of the following is a supervisor's effectiveness MOST likely to depend?
The

    8._____

    A. degree to which a supervisor allows subordinates to participate in the decision-making process and the setting of objectives
    B. degree to which a supervisor's style meets management's objectives and subordinates' needs
    C. strength and forcefulness of the supervisor in pursuing his objectives
    D. expertise and knowledge the supervisor has about the specific work to be done

9. For authority to be effective, which of the following is the MOST basic requirement?
Authority must be

    9._____

    A. absolute   B. formalized   C. accepted   D. delegated

10. Management no longer abhors the idea of employees taking daily work breaks, but prefers to schedule such breaks rather than to allot to each employee a standard amount of free time to be taken off during the day as he wishes. Which of the following BEST expresses the reason management theorists give for the practice of scheduling such breaks?

    10._____

    A. Many jobs fall into natural work units which are scheduled, and the natural time to take a break is at the end of the unit.

B. Taking a scheduled break permits socialization and a feeling of accomplishment.
C. Managers have concluded that scheduling rest periods seems to reduce the incidence of unscheduled ones.
D. Many office workers who really need such breaks are hesitant about taking them unless they are scheduled.

11. The computer represents one of the major developments of modern technology. It is widely used in both scientific and managerial activities because of its many advantages. Which of the following is NOT an advantage gained by management in the use of the computer?
A computer   11._____

A. provides the manager with a greatly enlarged memory so that he can easily be provided with data for decision making
B. relieves the manager of basic decision-making responsibility, thereby giving him more time for directing and controlling
C. performs routine, repetitive calculations with greater precision and reliability than employees
D. provides a capacity for rapid simulations of alternative solutions to problem solving

12. A supervisor of a unit in a division is usually responsible for all of the following EXCEPT   12._____

A. the conduct of subordinates in the achievement of division objectives
B. maintaining quality standards in the unit
C. the protection and care of materials and equipment in the unit
D. performing the most detailed tasks in the unit himself

13. You have been assigned to teach a new employee the functions and procedures of your office.
In your introductory talk, which of the following approaches is PREFERABLE?   13._____

A. Advise the new employee of the employee benefits and services available to him, over and above his salary.
B. Discuss honestly the negative aspects of departmental procedures and indicate methods available to overcome them.
C. Give the new employee an understanding of the general purpose of office procedures and functions and of their relevance to departmental objectives.
D. Give a basic and detailed explanation of the operations of your office, covering all functions and procedures.

14. It is your responsibility to assign work to several clerks under your supervision. One of the clerks indignantly refuses to accept an assignment and asks to be given something else. He has not yet indicated why he does not want the assignment, but is sitting there glaring at you, awaiting your reaction.
Of the following, which is the FIRST action you should take?   14._____

A. Ask the employee into your office in order to reprimand him and tell him emphatically that he must accept the assignment.
B. Talk to the employee privately in an effort to find the reason for his indignation and refusal, and then base your action upon your findings.

C. Let the matter drop for a day or two to allow the employee to cool off before you insist that he accept the assignment.
D. Inform the employee quietly and calmly that as his supervisor you have selected him for this assignment and that you fully expect him to accept it.

15. Administrative officers are expected to be able to handle duties delegated to them by their supervisors and to be able, as they advance in status, to delegate tasks to assistants.
When considering whether to delegate tasks to a subordinate, which of the following questions should be LEAST important to an administrative officer?
In the delegated tasks,

    A. how significant are the decisions to be made, and how much consultation will be involved?
    B. to what extent is uniformity and close coordination of activity required?
    C. to what extent must speedy-on-the-spot decisions be made?
    D. to what extent will delegation relieve the administrative officer of his burden of responsibility?

15.____

16. A functional forms file is a collection of forms which are grouped by

    A. purpose   B. department   C. title   D. subject

16.____

17. All of the following are reasons to consult a records retention schedule except one.
Which one is that?
To determine

    A. whether something should be filed
    B. how long something should stay in file
    C. who should be assigned to filing
    D. when something on file should be destroyed

17.____

18. Listed below are four of the steps in the process of preparing correspondence for filing.
If they were to be put in logical sequence, the SECOND step would be

    A. preparing cross-reference sheets or cards
    B. coding the correspondence using a classification system
    C. sorting the correspondence in the order to be filed
    D. checking for follow-up action required and preparing a follow-up slip

18.____

19. New material added to a file folder should USUALLY be inserted

    A. in the order of importance (the most important in front)
    B. in the order of importance (the most important in back)
    C. chronologically (most recent in front)
    D. chronologically (most recent in back)

19.____

20. An individual is looking for a name in the white pages of a telephone directory.
Which of the following BEST describes the system of filing found there?
A(n)_____ file

    A. alphabetic   B. sequential
    C. locator   D. index

20.____

21. The MAIN purpose of a tickler file is to

    A. help prevent overlooking matters that require future attention
    B. check on adequacy of past performance
    C. pinpoint responsibility for recurring daily tasks
    D. reduce the volume of material kept in general files

21.____

22. Which of the following BEST describes the process of reconciling a bank statement?

    A. Analyzing the nature of the expenditures made by the office during the preceding month
    B. Comparing the statement of the bank with the banking records maintained in the office
    C. Determining the liquidity position by reading the bank statement carefully
    D. Checking the service charges noted on the bank statement

22.____

23. From the viewpoint of preserving agency or institutional funds, which of the following is the LEAST acceptable method for making a payment?
A check made out to

    A. cash
    C. an individual
    B. a company
    D. a partnership

23.____

24. In general, the CHIEF economy of using multicopy forms is in

    A. the paper on which the form is printed
    B. printing the form
    C. employee time
    D. carbon paper

24.____

25. Suppose your supervisor has asked you to develop a form to record certain information needed.
The FIRST thing you should do is to

    A. determine the type of data that will be recorded repeatedly so that it can be pre-printed
    B. study the relationship of the form to the job to be accomplished so that the form can be planned
    C. determine the information that will be recorded in the same place on each copy of the form so that it can be used as a check
    D. find out who will be responsible for supplying the information so that space can be provided for their signatures

25.____

26. An administrative officer in charge of a small fund for buying office supplies has just written a check to Charles Laird, a supplier, and has sent the check by messenger to him. A half-hour later, the messenger telephones the administrative officer. He has lost the check.
Which of the following is the MOST important action for the administrative officer to take under these circumstances?

    A. Ask the messenger to return and write a report describing the loss of the check.
    B. Make a note on the performance record of the messenger who lost the check.
    C. Take the necessary steps to have payment stopped on the check.
    D. Refrain from doing anyting since the check may be found shortly.

26.____

27. A petty cash fund is set up PRIMARILY to   27._____

    A. take care of small investments that must be made from time to time
    B. take care of small expenses that arise from time to time
    C. provide a fund to be used as the office wants to use it with little need to maintain records
    D. take care of expenses that develop during emergencies, such as machine breakdowns and fires

28. Of the following, which is usually the MOST important guideline in writing business letters?   28._____
A letter should be

    A. neat
    B. written in a formalized style
    C. written in clear language intelligible to the reader
    D. written in the past tense

29. Suppose you are asked to edit a policy statement. You note that personal pronouns like *you, we,* and *I* are used freely.   29._____
Which of the following statements BEST applies to this use of personal pronouns?
It

    A. is proper usage because written business language should not be different from carefully spoken business language
    B. requires correction because it is ungrammatical
    C. is proper because it is clearer and has a warmer tone
    D. requires correction because policies should be expressed in an impersonal manner

30. Good business letters are coherent.   30._____
To be coherent means to

    A. keep only one unifying idea in the message
    B. present the total message
    C. use simple, direct words for the message
    D. tie together the various ideas in the message

31. Proper division of a letter into paragraphs requires that the writer of business letters should, as much as possible, be sure that   31._____

    A. each paragraph is short
    B. each paragraph develops discussion of just one topic
    C. each paragraph repeats the theme of the total message
    D. there are at least two paragraphs for every message

32. An editor is given a letter with this initial paragraph: 32._____
We have received your letter, which we read with interest, and we are happy to respond to your question. In fact, we talked with several people in our office to get ideas to send to you.
Which of the following is it MOST reasonable for the editor to conclude?
The paragraph is

A. concise
B. communicating something of value
C. unnecessary
D. coherent

33. As soon as you pick up the phone, a very angry caller begins immediately to complain   33.____
about city agencies and *red tape.* He says that he has been shifted to two or three different offices. It turns out that he is seeking information which is not immediately available
to you. You believe you know, however, where it can be found. Which of the following
actions is the BEST one for you to take?

   A. To eliminate all confusion, suggest that the caller write the mayor stating explicitly
what he wants.
   B. Apologize by telling the caller how busy city agencies now are, but also tell him
directly that you do not have the information he needs.
   C. Ask for the caller's telephone number and assure him you will call back after you
have checked further.
   D. Give the caller the name and telephone number of the person who might be able to
help, but explain that you are not positive he will get results.

34. Suppose that one of your duties is to dictate responses to routine requests from the pub-   34.____
lic for information. A letter writer asks for information which, as expressed in a one-sen-
tence, explicit agency rule, cannot be given out to the public.
Of the following ways of answering the letter, which is the MOST efficient?

   A. Quote verbatim that section of the agency rules which prohibits giving this information to the public.
   B. Without quoting the rule, explain why you cannot accede to the request and suggest alternative sources.
   C. Describe how carefully the request was considered before classifying it as subject
to the rule forbidding the issuance of such information.
   D. Acknowledge receipt of the letter and advise that the requested information is not
released to the public.

35. Suppose you assist in supervising a staff which has rather high morale, and your own   35.____
supervisor asks you to poll the staff to find out who will be able to work overtime this particular evening to help complete emergency work.
Which of the following approaches would be MOST likely to win their cooperation while
maintaining their morale?

   A. Tell them that the better assignments will be given only to those who work over-
time.
   B. Tell them that occasional overtime is a job requirement .
   C. Assure them they'll be doing you a personal favor.
   D. Let them know clearly why the overtime is needed.

36. Suppose that you have been asked to write and to prepare for reproduction new depart-   36.____
mental vacation leave regulations.
After you have written the new regulations, all of which fit on one page, which one of
the following would be the BEST method of reproducing 1000 copies?

   A. An outside private printer, because you can best maintain confidentiality using this
technique
   B. Xeroxing, because the copies will have the best possible appearance

C. Typing copies, because you will be certain that there are the fewest possible errors
D. Including it in the next company newsletter

37. Administration is the center, but not necessarily the source, of all ideas for procedural improvement.
The MOST significant implication that this principle bears for the administrative officer is that

    A. before procedural improvements are introduced, they should be approved by a majority of the staff
    B. it is the unique function of the administrative officer to derive and introduce procedural improvements
    C. the administrative officer should derive ideas and suggestions for procedural improvement from all possible sources, introducing any that promise to be effective
    D. the administrative officer should view employee grievances as the chief source of procedural improvements

37.____

38. Your bureau is assigned an important task.
Of the following, the function that you, as an administrative officer, can LEAST reasonably be expected to perform under these circumstances is

    A. division of the large job into individual tasks
    B. establishment of *production lines* within the bureau
    C. performance personally of a substantial share of all the work
    D. check-up to see that the work has been well done

38.____

39. Suppose that you have broken a complex job into its smaller components before making assignments to the employees under your jurisdiction.
Of the following, the LEAST advisable procedure to follow from that point is to

    A. give each employee a picture of the importance of his work for the success of the total job
    B. establish a definite line of work flow and responsibility
    C. post a written memorandum of the best method for performing each job
    D. teach a number of alternative methods for doing each job

39.____

40. As an administrative officer, you are requested to draw up an organization chart of the whole department.
Of the following, the MOST important characteristic of such a chart is that it will

    A. include all peculiarities and details of the organization which distinguish it from any other
    B. be a schematic representation of purely administrative functions within the department
    C. present a modification of the actual departmental organization in the light of principles of scientific management
    D. present an accurate picture of the lines of authority and responsibility

40.____

KEY (CORRECT ANSWERS)

1.	A	11.	B	21.	A	31.	B
2.	C	12.	D	22.	B	32.	C
3.	C	13.	C	23.	A	33.	C
4.	D	14.	B	24.	C	34.	A
5.	D	15.	D	25.	B	35.	D
6.	C	16.	A	26.	C	36.	B
7.	D	17.	C	27.	B	37.	C
8.	B	18.	A	28.	C	38.	C
9.	C	19.	C	29.	D	39.	D
10.	C	20.	A	30.	D	40.	D

TEST 2

DIRECTIONS: Each question or incomplete statement is followed by several suggested answers or completions. Select the one that BEST answers the question or completes the statement. *PRINT THE LETTER OF THE CORRECT ANSWER IN THE SPACE AT THE RIGHT.*

Questions 1-10.

DIRECTIONS: In each of Questions 1 through 10, a pair of related words written in capital letters is followed by four other pairs of words. For each question, select the pair of words which MOST closely expresses a relationship similar to that of the pair in capital letters.

SAMPLE QUESTION:

BOAT - DOCK
    A. airplane - hangar   B. rain - snow
    C. cloth - cotton   D. hunger - food

Choice A is the answer to this sample question since, of the choices given, the relationship between airplane and hangar is most similar to the relationship between boat and dock.

1. AUTOMOBILE - FACTORY   1.____

    A. tea - lemon   B. wheel - engine
    C. pot - flower   D. paper - mill

2. GIRDER - BRIDGE   2.____

    A. petal - flower   B. street - sidewalk
    C. meat - vegetable   D. sun - storm

3. RADIUS - CIRCLE   3.____

    A. brick - building   B. tie - tracks
    C. spoke - wheel   D. axle - tire

4. DISEASE - RESEARCH   4.____

    A. death - poverty   B. speech - audience
    C. problem - conference   D. invalid - justice

5. CONCLUSION - INTRODUCTION   5.____

    A. commencement - beginning   B. housing - motor
    C. caboose - engine   D. train - cabin

6. SOCIETY - LAW   6.____

    A. baseball - rules   B. jury - law
    C. cell - prisoner   D. sentence - jury

7. PLAN - ACCOMPLISHMENT   7.____

    A. deed - fact   B. method - success
    C. graph - chart   D. rules - manual

8. ORDER - GOVERNMENT   8.____

    A. chaos - administration   B. confusion - pandemonium
    C. rule - stability   D. despair - hope

9. TYRANNY - FREEDOM   9.____

    A. despot - mob   B. wealth - poverty
    C. nobility - commoners   D. dictatorship - democracy

10. FAX - LETTER   10.____

    A. hare - tortoise   B. lie - truth
    C. number - word   D. report - research

Questions 11-16.

DIRECTIONS: Answer Questions 11 through 16 SOLELY on the basis of the information given in the passage below.

Inherent in all organized endeavors is the need to resolve the individual differences involved in conflict. Conflict may be either a positive or negative factor, since it may lead to creativity, innovation, and progress, on the one hand, or it may result, on the other hand, in a deterioration or even destruction of the organization. Thus, some forms of conflict are desirable, whereas others are undesirable and ethically wrong.

There are three management strategies which deal with interpersonal conflict. In the "divide-and-rule strategy", management attempts to maintain control by limiting the conflict to those directly involved and preventing their disagreement from spreading to the larger group. The "suppression-of-differences strategy" entails ignoring conflicts or pretending they are irrelevant. In the "working-through-differences strategy", management actively attempts to solve or resolve intergroup or interpersonal conflicts. Of the three strategies, only the last directly attacks and has the potential for eliminating the causes of conflict. An essential part of this strategy, however, is its employment by a committed and relatively mature management team.

11. According to the above passage, the *divide-and-rule strategy* for dealing with conflict is   11.____
the attempt to

    A. involve other people in the conflict
    B. restrict the conflict to those participating in it
    C. divide the conflict into positive and negative factors
    D. divide the conflict into a number of smaller ones

12. The word *conflict* is used in relation to both positive and negative factors in this passage.   12.____
Which one of the following words is MOST likely to describe the activity which the word *conflict*, in the sense of the passage, implies?

    A. Competition   B. Cooperation
    C. Confusion   D. Aggression

13. According to the above passage, which one of the following characteristics is shared by   13.____
both the *suppression-of-differences strategy* and the *divide-and-rule strategy?*

    A. Pretending that conflicts are irrelevant
    B. Preventing conflicts from spreading to the group situation

C. Failure to directly attack the causes of conflict
D. Actively attempting to resolve interpersonal conflict

14. According to the above passage, the successful resolution of interpersonal conflict requires   14.____

    A. allowing the group to mediate conflicts between two individuals
    B. division of the conflict into positive and negative factors
    C. involvement of a committed, mature management team
    D. ignoring minor conflicts until they threaten the organization

15. Which can be MOST reasonably inferred from the above passage?   15.____
A conflict between two individuals is LEAST likely to continue when management uses

    A. the *working-through-differences strategy*
    B. the *suppression-of-differences strategy*
    C. the *divide-and-rule strategy*
    D. a combination of all three strategies

16. According to the above passage, a desirable result of conflict in an organization is when conflict   16.____

    A. exposes production problems in the organization
    B. can be easily ignored by management
    C. results in advancement of more efficient managers
    D. leads to development of new methods

Questions 17-23.

DIRECTIONS: Answer Questions 17 through 23 SOLELY on the basis of the information given in the passage below.

Modern management places great emphasis on the concept of communication. The communication process consists of the steps through which an idea or concept passes from its inception by one person, the sender, until it is acted upon by another person, the receiver. Through an understanding of these steps and some of the possible barriers that may occur, more effective communication may be achieved. The first step in the communication process is ideation by the sender. This is the formation of the intended content of the message he wants to transmit. In the next step, encoding, the sender organizes his ideas into a series of symbols designed to communicate his message to his intended receiver. He selects suitable words or phrases that can be understood by the receiver, and he also selects the appropriate media to be used-for example, memorandum, conference, etc. The third step is transmission of the encoded message through selected channels in the organizational structure. In the fourth step, the receiver enters the process by tuning in to receive the message. If the receiver does not function, however, the message is lost. For example, if the message is oral, the receiver must be a good listener. The fifth step is decoding of the message by the receiver, as for example, by changing words into ideas. At this step, the decoded message may not be the same idea that the sender originally encoded because the sender and receiver have different perceptions regarding the meaning of certain words.

Finally, the receiver acts or responds. He may file the information, ask for more information, or take other action. There can be no assurance, however, that communication has taken place unless there is some type of feedback to the sender in the form of an acknowledgement that the message was received.

17. According to the above passage, *ideation* is the process by which the   17._____

    A. sender develops the intended content of the message
    B. sender organizes his ideas into a series of symbols
    C. receiver tunes in to receive the message
    D. receiver decodes the message

18. In the last sentence of the passage, the word *feedback* refers to the process by which the   18._____
sender is assured that the

    A. receiver filed the information
    B. receiver's perception is the same as his own
    C. message was received
    D. message was properly interpreted

19. Which one of the following BEST shows the order of the steps in the communication pro-   19._____
cess as described in the passage?

    A. 1- ideation   2- encoding
          3- decoding   4- transmission
          5- receiving   6- action
          7- feedback to the sender

    B. 1- ideation   2- encoding
          3- transmission   4- decoding
          5- receiving   6- action
          7- feedback to the sender

    C. 1- ideation   2- decoding
          3- transmission   4- receiving
          5- encoding   6- action
          7- feedback to the sender

    D. 1- ideation   2- encoding
          3- transmission   4- receiving
          5- decoding   6- action
          7- feedback to the sender

20. Which one of the following BEST expresses the main theme of the passage?   20._____

    A. Different individuals have the same perceptions regarding the meaning of words.
    B. An understanding of the steps in the communication process may achieve better
       communication.
    C. Receivers play a passive role in the communication process.
    D. Senders should not communicate with receivers who transmit feedback.

21. The above passage implies that a receiver does NOT function properly when he   21._____

    A. transmits feedback   B. files the information
    C. is a poor listener   D. asks for more information

22. Which of the following, according to the above passage, is included in the SECOND step   22._____
of the communication process?

    A. Selecting the appropriate media to be used in transmission
    B. Formulation of the intended content of the message
    C. Using appropriate media to respond to the receiver's feedback
    D. Transmitting the message through selected channels in the organization

23. The above passage implies that the *decoding process* is MOST NEARLY the reverse of   23._____
the _____ process.

    A. transmission   B. receiving
    C. feedback   D. encoding

Questions 24-27.

DIRECTIONS: Answer Questions 24 through 27 SOLELY on the basis of the information
                       given in the paragraph below.

A personnel researcher has at his disposal various approaches for obtaining information, analyzing it, and arriving at conclusions that have value in predicting and affecting the behavior of people at work. The type of method to be used depends on such factors as the nature of the research problem, the available data, and the attitudes of those people being studied to the various kinds of approaches. While the experimental approach, with its use of control groups, is the most refined type of study, there are others that are often found useful in personnel research. Surveys, in which the researcher obtains facts on a problem from a variety of sources, are employed in research on wages, fringe benefits, and labor relations. Historical studies are used to trace the development of problems in order to understand them better and to isolate possible causative factors. Case studies are generally developed to explore all the details of a particular problem that is representative of other similar problems. A researcher chooses the most appropriate form of study for the problem he is investigating. He should recognize, however, that the experimental method, commonly referred to as the scientific method, if used validly and reliably, gives the most conclusive results.

24. The above statement discusses several approaches used to obtain information on partic-   24._____
ular problems.
Which of the following may be MOST reasonably concluded from the paragraph?
A(n)

    A. historical study cannot determine causative factors
    B. survey is often used in research on fringe benefits
    C. case study is usually used to explore a problem that is unique and unrelated to
        other problems
    D. experimental study is used when the scientific approach to a problem fails

25. According to the above paragraph, all of the following are factors that may determine the   25._____
type of approach a researcher uses EXCEPT

    A. the attitudes of people toward being used in control groups
    B. the number of available sources
    C. his desire to isolate possible causative factors
    D. the degree of accuracy he requires

26. The words *scientific method,* used in the last sentence of the paragraph, refer to a type of study which, according to the paragraph,   26.____

    A. uses a variety of sources
    B. traces the development of problems
    C. uses control groups
    D. analyzes the details of a representative problem

27. Which of the following can be MOST reasonably concluded from the above paragraph?   27.____
In obtaining and analyzing information on a particular problem, a researcher employs the method which is the

    A. most accurate   B. most suitable
    C. least expensive   D. least time-consuming

Questions 28-31.

DIRECTIONS: The graph below indicates at 5-year intervals the number of citations issued for various offenses from the year 1990 to the year 2010. Answer Questions 28 through 31 according to the information given in this graph.

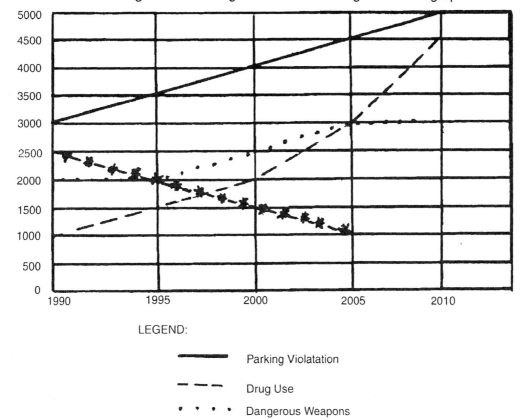

LEGEND:

———— Parking Violatation

– – – Drug Use

• • • • Dangerous Weapons

Improper Dress

28. Over the 20-year period, which offense shows an AVERAGE rate of increase of more than 150 citations per year?   28.____

    A. Parking Violations   B. Dangerous Weapons
    C. Drug Use   D. None of the above

29. Over the 20-year period, which offense shows a CONSTANT rate of increase or decrease?
    29.____

    A. Parking Violations   B. Drug Use
    C. Dangerous Weapons   D. Improper Dress

30. Which offense shows a TOTAL INCREASE OR DECREASE of 50% for the full 20-year period?
    30.____

    A. Parking Violations   B. Drug Use
    C. Dangerous Weapons   D. Improper Dress

31. The percentage increase in total citations issued from 1995 to 2000 is MOST NEARLY
    31.____

    A. 7%   B. 11%   C. 21%   D. 41%

Questions 32-35.

DIRECTIONS: The chart below shows the annual average number of administrative actions completed for the four divisions of a bureau. Assume that the figures remain stable from year to year.

Answer Questions 32 through 35 SOLELY on the basis of information given in the chart.

Administrative Actions	DIVISIONS				
	W	X	Y	Z	Totals
Telephone Inquiries Answered	8,000	6,800	7,500	4,800	27,100
Interviews Conducted	500	630	550	500	2,180
Applications Processed	15,000	18,000	14,500	9,500	57,000
Letters Typed	2,500	4,400	4,350	3,250	14,500
Reports Completed	200	250	100	50	600
Totals	26,200	30,080	27,000	18,100	101,380

32. In which division is the number of Applications Processed the GREATEST percentage of the total Administrative Actions for that division?
    32.____

    A. W   B. X   C. Y   D. Z

33. The bureau chief is considering a plan that would consolidate the typing of letters in a separate unit. This unit would be responsible for the typing of letters for all divisions in which the number of letters typed exceeds 15% of the total number of Administrative Actions. Under this plan, which of the following divisions would CONTINUE to type its own letters?
    33.____

    A. W and X   B. W, X, and Y
    C. X and Y   D. X and Z

34. The setting up of a central information service that would be capable of answering 25% of the whole bureau's telephone inquiries is under consideration. Under such a plan, the divisions would gain for other activities that time previously spent on telephone inquiries. Approximately how much total time would such a service gain for all four divisions if it requires 5 minutes to answer the average telephone inquiry? _____ hours.

34._____

    A. 500   B. 515   C. 565   D. 585

35. Assume that the rate of production shown in the table can be projected as accurate for the coming year and that monthly output is constant for each type of administrative action within a division. Division Y is scheduled to work exclusively on a 4-month long special project during that year. During the period of the project, Division Y's regular workload will be divided evenly among the remaining divisions.
Using the figures in the table, what would be MOST NEARLY the percentage increase in the total Administrative Actions completed by Division Z for the year?

35._____

    A. 8%   B. 16%   C. 25%   D. 50%

36. You have conducted a traffic survey at 10 two-lane bridges and find the traffic between 4:30 and 5:30 P.M. averages 665 cars per bridge that hour. You can't find the tabulation sheet for Bridge #7, but you know that 6066 cars were counted at the other 9 bridges. Determine from this how many must have been counted at Bridge #7.

36._____

    A. 584   B. 674   C. 665   D. 607

37. You pay temporary help $11.20 per hour and regular employees $12.00 per hour. Your workload is temporarily heavy, so you need 20 hours of extra regular employees' time to catch up. If you do this on overtime, you must pay time-and-a-half. If you use temporary help, it takes 25% more time to do the job.
What is the difference in cost between the two alternatives?

37._____

    A. $20 more for temporary   B. $40 more for temporary
    C. $80 more for regular   D. $136 more for regular

38. An experienced clerk can process the mailing of annual forms in 9 days. A new clerk takes 14 days to process them.
If they work together, how many days MOST NEARLY will it take to do the processing?

38._____

    A. $4\frac{1}{2}$ B. $5\frac{1}{2}$ C. $6\frac{1}{2}$ D. 7

39. A certain administrative aide is usually able to successfully handle 27% of all telephone inquiries without assistance. In a particular month, he receives 1200 inquiries and handles 340 of them successfully on his own. How many more inquiries has he handled successfully in that month than would have been expected of him based on his usual rate?

39._____

    A. 10   B. 16   C. 24   D. 44

40. Suppose that on a scaled drawing of an office building floor, 1/2 inch represents three feet of actual floor dimensions.
A floor which is, in fact, 75 feet wide and 132 feet long has which of the following dimensions on this scaled drawing? _____ inches wide and _____ inches long.

40._____

    A. 9.5; 20.5   B. 12.5; 22
    C. 17; 32   D. 25; 44

41. In a division of clerks and stenographers, 15 people are currently employed, 20% of whom are stenographers.
If management plans are to maintain the current number of stenographers, but to increase the clerical staff to the point where 12% of the total staff are stenographers, what is the MAXIMUM number of additional clerks that should be hired to meet these plans?

    A. 3   B. 8   C. 10   D. 12

41.____

42. Suppose that a certain agency had a 2005 budget of $1,100,500. The 2006 budget was 7% higher than that of 2005, and the 2007 budget was 8% higher than that of 2006. Of the following, which one is MOST NEARLY that agency's budget for 2007?

    A. $1,117,624   B. $1,261,737
    C. $1,265,575   D. $1,271,738

42.____

Question's 43-50.

DIRECTIONS: Your office keeps a file card record of the work assignments for all the employees in a certain bureau. On each card is the employee's name, a work assignment code number, and the date of this assignment. In this filing system, the employee's name is filed alphabetically, the work assignment code is filed numerically, and the date of the assignment is filed chronologically (earliest date first).

Each of Questions 43 through 50 represents five cards to be filed, numbered (1) through (5) shown in Column I. Each card is made up of the employee's name, a work assignment code number shown in parentheses, and the date of this assignment. The cards are to be filed according to the following rules:

First: File in alphabetical order;

Second: When two or more cards have the same employee's name, file according to the work assignment number, beginning with the lowest number.

Third: When two or more cards have the same employee's name and same assignment number, file according to the assignment date beginning with earliest date.

Column II shows the cards arranged in four different orders. Pick the answer (A, B, C, or D) in Column II which shows the cards arranged correctly according to the above filing rules.

SAMPLE QUESTION:

Column I				Column II				
(1) Cluney	(486503)	6/17/07	A.	2,	3,	4,	1,	5
(2) Roster	(246611)	5/10/06	B.	2,	5,	1,	3,	4
(3) Altool	(711433)	10/15/07	C.	3,	2,	1,	4,	5
(4) Cluney	(527610)	12/18/06	D.	3,	5,	1,	4,	2
(5) Cluney	(486500)	4/8/07						

The correct way to file the cards is:

(3) Altool	(711433)	10/15/07
(5) Cluney	(486500)	4/8/07
(1) Cluney	(486503)	6/17/07
(4) Cluney	(527610)	12/18/06
(2) Roster	(246611)	5/10/06

The correct filing order is shown by the numbers in front of each name (3, 5, 1, 4, 2). The answer to the sample question is the letter in Column II in front of the numbers 3, 5, 1, 4, 2. This answer is D.

43.   43.____

		Column I			Column II				
(1)	Prichard	(013469)	4/6/06	A.	5,	4,	3,	2,	1
(2)	Parks	(678941)	2/7/06	B.	1,	2,	5,	3,	4
(3)	Williams	(551467)	3/6/05	C.	2,	1,	5,	3,	4
(4)	Wilson	(551466)	8/9/02	D.	1,	5,	4,	3,	2
(5)	Stanhope	(300014)	8/9/02						

44.   44.____

(1)	Ridgeway	(623809)	8/11/06	A.	5,	1,	3,	4,	2
(2)	Travers	(305439)	4/5/02	B.	5,	1,	3,	2,	4
(3)	Tayler	(818134)	7/5/03	C.	1,	5,	3,	2,	4
(4)	Travers	(305349)	5/6/05	D.	1,	5,	4,	2,	3
(5)	Ridgeway	(623089)	10/9/06						

45.   45.____

(1)	Jaffe	(384737)	2/19/06	A.	3,	5,	2,	4,	1
(2)	Inez	(859176)	8/8/07	B.	3,	5,	2,	1,	4
(3)	Ingrahm	(946460)	8/6/04	C.	2,	3,	5,	1,	4
(4)	Karp	(256146)	5/5/05	D.	2,	3,	5,	4,	1
(5)	Ingrahm	(946460)	6/4/05						

46.   46.____

(1)	Marrano	(369421)	7/24/04	A.	1,	5,	3,	4,	2
(2)	Marks	(652910)	2/23/06	B.	3,	5,	4,	2,	1
(3)	Netto	(556772)	3/10/07	C.	2,	4,	1,	5,	3
(4)	Marks	(652901)	2/17/07	D.	4,	2,	1,	5,	3
(5)	Netto	(556772)	6/17/05						

47.   47.____

(1)	Abernathy	(712467)	6/23/05	A.	5,	3,	1,	2,	4
(2)	Acevedo	(680262)	6/23/03	B.	5,	4,	2,	3,	1
(3)	Aaron	(967647)	1/17/04	C.	1,	3,	5,	2,	4
(4)	Acevedo	(680622)	5/14/02	D.	2,	4,	1,	5,	3
(5)	Aaron	(967647)	4/1/00						

48.   48.____

(1)	Simon	(645219)	8/19/05	A.	4,	1,	2,	5,	3
(2)	Simon	(645219)	9/2/03	B.	4,	5,	2,	1,	3
(3)	Simons	(645218)	7/7/05	C.	3,	5,	2,	1,	4
(4)	Simms	(646439)	10/12/06	D.	5,	1,	2,	3,	4
(5)	Simon	(645219)	10/16/02						

49.   49.____

(1)	Rappaport	(312230)	6/11/06	A.	4,	3,	1,	2,	5
(2)	Rascio	(777510)	2/9/05	B.	4,	3,	1,	5,	2
(3)	Rappaport	(312230)	7/3/02	C.	3,	4,	1,	5,	2
(4)	Rapaport	(312330)	9/6/05	D.	5,	2,	4,	3,	1
(5)	Rascio	(777501)	7/7/05						

50.   50._____

(1)	Johnson	(843250)	6/8/02	A.	1,	3,	2,	4,	5
(2)	Johnson	(843205)	4/3/05	B.	1,	3,	2,	5,	4
(3)	Johnson	(843205)	8/6/02	C.	3,	2,	1,	4,	5
(4)	Johnson	(843602)	3/8/06	D.	3,	2,	1,	5,	4
(5)	Johnson	(843602)	8/3/05						

KEY (CORRECT ANSWERS)

1.	D	11.	B	21.	C	31.	B	41.	C
2.	A	12.	A	22.	A	32.	B	42.	D
3.	C	13.	C	23.	D	33.	A	43.	C
4.	C	14.	C	24.	B	34.	C	44.	A
5.	C	15.	A	25.	D	35.	B	45.	C
6.	A	16.	D	26.	C	36.	A	46.	D
7.	B	17.	A	27.	B	37.	C	47.	A
8.	C	18.	C	28.	C	38.	B	48.	B
9.	D	19.	D	29.	A	39.	B	49.	B
10.	A	20.	B	30.	C	40.	B	50.	D

EXAMINATION SECTION

DIRECTIONS: Each question or incomplete statement is followed by several suggested answers or completions. Select the one that BEST answers the question or completes the statement. *PRINT THE LETTER OF THE CORRECT ANSWER IN THE SPACE AT THE RIGHT.*

Questions 1-5.

DIRECTIONS: Each of Questions 1 through 5 consists of a passage which contains one word that is incorrectly used because it is not in keeping with the meaning that the quotation is evidently intended to convey. Determine which word is incorrectly used. Select from the choices lettered A, B, C, and D the word which, when substituted for the incorrectly used word, would BEST help to convey the meaning of the quotation.

1. Whatever the method, the necessity to keep up with the dynamics of an organization is the point on which many classification plans go awry. The budgetary approach to "positions," for example, often leads to using for recruitment and pay purposes a position authorized many years earlier for quite a different purpose than currently contemplated – making perhaps the title, the class, and the qualifications required inappropriate to the current need. This happens because executives overlook the stability that takes place in job duties and fail to reread an initial description of the job before saying, as they scan a list of titles, "We should fill this position right away." Once a classification plan is adopted, it is pointless to do anything less than provide for continuous, painstaking maintenance on a current basis, else once different positions that have actually become similar to each other remain in different classes, and some former cognates that have become quite different continue in the same class. Such a program often seems expensive. But to stint too much on this out-of-pocket cost may create still higher hidden costs growing out of lowered morale, poor production, delayed operating programs, excessive pay for simple work, and low pay for responsible work (resulting in poorly qualified executives and professional men) – all normal concomitants of inadequate, hasty, or out-of-date classification.

    A. evolution   B. personnel
    C. disapproved   D. forward

1.____

2. At first sight, it may seem that there is little or no difference between the usableness of a manual and the degree of its use. But there is a difference. A manual may have all the qualities which make up the usable manual and still not be used. Take this instance as an example: Suppose you have a satisfactory manual but issue instructions from day to day through the avenue of bulletins, memorandums, and other informational releases. Which will the employee use, the manual or the bulletin which passes over his desk? He will, of course, use the latter, for some obsolete material will not be contained in this manual. Here we have a theoretically usable manual which is unused because of the other avenues by which procedural information may be issued.

    A. countermand   B. discard
    C. intentional   D. worthwhile

2.____

3. By reconcentrating control over its operations in a central headquarters, a firm is able to extend the influence of automation to many, if not all, of its functions – from inventory and payroll to production, sales, and personnel. In so doing, businesses freeze all the elements of the corporate function in their relationship to one another and to the overall objectives of the firm. From this total systems concept, companies learn that computers can accomplish much more than clerical and accounting jobs. Their capabilities can be tapped to perform the traditional applications (payroll processing, inventory control, accounts payable, and accounts receivable) as well as newer applications such as spotting deviations from planned programs (exception reporting), adjusting planning schedules, forecasting business trends, simulating market conditions, and solving production problems. Since the office manager is a manager of information and each of these applications revolves around the processing of data, he must take an active role in studying and improving the system under his care.

3.____

   A. maintaining
   C. limited
   B. inclusion
   D. visualize

4. In addition to the formal and acceptance theories of the source of authority, although perhaps more closely related to the latter, is the belief that authority is generated by personal qualifies of technical competence. Under this heading is the individual who has made, in effect, subordinates of others through sheer force of personality, and the engineer or economist who exerts influence by furnishing answers or sound advice. These may have no actual organizational authority, yet their advice may be so eagerly sought and so unerringly followed that it appears to carry the weight of an order.
   But, above all, one cannot discount the importance of formal authority with its institutional foundations. Buttressed by the qualities of leadership implicit in the acceptance theory, formal authority is basic to the managerial job. Once abrogated, it may be delegated or withheld, used or misused, and be effective in capable hands or be ineffective in inept hands.

4.____

   A. selected
   C. limited
   B. delegation
   D. possessed

5. Since managerial operations in organizing, staffing, directing, and controlling are designed to support the accomplishment of enterprise objectives, planning logically precedes the execution of all other managerial functions. Although all the functions intermesh in practice, planning is unique in that it establishes the objectives necessary for all group effort. Besides, plans must be made to accomplish these objectives before the manager knows what kind of organization relationships and personal qualifications are needed, along which course subordinates are to be directed, and what kind of control is to be applied. And, of course, each of the other managerial functions must be planned if they are to be effective.
   Planning and control are inseparable – the Siamese twins of management. Unplanned action cannot be controlled, for control involves keeping activities on course by correcting deviations from plans. Any attempt to control without plans would be meaningless, since there is no way anyone can tell whether he is going where he wants to go – the task of control – unless first he knows where he wants to go – the task of planning. Plans thus preclude the standards of control.

5.____

   A. coordinating
   C. furnish
   B. individual
   D. follow

Questions 6-7.

DIRECTIONS: Answer Questions 6 and 7 SOLELY on the basis of information given in the following paragraph.

In-basket tests are often used to assess managerial potential. The exercise consists of a set of papers that would be likely to be found in the in-basket of an administrator or manager at any given time, and requires the individuals participating in the examination to indicate how they would dispose of each item found in the in-basket. In order to handle the in-basket effectively, they must successfully manage their time, refer and assign some work to subordinates, juggle potentially conflicting appointments and meetings, and arrange for follow-up of problems generated by the items in the in-basket. In other words, the in-basket test is attempting to evaluate the participants' abilities to organize their work, set priorities, delegate, control, and make decisions.

6. According to the above paragraph, to succeed in an in-basket test, an administrator must   6.____

   A. be able to read very quickly
   B. have a great deal of technical knowledge
   C. know when to delegate work
   D. arrange a lot of appointments and meetings

7. According to the above paragraph, all of the following abilities are indications of managerial potential EXCEPT the ability to   7.____

   A. organize and control   B. manage time
   C. write effective reports   D. make appropriate decisions

Questions 8-9.

DIRECTIONS: Answer Questions 8 and 9 SOLELY on the basis of information given in the following paragraph.

One of the biggest mistakes of government executives with substantial supervisory responsibility is failing to make careful appraisals of performance during employee probationary periods. Many a later headache could have been avoided by prompt and full appraisal during the early months of an employee's assignment. There is not much more to say about this except to emphasize the common prevalence of this oversight, and to underscore that for its consequences, which are many and sad, the offending managers have no one to blame but themselves.

8. According to the above passage, probationary periods are   8.____

   A. a mistake, and should not be used by supervisors with large responsibilities
   B. not used properly by government executives
   C. used only for those with supervisory responsibility
   D. the consequence of management mistakes

4

9. The one of the following conclusions that can MOST appropriately be drawn from the above passage is that

    A. management's failure to appraise employees during their probationary period is a common occurrence
    B. there is not much to say about probationary periods, because they are unimportant
    C. managers should blame employees for failing to use their probationary periods properly
    D. probationary periods are a headache to most managers

9.____

Questions 10-12.

DIRECTIONS: Answer Questions 10 through 12 SOLELY on the basis of information given in the following paragraph.

The common sense character of the merit system seems so natural to most Americans that many people wonder why it should ever have been inoperative. After all, the American economic system, the most phenomenal the world has ever known, is also founded on a rugged selective process which emphasizes the personal qualities of capacity, industriousness, and productivity. The criteria may not have always been appropriate and competition has not always been fair, but competition there was, and the responsibilities and the rewards – with exceptions, of course – have gone to those who could measure up in terms of intelligence, knowledge, or perseverance. This has been true not only in the economic area, in the money-making process, but also in achievement in the professions and other walks of life.

10. According to the above paragraph, economic rewards in the United States have

    A. always been based on appropriate, fair criteria
    B. only recently been based on a competitive system
    C. not gone to people who compete too ruggedly
    D. usually gone to those people with intelligence, knowledge, and perseverance

10.____

11. According to the above passage, a merit system is

    A. an unfair criterion on which to base rewards
    B. unnatural to anyone who is not American
    C. based only on common sense
    D. based on the same principles as the American economic system

11.____

12. According to the above passage, it is MOST accurate to say that

    A. the United States has always had a civil service merit system
    B. civil service employees are very rugged
    C. the American economic system has always been based on a merit objective
    D. competition is unique to the American way of life

12.____

Questions 13-15.

DIRECTIONS: The management study of employee absence due to sickness is an effective tool in planning. Answer Questions 13 through 15 SOLELY on the data given below.

Number of days absent per worker (sickness)	1	2	3	4	5	6	7	8 or Over
Number of workers	76	23	6	3	1	0	1	0

Total Number of Workers: 400
Period Covered: January 1 - December 31

13. The total number of man days lost due to illness was   13._____

    A. 110   B. 137   C. 144   D. 164

14. What percent of the workers had 4 or more days absence due to sickness?   14._____

    A. .25%   B. 2.5%   C. 1.25%   D. 12.5%

15. Of the 400 workers studied, the number who lost no days due to sickness was   15._____

    A. 190   B. 236   C. 290   D. 346

Questions 16-18.

DIRECTIONS: In the graph below, the lines labeled "A" and "B" represent the cumulative progress in the work of two file clerks, each of whom was given 500 consecutively numbered applications to file in the proper cabinets over a five-day work week. Answer Questions 16 through 18 SOLELY upon the data provided in the graph.

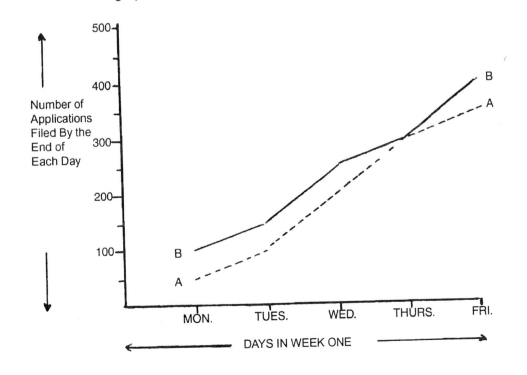

16. The day during which the LARGEST number of applications was filed by both clerks was   16.____

    A. Monday   B. Tuesday   C. Wednesday   D. Friday

17. At the end of the second day, the percentage of applications STILL to be filed was   17.____

    A. 25%   B. 50%   C. 66%   D. 75%

18. Assuming that the production pattern is the same the following week as the week shown   18.____
in the chart, the day on which the file clerks will FINISH this assignment will be

    A. Monday   B. Tuesday   C. Wednesday   D. Friday

Questions 19-21.

DIRECTIONS: The following chart shows the differences between the rates of production of employees in Department D in 1996 and 2006. Answer Questions 19 through 21 SOLELY on the basis of the information given in the chart.

Number of Employees Producing Work-Units Within Range in 1996	Number of Work-Units Produced	Number of Employees Producing Work-Units Within Range in 2006
7	500 - 1000	4
14	1001 - 1500	11
26	1501 - 2000	28
22	2001 - 2500	36
17	2501 - 3000	39
10	3001 - 3500	23
4	3501 - 4000	9

19. Assuming that within each range of work-units produced the average production was at   19.____
the mid-point at that range (e.g., category 500 - 1000 = 750), then the AVERAGE number
of work-units produced per employee in 1996 fell into the range

    A. 1001 - 1500   B. 1501 - 2000
    C. 2001 - 2500   D. 2501 - 3000

20. The ratio of the number of employees producing more than 2000 work-units in 1996 to   20.____
the number of employees producing more than 2000 work-units in 2006 is *most nearly*

    A. 1:2   B. 2:3   C. 3:4   D. 4:5

21. In Department D, which of the following were GREATER in 2006 than in 1996?   21.____
    I.   Total number of employees
    II. Total number of work-units produced
    III. Number of employees producing 2000 or fewer work-units
The CORRECT answer is:

    A. I, II, III   B. I, II
    C. I, III   D. II, III

22. Unit S's production fluctuated substantially from one year to another. In 2004, Unit S's production was 100% greater than in 2003. In 2005, production decreased by 25% from 2004. In 2006, Unit S's production was 10% greater than in 2005.
On the basis of this information, it is CORRECT to conclude that Unit S's production in 2006 exceeded Unit S's production in 2003 by

    A. 65%   B. 85%   C. 95%   D. 135%

22.____

23. Agency "X" is moving into a new building. It has 1500 employees presently on its staff and does not contemplate much variance from this level. The new building contains 100 available offices, each with a maximum capacity of 30 employees. It has been decided that only 2/3 of the maximum capacity of each office will be utilized. The TOTAL number of offices that will be occupied by Agency "X" is

    A. 30   B. 66   C. 75   D. 90

23.____

24. One typist completes a form letter every 5 minutes and another typist completes one every 6 minutes.
If the two typists start together, they will again start typing new letters simultaneously _____ minutes later and will have completed ____ letters by that time.

    A. 11; 30   B. 12; 24   C. 24; 12   D. 30; 11

24.____

25. During one week, a machine operator produces 10 fewer pages per hour of work than he usually does. If it ordinarily takes him six hours to produce a 300-page report, it will take him____hours LONGER to produce that same 300-page report during the week when he produces MORE slowly.

    A. $1\frac{1}{2}$ B. $1\frac{2}{3}$ C. 2   D. $2\frac{3}{4}$

25.____

KEY (CORRECT ANSWERS)

<u>Incorrect Words</u>

1.	A	stability
2.	D	obsolete
3.	D	freeze
4.	D	abrogated
5.	C	preclude

6.	C	16.	C
7.	C	17.	D
8.	B	18.	B
9.	A	19.	C
10.	D	20.	A
11.	D	21.	B
12.	C	22.	A
13.	D	23.	C
14.	C	24.	D
15.	C	25.	A

———

EXAMINATION SECTION
TEST 1

DIRECTIONS: Each question or incomplete statement is followed by several suggested answers or completions. Select the one that BEST answers the question or completes the statement. *PRINT THE LETTER OF THE CORRECT ANSWER IN THE SPACE AT THE RIGHT.*

1. As a supervisor in a bureau, you have been asked by the head of the bureau to recom-   1._____
   mend whether or not the work of the bureau requires an increase in the permanent staff
   of the bureau.
   Of the following questions, the one whose answer would MOST likely assist you in
   making your recommendation is: Are

   A. some permanent employees working irregular hours because they occasionally
      work overtime?
   B. the present permanent employees satisfied with their work assignments?
   C. temporary employees hired to handle seasonal fluctuations in work load?
   D. the present permanent employees keeping the work of the bureau current?

2. In making job assignments to his subordinates, a supervisor should follow the principle   2._____
   that each individual GENERALLY is capable of

   A. performing one type of work well and less capable of performing other types well
   B. learning to perform a wide variety of different types of work
   C. performing best the type of work in which he has had experience
   D. learning to perform any type of work in which he is given training

3. Assume that you are the supervisor of a large number of clerks in a unit in a city agency.   3._____
   Your unit has just been given an important assignment which must be completed a week
   from now. You know that, henceforth, your unit will be given this assignment every six
   months.
   You or any one of your subordinates who has been properly instructed can complete
   this assignment in one day. This assignment is of a routine type which is ordinarily
   handled by clerks. There is enough time for you to train one of your subordinates to
   handle the assignment and then have him do it. However, it would take twice as much
   time for you to take this course of action as it would for you to do the assignment yourself. The one of the following courses of action which you should take in this situation
   is to

   A. do the assignment yourself as soon as possible without discussing it with any of
      your subordinates at this time
   B. do the assignment yourself and then train one of your subordinates to handle it in
      the future
   C. give the assignment to one of your subordinates after training him to handle it
   D. train each of your subordinates to do the assignment on a rotating basis after you
      have done it yourself the first time

4. You are in charge of an office in which each member of the staff has a different set of duties, although each has the same title. No member of the staff can perform the duties of any other member of the staff without first receiving extensive training. Assume that it is necessary for one member of the staff to take on, in addition to his regular work, an assignment which any member of the staff is capable of carrying out.
The one of the following considerations which would have the MOST weight in determining which staff member is to be given the additional assignment is the

    A. quality of the work performed by the individual members of the staff
    B. time consumed by individual members of the staff in performing their work
    C. level of difficulty of the duties being performed by individual members of the staff
    D. relative importance of the duties being performed by individual members of the staff

5. The one of the following causes of clerical error which is usually considered to be LEAST attributable to faulty supervision or inefficient management is

    A. inability to carry out instructions
    B. too much work to do
    C. an inappropriate recordkeeping system
    D. continual interruptions

6. Suppose you are in charge of a large unit in which all of the clerical staff perform similar tasks.
In evaluating the relative accuracy of the clerks, the clerk who should be considered to be the LEAST accurate is the one

    A. whose errors result in the greatest financial loss
    B. whose errors cost the most to locate
    C. who makes the greatest percentage of errors in his work
    D. who makes the greatest number of errors in the unit

7. Assume that under a proposed procedure for handling employee grievances in a public agency, the first step to be taken is for the aggrieved employee to submit his grievance as soon as it arises to a grievance board set up to hear all employee grievances in the agency. The board, which is to consist of representatives of management and of rank and file employees, is to consider the grievance, obtain all necessary pertinent information, and then render a decision on the matter. Thus, the first-line supervisor would not be involved in the settlement of any of his subordinates' grievances except when asked by the board to submit information.
This proposed procedure would be generally UNDESIRABLE chiefly because the

    A. board may become a bottleneck to delay the prompt disposition of grievances
    B. aggrieved employees and their supervisors have not been first given the opportunity to resolve the grievances themselves
    C. employees would be likely to submit imaginary, as well as real, grievances to the board
    D. board will lack first-hand, personal knowledge of the factors involved in grievances

8. Sometimes jobs in private organizations and public agencies are broken down so as to permit a high degree of job specialization.
Of the following, an IMPORTANT effect of a high degree of job specialization in a public agency is that employees performing

A. highly specialized jobs may not be readily transferable to other jobs in the agency
B. similar duties may require closer supervision than employees performing unrelated functions
C. specialized duties can be held responsible for their work to a greater extent than can employees performing a wide variety of functions
D. specialized duties will tend to cooperate readily with employees performing other types of specialized duties

9. Assume that you are the supervisor of a clerical unit in an agency. One of your subordinates violates a rule of the agency, a violation which requires that the employee be suspended from his work for one day. The violated rule is one that you have found to be unduly strict, and you have recommended to the management of the agency that the rule be changed or abolished. The management has been considering your recommendation but has not yet reached a decision on the matter.
In these circumstances, you should

   9._____

A. not initiate disciplinary action but, instead, explain to the employee that the rule may be Changed shortly
B. delay disciplinary action on the violation until the management has reached a decision on changing the rule
C. modify the disciplinary action by reprimanding the employee and informing him that further action may be taken when the management has reached a decision on changing the rule
D. initiate the prescribed disciplinary action without commenting on the strictness of the rule or on your recommendation

10. Assume that a supervisor praises his subordinates for satisfactory aspects of their work only when he is about to criticize them for unsatisfactory aspects of their work.
Such a practice is UNDESIRABLE primarily because

   10._____

A. his subordinates may expect to be praised for their work even if it is unsatisfactory
B. praising his subordinates for some aspects of their work while criticizing other aspects will weaken the effects of the criticisms
C. his subordinates would be more receptive to criticism if it were followed by praise
D. his subordinates may come to disregard praise and wait for criticism to be given

11. The one of the following which would be the BEST reason for an agency to eliminate a procedure for obtaining and recording certain information is that

   11._____

A. it is no longer legally required to obtain the information
B. there is no advantage in obtaining the information
C. the information could be compiled on the basis of other information available
D. the information obtained is sometimes incorrect

12. In determining the type and number of records to be kept in an agency, it is important to recognize that records are of value PRIMARILY as

   12._____

A. raw material to be used in statistical analysis
B. sources of information about the agency's activities
C. by-products of the activities carried on by the agency
D. data for evaluating the effectiveness of the agency

13. Aside from requirements imposed by authority, the frequency with which reports are sub- 13.____
mitted or the length of the interval which they cover should depend PRINCIPALLY on the

    A. availability of the data to be included in the reports
    B. amount of time required to prepare the reports
    C. extent of the variations in the data with the passage of time
    D. degree of comprehensiveness required in the reports

14. Organizations that occupy large, general, open-area offices sometimes consider it desir- 14.____
able to build private offices for the supervisors of large bureaus.
The one of the following which is generally NOT considered to be a justification of the
use of private offices is that they

    A. lend prestige to the person occupying the office
    B. provide facilities for private conferences
    C. achieve the maximum use of office space
    D. provide facilities for performing work requiring a high degree of concentration

15. The LEAST important factor to be considered in planning the layout of an office is the 15.____

    A. relative importance of the different types of work to be done
    B. convenience with which communication can be achieved
    C. functional relationships of the activities of the office
    D. necessity for screening confidential activities from unauthorized persons

16. The one of the following which is generally considered to be the CHIEF advantage of 16.____
using data processing equipment in modern offices is to

    A. facilitate the use of a wide variety of sources of information
    B. supply management with current information quickly
    C. provide uniformity in the processing and reporting of information
    D. broaden the area in which management decisions can be made

17. In the box design of office forms, the spaces in which information is to be entered are 17.____
arranged in boxes containing captions.
Of the following, the one which is generally NOT considered to be an acceptable rule in
employing box design is that

    A. space should be allowed for the lengthiest anticipated entry in a box
    B. the caption should be located in the upper left corner of the box
    C. the boxes on a form should be of the same size and shape
    D. boxes should be aligned vertically whenever possible

18. As a management tool, the work count would generally be of LEAST assistance to a unit 18.____
supervisor in

    A. scheduling the work of his unit
    B. locating bottlenecks in the work of his unit
    C. ascertaining the number of subordinates he needs
    D. tracing the flow of work in the unit

19. Of the following, the FIRST step that should be taken in a forms simplification program is 19.____
to make a

A. detailed analysis of the items found on current forms
B. study of the amount of use made of existing forms
C. survey of the amount of each kind of form on hand
D. survey of the characteristics of the more effective forms in use

20. The work-distribution chart is a valuable tool for an office supervisor to use in conducting work'simplification programs.   20.____
Of the following questions, the one which a work-distribution chart would generally be LEAST useful in answering is:

A. What activities take the most time?
B. Are the employees doing many unrelated tasks?
C. Is work being distributed evenly among the employees?
D. Are activities being performed in proper sequence?

21. Assume that, as a supervisor, you conduct, from time to time, work-performance studies   21.____
in various sections of your agency. The units of measurement used in any study depend on the particular study and may be number of letters typed, number of papers filed, or other suitable units.
It is MOST important that the units of measurement to be used in a study conform to the units used in similar past studies when the

A. units of measurement to be used in the study cannot be defined sharply
B. units of measurement used in past studies were satisfactory
C. results of the study are to be compared with those of past studies
D. results of the study are to be used for the same purpose as were those of past studies

22. As it is used in auditing, an internal check is a   22.____

A. procedure which is designed to guard against fraud
B. periodic audit by a public accounting firm to verify the accuracy of the internal transactions of an organization
C. document transferring funds from one section to another within an organization
D. practice of checking documents twice before they are transmitted outside an organization

23. Of the following, the one which can LEAST be considered to be a proper function of an   23.____
accounting system is to

A. indicate the need to curtail expenditures
B. provide information for future fiscal programs
C. record the expenditure of funds from special appropriations
D. suggest methods to expedite the collection of revenues

24. Assume that a new unit is to be established in an agency. The unit is to compile and tab-   24.____
ulate data so that it will be of the greatest usefulness to the high-level administrators in the agency in making administrative decisions. In planning the organization of this unit, the question that should be answered FIRST is:

A. What interpretations are likely to be made of the data by the high-level administrators in making decisions?
B. At what point in the decision-making process will it be most useful to inject the data?
C. What types of data will be required by high-level administrators in making decisions?
D. What criteria will the high-level administrators use to evaluate the decisions they make?

25. The one of the following which is the CHIEF limitation of the organization chart as it is generally used in business and government is that the chart   25.____

A. engenders within incumbents feelings of rights to positions they occupy
B. reveals only formal authority relationships, omitting the informal ones
C. shows varying degrees of authority even though authority is not subject to such differentiation
D. presents organizational structure as it is rather than what it is supposed to be

26. The degree of decentralization that is effective and economical in an organization tends to vary INVERSELY with the   26.____

A. size of the organization
B. availability of adequate numbers of competent personnel
C. physical dispersion of the organization's activities
D. adequacy of the organization's communications system

27. The one of the following which usually can LEAST be considered to be an advantage of committees as they are generally used in government and business is that they   27.____

A. provide opportunities for reconciling varying points of view
B. promote coordination by the interchange of information among the members of the committee
C. act promptly in situations requiring immediate action
D. use group judgment to resolve questions requiring a wide range of experience

28. Managerial decentralization is defined as the decentralization of decision-making authority.
The degree of managerial decentralization in an organization varies INVERSELY with the   28.____

A. number of decisions made lower down the management hierarchy
B. importance of the decisions made lower down the management hierarchy
C. number of major organizational functions affected by decisions made at lower management levels
D. amount of review to which decisions made at lower management levels are subjected

29. Some policy-making commissions are composed of members who are appointed to overlapping terms.
Of the following, the CHIEF advantage of appointing members to overlapping terms in such commissions is that   29.____

A. continuity of policy is promoted
B. the likelihood of compromise policy decisions is reduced
C. responsibility for policy decisions can be fixed upon individual members
D. the likelihood of unanimity of opinion is increased

30. If a certain public agency with a fixed number of employees has a line organizational structure, then the width of the span of supervision is   30._____

A. inversely proportional to the length of the chain of command in the organization
B. directly proportional to the complexity of tasks performed in the organization
C. inversely proportional to the competence of the personnel in the organization
D. directly proportional to the number of levels of supervision existing in the organization

31. Mr. Brown is a supervisor in charge of a section of clerical employees in an agency. The   31._____
section consists of four units, each headed by a unit supervisor. From time to time, he
makes tours of his section for the purpose of maintaining contact with the rank and file
employees. During these tours, he discusses with these employees their work production, work methods, work problems, and other related topics. The information he obtains
in this manner is often incomplete or inaccurate. At meetings with the unit supervisors,
he questions them on the information acquired during his tours. The supervisors are
often unable to answer the questions immediately because they are based on incomplete or inaccurate information. When the supervisors ask that they be permitted to
accompany Mr. Brown on his tours and thus answer his questions on the spot, Mr. Brown
refuses, explaining that a rank and file employee might be reluctant to speak freely in the
presence of his supervisor. This situation may BEST be described as a violation of the
principle of organization called

A. span of control   B. delegation of authority
C. specialization of work   D. unity of command

Questions 32-36.

DIRECTIONS: Each of Questions 32 through 36 consists of a statement which contains one
word that is incorrectly used because it is not in keeping with the meaning that
the quotation is evidently intended to convey. For each of these questions, you
are to select the INCORRECTLY used word and substitute for it one of the
words lettered A, B, C, or D, which helps BEST to convey the meaning of the
statement.

32. There has developed in recent years an increasing awareness of the need to measure   32._____
the quality of management in all enterprises and to seek the principles that can serve as
a basis for this improvement.

A. growth   B. raise   C. efficiency   D. define

33. It is hardly an exaggeration to deny that the permanence, productivity, and humanity of   33._____
any industrial system depend upon its ability to utilize the positive and constructive
impulses of all who work and upon its ability to arouse and continue interest in the necessary activities.

A. develop   B. efficiency
C. state   D. inspirational

34. The selection of managers on the basis of technical knowledge alone seems to recognize that the essential characteristic of management is getting things done through others, thereby demanding skills that are essential in coordinating the activities of subordinates.

    A. training   B. fails
    C. organization   D. improving

34.____

35. Only when it is deliberate and when it is clearly understood what impressions the ease of communication will probably create in the minds of employees and subordinate management, should top management refrain from commenting on a subject that is of general concern.

    A. obvious   B. benefit   C. doubt   D. absence

35.____

36. Scientific planning of work requires careful analysis of facts and a precise plan of action for the whims and fancies of executives that often provide only a vague indication of the work to be done.

    A. substitutes   B. development
    C. preliminary   D. comprehensive

36.____

37. Within any single level of government, as a city or a state, the administrative authority may be concentrated or dispersed.
    Of the following plans of government, the one in which administrative authority would be dispersed the MOST is the _____ plan.

    A. mayor   B. mayor-council
    C. commission   D. city manager

37.____

38. In general, the courts may review a decision of an administrative agency with rule-making powers. However, the courts will usually REFUSE to review a decision of such an agency if the only question raised concerning the decision is whether or not the

    A. decision contravenes public policy
    B. agency has abused the powers conferred upon it
    C. decision deals with an issue which is within the jurisdiction of the agency
    D. agency has applied the same rules of evidence as are used in the courts

38.____

39. A legislature sometimes delegates rule-making powers to the administrators of a public agency.
    Of the following, the CHIEF advantage of such delegation is that

    A. the frequency with which the legality of the agency's rules is contested in court will be reduced
    B. the agency will have the flexibility to adjust to changing conditions and problems
    C. mistakes made by the administrators or the legislature in defining the scope of the agency's program may be easily corrected
    D. the legislature will not be required to approve the rules formulated by the agency

39.____

40. Some municipalities have delegated the functions of budget preparation and personnel selection to central agencies, thus removing these functions from operating departments.
    Of the following, the MOST important reason why municipalities have delegated these functions to central agencies is that

40.____

A. the performance of these functions presents problems that vary from one operating department to another
B. operating departments often lack sufficient funds to perform these functions adequately
C. the performance of these functions by a central agency produces more uniform policies than if these functions are performed by the operating departments
D. central agencies are not controlled as closely as are operating departments and so have greater freedom in formulating new policies and procedures to deal with difficult budget and personnel problems

41. Of the following, the MOST fundamental reason for the use of budgets in governmental administration is that budgets   41._____

A. minimize seasonal variations in work loads and expenditures of public agencies
B. facilitate decentralization of functions performed by public agencies
C. provide advance control on the expenditure of funds
D. establish valid bases for comparing present governmental activities with corresponding activities in previous periods

42. In some governmental jurisdictions, the chief executive prepares the budget for a fiscal   42._____
period and presents it to the legislative branch of government for adoption. In other jurisdictions, the legislative branch prepares and adopts the budget.
Preparation of the budget by the chief executive rather than by the legislative branch is

A. *desirable*, primarily because the chief executive is held largely accountable by the public for the results of fiscal operations and should, therefore, be the one to prepare the budget
B. *undesirable,* primarily because such a separation of the legislative and executive branches leads to the enactment of a budget that does not consider the overall needs of the government
C. *desirable,* primarily because the preparation of the budget by the chief executive limits legislative review and evaluation of operating programs
D. *undesirable,* primarily because responsibility for budget preparation should be placed in the branch that must eventually adopt the budget and appropriate the funds for it

43. The one of the following which is generally the FIRST step in the budget-making process   43._____
of a municipality that has a central budget agency is

A. determination of available sources of revenue within the municipality
B. establishment of tax rates at levels sufficient to achieve a balanced budget in the following fiscal period
C. evaluation by the central budget agency of the adequacy of the municipality's previous budgets
D. assembling by the central budget agency of the proposed expenditures of each agency in the municipality for the following fiscal period

44. It is advantageous for a municipality to issue serial bonds rather than sinking fund bonds   44._____
CHIEFLY because

A. an issue of serial bonds usually includes a wider range of maturity dates than does an issue of sinking fund bonds
B. appropriations set aside periodically to retire serial bonds as they fall due are more readily invested in long-term securities at favorable rates of interest than are appropriations earmarked for redemption of sinking fund bonds
C. serial bonds are sold at regular intervals while sinking fund bonds are issued as the need for funds arises
D. a greater variety of interest rates is usually offered in an issue of serial bonds than in an issue of sinking fund bonds

45. Studies conducted by the Regional Plan Association of the 22-county New York Metropolitan Region, comprising New York City and surrounding counties in New York, New Jersey, and Connecticut, have defined Manhattan, Brooklyn, Queens, the Bronx, and Hudson County in New Jersey as the *core*. Such studies have examined the per capita personal income of the core as a percent of the per capita personal income of the entire Region, and the population of the core as a percent of the total population of the entire Region.
These studies support the conclusion that, as a percent of the entire Region,   45.____

A. both population and per capita personal income in the core were higher in 1970 than in 1940
B. both population and per capita personal income in the core were lower in 1970 than in 1940
C. population was higher and per capita personal income was lower in the core in 1970 than in 1940
D. population was lower and per capita personal income was higher in the core in 1970 than in 1940

KEY (CORRECT ANSWERS)

1. D	11. B	21. C	31. D	41. C
2. B	12. B	22. A	32. B	42. A
3. C	13. C	23. D	33. C	43. D
4. B	14. C	24. C	34. B	44. A
5. A	15. A	25. B	35. D	45. B
6. C	16. B	26. D	36. A	
7. B	17. C	27. C	37. C	
8. A	18. D	28. D	38. D	
9. D	19. B	29. A	39. B	
10. D	20. D	30. A	40. C	

EXAMINATION SECTION
TEST 1

DIRECTIONS: Each question or incomplete statement is followed by several suggested answers or completions. Select the one that BEST answers the question or completes the statement. *PRINT THE LETTER OF THE CORRECT ANSWER IN THE SPACE AT THE RIGHT.*

1. In performing a systems study, the analyst may find it necessary to prepare an accurate record of working statistics from departmental forms, questionnaires, and information gleaned in interviews.
    Which one of the following statements dealing with the statistical part of the study is the MOST valid?

    A. The emphasis of every survey is data collection.
    B. Data should not be represented in narrative form.
    C. The statistical report should include the titles of personnel required for each processing task.
    D. In gathering facts, the objective of a systems study should be the primary consideration.

    1.____

2. The most direct method of obtaining information about activities in the area under study is by observation. There are several general rules for an analyst that are essential for observing and being accepted as an observer.
    The one of the following statements relating to this aspect of an analyst's responsibility that is most valid in the initial phase is that the analyst should NOT

    A. limit himself to observing only; he may criticize operations and methods
    B. prepare himself for what he is about to observe
    C. obtain permission of the department's management to actually perform some of the clerical tasks himself
    D. offer views of impending charges regarding new staff requirements, equipment, or procedures

    2.____

3. The active concern of the systems analyst is the study and documentation of what he observes as it exists. Before attempting the actual study and documentation, the analyst should comply with certain generally accepted procedures.
    Of the following, the step the analyst should *generally* take FIRST is to

    A. define the problem and prepare a statement of objectives
    B. confer with the project director concerning persons to be interviewed
    C. accumulate data from all available sources within the area under study
    D. meet with operations managers to enlist their cooperation

    3.____

4. During the course of any systems study, the analyst will have to gather some statistics if the operation model is to be realistic and meaningful.
    With respect to the statistical report part of the study, it is MOST valid to say that

    A. it must follow a standard format since there should be no variation from one study to the next
    B. the primary factor to be considered is the volume of work in the departmental unit at each stage of completion
    C. only variations that occur during peak and slow periods should be recorded
    D. unless deadlines in the departmental units studied by the analyst occur constantly, they should not be taken into account

    4.____

5. In systems analysis, the interview is one of the analyst's major sources of information. In   5.____
   conducting an interview, he should strive for immediate rapport with the operations manager or department head with whom he deals.
   With respect to his responsibility in this area, it is considered LEAST appropriate for
   the analyst to

   A. explain the full background of the study and the scope of the investigation
   B. emphasize the importance of achieving the stated objectives and review the plan
      of the project
   C. assume that the attitudes of the workers are less important than those of the exec-
      utives
   D. request the manager's assistance in the form of questions, suggestions, and gen-
      eral cooperation

6. Large, complex endeavors often take a long time to implement. The following statements   6.____
   relate to long lead times imposed by large-scale endeavors.
   Select the one usually considered to be LEAST valid.

   A. Where there are external sponsors who provide funds or political support, they
      should be provided with some demonstration of what is being accomplished.
   B. Long lead times simplify planning and diminish the threat of obsolescence by
      assuring that objectives will be updated by the time the project is nearing comple-
      tion.
   C. During the period when no tangible results are forthcoming, techniques must be
      found to assess progress.
   D. Employees, particularly scientific personnel, should feel a sense of accomplish-
      ment or they may shy away from research which involves long-term commitments.

7. In traditional management theory, administrators are expected to collect and weigh facts   7.____
   and probabilities, make an optimal decision and see that it is carried out.
   In the management of large-scale development projects, such a clear sequence of
   action is *generally* NOT possible because of

   A. their limited duration
   B. the static and fixed balance of power among interest groups
   C. continuous suppression of new facts
   D. constantly changing constraints and pressures

Questions 8–10.

DIRECTIONS: One of the most valuable parts of the systems package is the systems flow-chart, a technique that aids understanding of the work flow. A flowchart should depict all the intricacies of the work flow from start to finish in order to give the onlooker a solid picture at a glance. The table below contains symbols used by the analyst in flowcharting. In answering Questions 8 through 10, refer to the following figures.

Figure I	Figure VI	Figure XI
Figure II	Figure VII	Figure XII
Figure III	Figure VIII	Figure XIII
Figure IV	Figure IX	
Figure V	Figure X	

8. The symbol that is COMMONLY used to specify clerical procedures which are not essen-tial to the main processing function and yet are part of the overall procedure is repre-sented by Figure

    A. III   B. VI   C. XII   D. XIII

8._____

9. An analyst wishes to designate the following activities:
    File reports; Calculate average; Attach labels.
    The MOST APPROPRIATE symbol to use is represented by Figure

    A. V   B. VI   C. VII   D. II

9._____

10. A *Report, Journal,* or *Record* should be represented by Figure

    A. I   B. III   C. IX   D. XI

10._____

Question 11.

DIRECTIONS: The following figures are often used in program and systems flowcharting.

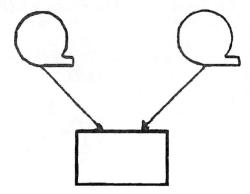

11.   The above figures represent   11.____

    A.   two magnetic tapes incorporated in a processing function
    B.   two report papers to be put in a cabinet in chronological order
    C.   two transmittal tapes–both externally generated–routed to a vault
    D.   an auxiliary operation involving two sequential decisions

12.   When research and analysis of government programs, e.g., pest control, drug rehabilita-   12.____
    tion, etc., is sponsored and conducted within a government unit, the scope of the analy-
    sis should *generally* be _____ the scope of the authority of the manager to whom the
    analyst is responsible.

    A.   less than   B.   less than or equal to
    C.   greater than or equal to   D.   greater than

13.   In recent years, there has been an increasing emphasis on outputs–the goods and ser-   13.____
    vices that a program produces. This emphasis on outputs imposes an information
    requirement. The one of the following which would MOST likely NOT be considered out-
    put information in a hospital or health care program is the

    A.   number of patients cared for
    B.   number of days patients were hospitalized
    C.   budgeted monies for hospital beds
    D.   quality of the service

14.   Which one of the following statements pertaining to management information systems is   14.____
    generally considered to be LEAST valid?

    A.   A management information system is a network of related subsystems developed
        according to an integrated scheme for evaluating the activities of an agency.
    B.   A management information system specifies the content and format, the prepara-
        tion and integration of information for all various functions within an agency that will
        best satisfy needs at various levels of management.
    C.   To operate a successful management information system, an agency will require a
        complex electronic computer installation.
    D.   The five elements which compose a management information system are: data
        input, files, data processing, procedures, and data output.

15. In the field of records management, electronic equipment is being used to handle office   15._____
paperwork or data processing. With respect to such use, of the following, it is MOST valid
to say that

    A. electronic equipment is not making great strides in the achievement of speed and
economy in office paperwork
    B. electronic equipment accelerates the rate at which office paperwork is completed
    C. paperwork problems can be completely solved through mechanization
    D. introduction of electronic data processing equipment cuts down on the paper con-
sumed in office processes

16. A reports control program evaluates the reporting requirements of top management so   16._____
that reviews can be made of the existing reporting system to determine its adequacy.
Of the following statements pertaining to reports control, which is the MOST likely to
be characteristic of such a program?

    A. Only the exception will be reported
    B. Preparation of daily reports will be promoted
    C. Executives will not delegate responsibility for preparing reports
    D. Normal conditions are reported

17. Which of the following types of work measurement techniques requires the HIGHEST   17._____
degree of training and skill of technicians and supervisors and is MOST likely to involve
the HIGHEST original cost?

    A. Work sampling
    B. Predetermined time standards
    C. The time study (stopwatch timing)
    D. Employee reporting

18. Which of the following types of work measurement techniques *generally* requires the   18._____
LEAST amount of time to measure and establish standards?

    A. Work sampling
    B. Predetermined time standards
    C. The time study (stopwatch timing)
    D. Employee reporting

19. Assume that you, as an analyst, have been assigned to formally organize small work   19._____
groups within a city department to perform a special project. After studying the project,
you find you must choose between two possible approaches–either task teams or highly
functionalized groups.
What would be one of the advantages of choosing the task-team approach over the
highly functionalized organization?

    A. Detailed, centralized planning would be encouraged.
    B. Indifference to city goals and restrictions on output would be lessened.
    C. Work would be divided into very specialized areas.
    D. Superiors would be primarily concerned with seeing that subordinates do not devi-
ate from the project.

20. In systems theory, there is a *what-if* method of treating uncertainty that explores the   20._____
    effect on the alternatives of environmental change. This method is generally referred to
    as _____ analysis.

    A.   sensitivity   B.   contingency
    C.   a fortiori   D.   systems

KEY (CORRECT ANSWERS)

1.	D	11.	A
2.	D	12.	B
3.	A	13.	C
4.	B	14.	C
5.	C	15.	B
6.	B	16.	A
7.	D	17.	B
8.	D	18.	A
9.	A	19.	B
10.	B	20.	B

TEST 2

DIRECTIONS: Each question or incomplete statement is followed by several suggested answers or completions. Select the one that BEST answers the question or completes the statement. *PRINT THE LETTER OF THE CORRECT ANSWER IN THE SPACE AT THE RIGHT.*

1. Which of the following systems exists at the strategic level of an organization?   1.____

   A. Decision support system (DSS)
   B. Executive support system (ESS)
   C. Knowledge work system (KWS)
   D. Management information system (MIS)

2. The functions of knowledge workers in an organization generally include each of the following EXCEPT   2.____

   A. updating knowledge
   B. managing documentation of knowledge
   C. serving as internal consultants
   D. acting as change agents

3. Which of the following is not a management benefit associated with end-user development of information systems?   3.____

   A. Reduced application backlog
   B. Increased user satisfaction
   C. Simplified testing and documentation procedures
   D. Improved requirements determination

4. Assume that an analyst is preparing an analysis of a departmental program. His investigation leads him to a potential problem relating to the program. The analyst thinks the potential problem is so serious that he cannot rely on preventive actions to remove the cause or significantly reduce the probability of its occurrence.
   Of the following, the MOST appropriate way for the analyst to promptly handle this serious matter described above would be to   4.____

   A. apply systematic afterthought to the achievement of objectives by analysis of the problem
   B. compare actual performance with the expected standard of performance
   C. prepare contingency actions to be adopted immediately if the problem does occur
   D. identify, locate, and describe the deviation from the standard

5. Assume that an analyst is directed to investigate a problem relating to organizational behavior in his agency and to prepare a report thereon. After reviewing the preliminary draft, his superior cautions him to overcome his tendency to misuse and overgeneralize his interpretation of existing knowledge.
   Which one of the following statements appearing in the draft is MOST *usually* considered to be a common distortion of behavioral science knowledge?   5.____

   A. Pay—even incentive pay—isn't very important anymore.
   B. There are nonrational aspects to people's behavior.
   C. The informal system exerts much control over organizational participants.
   D. Employees have many motives.

Questions 6-10.

DIRECTIONS: Each of Questions 6 through 10 consists of a statement which contains one word that is incorrectly used because it is not in keeping with the meaning that the quotation is evidently intended to convey. Determine which word is incorrectly used. Then select from the words lettered A, B, C, or D the word which, when substituted for the incorrectly used word, would BEST help to convey the meaning of the statement.

6. While the utilization of cost-benefit analysis in decision-making processes should be
encouraged, it must be well understood that there are many limitations on the constraints
of the analysis. One must be cautioned against using cost-benefit procedures automati-
cally and blindly. Still, society will almost certainly be better off with the application of
cost-benefit methods than it would be without them. As some authorities aptly point out,
an important advantage of a cost-benefit study is that it forces those responsible to
quantify costs and benefits as far as possible rather than rest content with vague qualita-
tive judgments or personal hunches. Also, such an analysis has the very valuable by-
product of causing questions to be asked which would otherwise not have been raised.
Finally, even if cost-benefit analysis cannot give the right answer, it can sometimes play
the purely negative role of screening projects and rejecting those answers which are
obviously less promising.

    A. precise   B. externally
    C. applicability   D. unresponsiveness

6.____

7. The programming method used by the government should attempt to assess the costs
and benefits of individual projects, in comparison with private and other public alternatives. The program, then, consists of the most meritorious projects that the budget will
design. Meritorious projects excluded from the budget provide arguments for increasing
its size. There are difficulties inherent in the specific project approach. The attempt is to
apply profit criteria in public projects analogous to those used in evaluating private
projects. This involves comparison of monetary values of present and future costs and
benefits. But, in many important cases, such as highways, parkways, and bridges, the
product of the government's investment does not directly enter the market economy.
Consequently, evaluation requires imputation of market values. For example, the returns
on a bridge have been estimated by attempting to value the time saved by users. Such
measurements necessarily contain a strong, element of artificiality.

    A. annulled   B. expedient   C. accommodate   D. marginally

7.____

8. Consider the problem of budgeting for activities designed to alleviate poverty and rooted
unemployment. Are skill retraining efforts better or worse investments than public works?
Are they better or worse than subsidies or other special incentives to attract new industry? Or, at an even more fundamental level, is a dollar invested in an attempt to rehabili-
tate a mature, technologically displaced, educationally handicapped, unemployed man a
better commitment than a comparable dollar invested in supporting the educational and
technical preparation of his son for employment in a different line of work? The questions
may look unreasonable, even unanswerable. But the fact is that they are implicitly
answered in any budget decision in the defined problem area. The only subordinate
issue is whether the answer rests on intuition and guess, or on a budget system that presents relevant information so organized as to contribute to rational analysis, planning,
and decision-making.

    A. incomplete   B. relevant
    C. significant   D. speculate

8.____

9. Choices among health programs, on the basis of cost-benefit analysis, raise another set   9.____
of ethical problems. Measuring discounted lifetime earnings does not reveal the value of
alleviating pain and suffering; some diseases have a high death rate, others are debilitat-
ing, others are merely uncomfortable. In general, choices among health and education
programs that are predicated on discounted lifetime earnings will structure the choice
against those who have low earnings, those whose earnings will materialize only at
some future point in time, or those whose participation in the labor force is limited. It may
be an appropriate economic policy to reduce expenditures in areas that maximize the
future level of national income. But the maximization of social welfare may dictate attention to considerations, such as equality of opportunity, that transcend the limitations of
values defined in such narrow terms.

   A. concentrate   B. divergent   C. enforcing   D. favorably

10. Without defined and time-phased objectives, it is difficult to be critical of administrative   10.____
performance. To level a charge of waste or malperformance at the managers of a public
program is, of course, one of the more popular pastimes of any administration's loyal
opposition. But it is a rare experience to find such a charge documented by the kind of
precise cost-effectiveness measures that are the common test of the quality of management performance in a well-run organization. Those who take a professional view of
management responsibility are even more concerned about the acceptance of the kind
of information that would enable a manager to assess the progress and quality of his own
performance and, as appropriate, to initiate corrective action before outside criticism can
even start.

   A. absence   B. rebut   C. withdraw   D. impeded

11. What is the relationship between the cost of inputs and the value of outputs when the   11.____
results obtained from a program can be measured in money? _____ ratio.

   A. Value administrative-cost   B. Break-even point
   C. Variable-direct   D. Cost-benefit

12. Some writers in the field of public expenditure have noted a disturbing tendency inherent   12.____
in cost-benefit analysis. Which one of the following statements MOST accurately
expresses their concern over the use of cost-benefit analysis? It

   A. encourages the attachment of monetary values to intangibles
   B. has a built-in neglect of measurable outcomes while emphasizing the nonmeasur-
      able
   C. consciously exaggerates social values and overstates political values
   D. encourages emphasis of those costs and benefits that cannot be measured rather
      than those that can

13. In private industry, budgetary control begins logically with an estimate of sales and the   13.____
income therefrom.
Of the following, the term used in government which is MOST analogous to that of
sales in private industry is

   A. borrowed funds   B. the amount appropriated
   C. general overhead   D. surplus funds

14. When constructing graphs of causally related variables, how should the variables be placed to conform to conventional use?

    A. The independent variable should be placed on the vertical axis and the dependent variable on the horizontal axis.
    B. The dependent variable should be placed on the vertical axis and the independent variable on the horizontal axis.
    C. Independent variables should be placed on both axes.
    D. Dependent variables should be placed on both axes.

14._____

Questions 15–18.

DIRECTIONS: Answer Questions 15 through 18 on the basis of the following graph describing the output of computer operators.

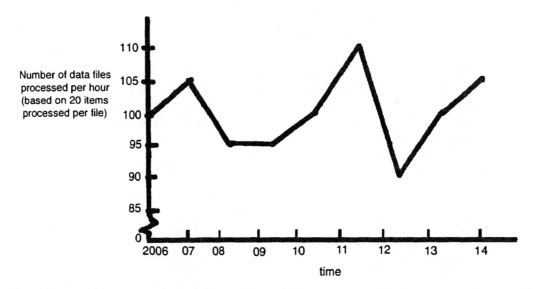

15. Of the following, during what four-year period did the AVERAGE OUTPUT of computer operators *fall below* 100 data files per hour?

    A. 2007-10   B. 2008-11   C. 2010-13   D. 2011-14

15._____

16. The AVERAGE PERCENTAGE CHANGE in output over the previous year's output for the years 2009 to 2012 is MOST NEARLY

    A. 2   B. 0   C. -5   D. -7

16._____

17. The DIFFERENCE between the actual output for 2012 and the projected figure based upon the average increase from 2006 to 2011 is MOST NEARLY

    A. 18   B. 20   C. 22   D. 24

17._____

18. Assume that after constructing the above graph, you, an analyst, discovered that the average number of items processed per file in 2012 was 25 (instead of 20) because of the complex nature of the work performed during that period.
The AVERAGE OUTPUT in files per hour for the period 2010 to 2013, expressed in terms of 20 items per file, would then be APPROXIMATELY

    A. 95   B. 100   C. 105   D. 110

18.____

19. Assume that Unit S's production fluctuated substantially from one year to another. In 2009, Unit S's production was 100% greater than in 2008; in 2010, it was 25% less than in 2009; and in 2011, it was 10% greater than in 2010. On the basis of this information, it is CORRECT to conclude that Unit S's production in 2011 exceeded its production in 2008 by

    A. 50%   B. 65%   C. 75%   D. 90%

19.____

20. Statistical sampling is often used in administrative operations primarily because it enables

    A. administrators to make staff selections
    B. decisions to be made based on mathematical and scientific fact
    C. courses of action to be determined by electronic data processing or computer programs
    D. useful predictions to be made from relatively small samples

20.____

KEY (CORRECT ANSWERS)

1.	B	11.	D
2.	B	12.	A
3.	C	13.	B
4.	C	14.	B
5.	A	15.	A
6.	C	16.	B
7.	C	17.	C
8.	C	18.	C
9.	A	19.	B
10.	A	20.	D

EXAMINATION SECTION
TEST 1

DIRECTIONS: Each question or incomplete statement is followed by several suggested
answers or completions. Select the one that BEST answers the question or
completes the statement. *PRINT THE LETTER OF THE CORRECT ANSWER
IN THE SPACE AT THE RIGHT.*

1. Of the following, the BEST statement concerning the placement of *Conclusions and Rec-*   1.____
ommendations in a management report is:

   A. Recommendations should always be included in a report unless the report presents the results of an investigation
   B. If a report presents conclusions, it must present recommendations
   C. Every statement that is a conclusion should grow out of facts given elsewhere in
the report
   D. Conclusions and recommendations should always conclude the report because
they depend on its contents

2. Assume you are preparing a systematic analysis of your agency's pest control program   2.____
and its effect on eliminating rodent infestation of premises in a specific region.
To omit from your report important facts which you originally received from the person
to whom you are reporting is GENERALLY considered to be

   A. *desirable;* anyone who is likely to read the report can consult his files for extra infor-
mation
   B. *undesirable;* the report should include major facts that are obtained as a result of
your efforts
   C. *desirable;* the person you are reporting to does not
   D. pass the report on to others who lack his own familiarity with the subject
   E. *undesirable;* the report should include all of the facts that are obtained as a result
of your efforts

3. Of all the nonverbal devices used in report writing, tables are used most frequently to   3.____
enable a reader to compare statistical information more easily. Hence, it is important that
an analyst know when to use tables.
Which one of the following statements that relate to tables is generally considered to
be LEAST valid?

   A. A table from an outside source must be acknowledged by the report writer.
   B. A table should be placed far in advance of the point where it is referred to or dis-
cussed in the report.
   C. The notes applying to a table are placed at the bottom of the table, rather than at
the bottom of the page on which the table is found.
   D. A table should indicate the major factors that effect the data it contains.

4. Assume that an analyst writes reports which contain more detail than might be needed to   4.____
serve their purpose.
Such a practice is GENERALLY considered to be

    A. *desirable* ; this additional detail permits maximized machine utilization

    B. *undesirable;* if specifications of reports are defined when they are first set up, loss of flexibility will follow

    C. *desirable;* everything ought to be recorded so it will be there if it is ever needed

    D. *undesirable;* recipients of these reports are likely to discredit them entirely

5. Assume that an analyst is gathering certain types of information which can be obtained only through interrogation of the clientele by means of a questionnaire.
Which one of the following statements that relate to construction of the questionnaire is the MOST valid?

    A. Stress, whenever possible, the use of leading questions.

    B. Avoid questions which touch on personal prejudice or pride.

    C. Opinions, as much as facts, should be sought.

    D. There is no psychological advantage for starting with a question of high interest value.

Questions 6-10.

DIRECTIONS: Questions 6 through 10 consist of sentences lettered A, B, C, and D. For each question, choose the sentence which is stylistically and grammatically MOST appropriate for a management report.

6.   A. For too long, the citizen has been forced to rely for his productivity information on the whims, impressions and uninformed opinion of public spokesmen.

    B. For too long, the citizen has been forced to base his information about productivity on the whims, impressions and uninformed opinion of public spokesmen.

    C. The citizen has been forced to base his information about productivity on the whims, impressions and uninformed opinion of public spokesmen for too long.

    D. The citizen has been forced for too long to rely for his productivity information on the whims, impressions and uninformed opinion of public spokesmen.

7.   A. More competition means lower costs to the city, thereby helping to compensate for inflation.

    B. More competition, helping to compensate for inflation, means lower costs to the city.

    C. Inflation may be compensated for by more competition, which will reduce the city's costs.

    D. The costs to the city will be lessened by more competition, helping to compensate for inflation.

8.   A. Some objectives depend on equal efforts from others, particularly private interests and the federal government; for example, technical advancement.

    B. Some objectives, such as technical advancement, depend on equal efforts from others, particularly private interests and the federal government.

    C. Some objectives depend on equal efforts from others, particularly private interests and the federal government, such as technical advancement.

    D. Some objectives depend on equal efforts from others (technical advancement, for example); particularly private interests and the federal government.

9. A. It has always been the practice of this office toeffectuate recruitment of prospective   9.____
        employees from other departments.
    B. This office has always made a practice of recruiting prospective employees from
        other departments.
    C. Recruitment of prospective employees from other departments has always been
        a practice which has been implemented by this office.
    D. Implementation of the policy of recruitment of prospective employees from other
        departments has always been a practice of this office.

10. A. These employees are assigned to the level of work evidenced by their efforts and   10.____
        skills during the training period.
    B. The level of work to which these employees is assigned is decided upon on the
        basis of the efforts and skills evidenced by them during the period in which they
        were trained.
    C. Assignment of these employees is made on the basis of the level of work their
        efforts and skills during the training period has evidenced.
    D. These employees are assigned to a level of work their efforts and skills during
        the training period have evidenced.

11. To overcome the manual collation problem, forms are frequently padded.   11.____
    Of the following statements which relate to this type of packaging, select the one that is
    MOST accurate.

    A. Typewritten forms which are prepared as padded forms are more efficient than all
        other packaging.
    B. Padded forms are best suited for handwritten forms.
    C. It is difficult for a printer to pad form copies of different colors.
    D. Registration problems increase when cut-sheet forms are padded.

12. Most forms are cut from a standard mill sheet of paper.   12.____
    This is the size on which forms dealers base their prices. Since an agency is paying for
    a full-size sheet of paper, it is the responsibility of the analyst to design forms so that
    as many as possible may be cut from the sheet without waste.
    Of the following sizes, select the one that will cut from a standard mill sheet with the
    GREATEST waste and should, therefore, be avoided if possible.

    A. 4" x 6"   B. 5" x 8"   C. 9" x 12"   D. 8 1/2" x 14"

13. Assume that you are assigned the task of reducing the time and costs involved in com-   13.____
    pleting a form that is frequently used in your agency. After analyzing the matter, you
    decide to reduce the writing requirements of the form through the use of ballot boxes and
    preprinted data.
    If exact copy-to-copy registration of this form is necessary, it is MOST advisable to

    A. vary the sizes of the ballot boxes
    B. stagger the ballot boxes
    C. place the ballot boxes as close together as possible
    D. have the ballot boxes follow the captions

14. To overcome problems that are involved in the use of cut-sheet and padded forms, spe-   14._____
cialty forms have been developed. Normally, these forms are commercially manufactured
rather than produced in-plant. Before designing a form as a specialty form, however, you
should be assured that certain factors are present.
Which one of the following factors deserves LEAST consideration?

   A. The form is to be used in quantities of 5,000 or more annually.
   B. The forms will be prepared on equipment using either a pinfeed device or pressure
rollers for continuous feed-through.
   C. Two or more copies of the form set must be held together for further processing
subsequent to the initial distribution of the form set.
   D. Copies of the form will be identical and no items of data will be selectively eliminated from one or more copies of the form.

15. Although a well-planned form should require little explanation as to its completion, there   15._____
are many occasions when the analyst will find it necessary to include instructions on the
form to assure that the person completing it does so correctly.
With respect to such instructions, it is usually considered to be LEAST appropriate to
place them

   A. in footnotes at the bottom of the form
   B. following the spaces to be completed
   C. directly under the form's title
   D. on the front of the form

16. One of the basic data-arrangement methods used in forms design is the *on-line* method.   16._____
When this method is used, captions appear on the same line as the space provided for
entry of the variable data.
This arrangement is NOT recommended because it

   A. forces the typist to make use of the typewriter's tab stops, thus increasing process-
ing time
   B. wastes horizontal space since the caption appears on the writing line
   C. tends to make the variable data become more dominant than the captions
   D. increases the form's processing time by requiring the typist to continually roll the
platen back and forth to expose the caption

17. Before designing a form for his agency, the analyst should be aware of certain basic   17._____
design standards.
Which one of the following statements relating to horizontal and vertical spacing
requirements is *generally* considered to be the MOST acceptable in forms design?

   A. If the form will be completed by typewriter, no more than four writing lines to the
vertical inch should be allowed.
   B. If the form will be completed by hand, allowance should not be made for the different sizes of individual handwriting.
   C. If the form will be completed partly by hand and partly by typewriter, the analyst
should provide the same vertical spacing as for typewriter completion
   D. The form should be designed with proportional spacing for pica and elite type.

18. As an analyst, you may be required to conduct a functional analysis of your agency's forms.
Which one of the following statements pertaining to this type of analysis is *generally* considered to be MOST valid?

    18.____

    A. Except for extremely low-volume forms, all forms should be functionally analyzed.
    B. To obtain maximum benefit from the analysis, functional re-analyses of all forms should be undertaken at least once every three to six months.
    C. All existing forms should be functionally analyzed before reorder.
    D. Only new forms should be functionally analyzed prior to being authorized for adoption.

19. The analyst must assure the users of a form that its construction provides for the most efficient method in terms of how data will be entered and processed subsequent to their initial entry.
While the simplest construction is the cut sheet, the GREATEST disadvantage of this type of construction is

    19.____

    A. the non-productive *makeready* time required if multiple copies of a form must be simultaneously prepared
    B. the difficulty experienced by users in filling in the forms solely by mechanical means
    C. its uneconomical cost of production
    D. the restrictions of limitations placed on the utilization of a variety of substances which may be used in form composition

20. Assume you have designed a form which requires data to be entered on multiple copies simultaneously. A determination has not yet been made whether to order the form as interleaved-carbon form sets or as carbonless forms.
The advantage of using carbonless forms is that they

    20.____

    A. permit more readable copies to be made at a single writing
    B. average about 30 percent lower in price than conventional interleaved-carbon form sets
    C. provide greater security if the information entered on the form is classified
    D. are not subject to accidental imaging

KEY (CORRECT ANSWERS)

1.	C	11.	B
2.	B	12.	C
3.	B	13.	B
4.	D	14.	D
5.	B	15.	A
6.	B	16.	B
7.	A	17.	C
8.	B	18.	C
9.	B	19.	A
10.	A	20.	C

———

TEST 2

DIRECTIONS: Each question or incomplete statement is followed by several suggested answers or completions. Select the one that BEST answers the question or completes the statement. *PRINT THE LETTER OF THE CORRECT ANSWER IN THE SPACE AT THE RIGHT.*

1. Many analysts lean toward the use of varying colors of paper in a multiple-part form set to indicate distribution. This usage is GENERALLY considered to be

    A. *desirable;* it is more effective than using white paper for all copies and imprinting the distribution in the margin of the copy
    B. *undesirable;* colored inks should be used instead to indicate distribution in a multi-part form set
    C. *desirable;* it will lead to lower costs of form production
    D. *undesirable;* it causes operational difficulties if the form is to be microfilmed or optically scanned

1.____

2. After a form has been reviewed and approved by the analyst, it should be given an identifying number. The following items pertain to the form number.
Which item is MOST appropriately included as a portion of the form number?

    A. Revision date
    B. Order quantity
    C. Retention period
    D. Organization unit responsible for the form

2.____

Questions 3-8

DIRECTIONS: Questions 3 through 8 should be answered on the basis of the following information.

Assume that the figure at the top of the next page is a systems flowchart specifically prepared for the purchasing department of a large municipal agency. Some of the symbols in the flowchart are incorrectly used. The symbols are numbered.

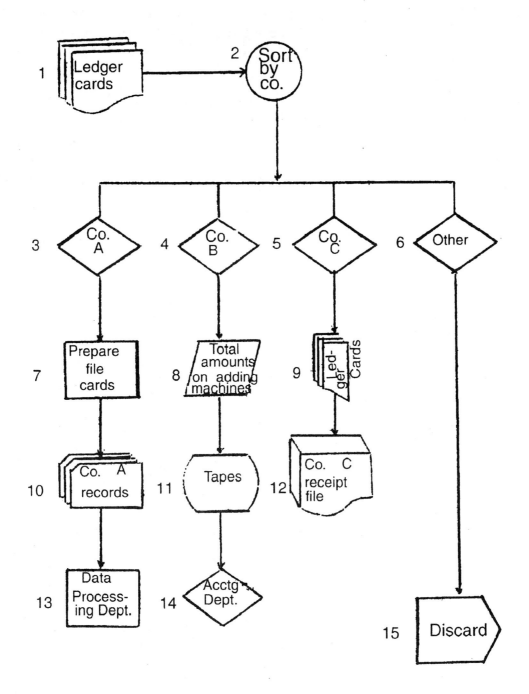

3. According to the flowchart, Number 2 is

    A. *correct*
    B. *incorrect;* the symbol should have six sides
    C. *incorrect;* the symbol should be the same as Number 7
    D. *incorrect;* the symbol should be the same as Number 8

3.____

4. According to the flowchart, Number 9 is

    A. *correct*
    B. *incorrect;* the symbol should be the same as Number 1

4.____

   C. *incorrect;* the symbol should be the same as Number 7
   D. *incorrect;* the symbol should be the same as Number 10

5. According to the flowchart, Number 11 is   5._____

   A. *correct*
   B. *incorrect;* the symbol should be the same as Number 13
   C. *incorrect;* the symbol should be the same as Number 10
   D. *incorrect;* the symbol should be the same as Number 9

6. According to the flowchart, Number 14 is   6._____

   A. *correct*
   B. *incorrect;* the symbol should have three sides
   C. *incorrect;* the symbol should have six sides
   D. *incorrect;* the symbol should have eight sides

7. According to the flowchart, Number 12 is   7._____

   A. *correct*
   B. *incorrect;* a *file* should be represented in the same form as the symbol which
       immediately precedes it
   C. *incorrect;* the symbol should be the same as Number 13
   D. *incorrect;* the symbol should be the same as Number 14

8. According to the flowchart, Number 15 is   8._____
   A. *correct*

   B. *incorrect;* the symbol should be

   C. *incorrect;* the symbol should be

   D. *incorrect;* the symbol should be

9. An agency expects to increase its services, the workload of the office will increase, and   9._____
    additional equipment and personnel will probably be required. Although there is no set
    formula for determining how much space will be required in an agency in a specific num-
    ber of years from now, certain guidelines have been developed to assist the analyst in
    dealing with the problem of providing expansion space.
    Which of the following statements pertaining to this aspect of space utilization is *gen-*
    erally considered to be the LEAST desirable practice?

   A. Spread the departments to fit into space that is temporarily surplus and awaiting
       the day when it is needed
   B. Place major departments where they can expand into the area of minor depart-
       ments
   C. Visualize the direction in which the expansion will go and avoid placing the rela-
       tively fixed installations in the way
   D. Lay out the departments economically and screen off the surplus areas, using
       them for storage or other temporary usage

Questions 10-11.

DIRECTIONS: Questions 10 and 11 are based on the following layout.

Layout of Conference Room
BUREAU OF RODENT CONTROL

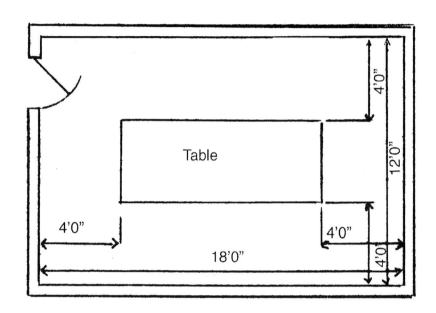

10.   The LARGEST number of persons that can be accommodated in the area shown in the   10.____
      layout is

      A. 16   B. 10   C. 8   D. 6

11.   Assume that the Bureau's programs undergo expansion and the Director indicates that   11.____
      the feasibility of increasing the size of the conference room should be explored.
      For every two additional persons that are to be accommodated, the analyst should rec-
      ommend that _____ be added to table length and _____ be added to room length.

      A. 2'-6";2'-6"   B. 5'-0"; 5'-0"
      C. 2'-6"; 5'-0"   D. 5'-0"; 2'-6"

Questions 12-14.

DIRECTIONS: Questions 12 through 14 are based on the following information.

SYMBOLS USED IN LAYOUT WORK

Figure I   ◯

Figure II   ⊸◯

Figure III   ⊙

Figure IV   ▣

Figure V   ⊸◯⊸

Figure VI   ◁

Figure VII   ▥

Figure VIII

Figure IX ——————————

Figure X   ⊠——⊠——⊠

Figure XI   ▱——▱——▱

Figure XII   ⊠ ≡

12. Figure XI is the symbol for   12.____

     A. a temporary partition   B. floor outlets
     C. ceiling outlets   D. a switch

13. A *solid post* is represented by Figure   13.____

     A. II   B. V   C. VIII   D. XII

14. Figure VI is the symbol for a(n)   14.____

     A. switch   B. intercom
     C. telephone outlet   D. railing

15. While there is no one office layout that will fit all organizations, there are some reason-   15.____
ably good principles of office layout by function that could be applied to any office situation.
Which one of the following statements relating to functions and locations is MOST
characteristic of a good layout?
The

     A. personnel department is usually close to the reception area
     B. purchasing department should be far from the entrance
     C. data processing activity and duplicating services are normally placed together
     D. top management group is usually dispersed throughout the general office group

16. Records are valuable to an organization becaused recorded information is more accu-   16.____
rate and enduring than oral information.
Of the following, the MOST important stage in records management is at the

     A. storage stage
     B. time when quality control principles are applied
     C. point of distribution
     D. source when records are created

17. The rough layout of an office can be made by sketching the office floor plan from actual measurements, or it can be copied from blueprints furnished by the building management.
    As an analyst assigned to improve an office layout, you should be aware that the experienced layout man prefers to make his sketch from

   A. a blueprint because it eliminates the extra work in checking a sketch made from it
   B. actual measurements because a blueprint is in a scale of 1/4 or 1/2 inch to a foot instead of the preferred 1/8 inch scale
   C. a blueprint because he can always trust the blueprint
   D. actual measurements because he has to sketch in the desks and other equipment

18. Planning the traffic flow and appropriate aisle space in an office are factors an analyst must consider in any desk arrangement.
    Of the following, it is *generally* the MOST desirable practice to

   A. deny requests to rearrange desks to give employees more working space if the space left for the aisle is more than needed for the traffic
   B. figure operating space and the open file drawer separately from the allowance for the aisle if files must open into the aisle
   C. conserve space by making the main aisle in an office no wider than 36 inches
   D. disregard the length of feeders to an aisle in determining the width of the aisle

19. Code systems which are used to mark records for long- or short-term retention are easy to devise and use.
    Accordingly, of the following situations, it would be MOST appropriate to use the *destroy code* for

   A. information that calls for action within 90 days and for which no record is necessary thereafter
   B. information that may be needed for evaluation of past agency activities
   C. records which contain information that is readily available elsewhere
   D. records that contain information necessary for audit requirements

20. Assume your agency is moving into new quarters and you will assist your superior in assigning space to the various offices. The offices will be air-conditioned. The interior of the space to be assigned is located away from windows.
    Of the following, it is MOST appropriate for you to recommend that the interior of the space be set aside for

   A. legal offices and confidential investigation sections
   B. visitors to the agency
   C. conference and training rooms
   D. typing and stenographic pools

17.____

18.____

19.____

20.____

KEY (CORRECT ANSWERS)

1.	D	11.	A
2.	A	12.	A
3.	A	13.	D
4.	B	14.	C
5.	D	15.	A
6.	C	16.	D
7.	A	17.	D
8.	C	18.	B
9.	A	19.	C
10.	B	20.	C

———

EXAMINATION SECTION
TEST 1

DIRECTIONS: Each question or incomplete statement is followed by several suggested answers or completions. Select the one that BEST answers the question or completes the statement. *PRINT THE LETTER OF THE CORRECT ANSWER IN THE SPACE AT THE RIGHT.*

1. The budget which shows the money to be spent to build and equip a new hospital is known as the _____ budget. 1._____

   A. capital   B. expense   C. planned   D. program

2. A significant characteristic of the program budget is that it lends itself to review and analysis. 2._____
   Why?

   A. The budget has a built-in accounting system that makes close control possible.
   B. The budget includes measurable objectives.
   C. It is possible to review performance based on units of service.
   D. All of the above

3. The advantages of program budgeting over line item and performance budgeting is: 3._____
      I. Tight, administrative control
      II. Forces the administrator to think through his total operation
      III. Measurable objectives
      IV. Simplicity of development
      V. Closer estimates of future costs
   The CORRECT answer is:

   A. I, II   B. II, III, IV
   C. II, III, V   D. III, IV, V

4. Of the following considerations, the one which is LEAST important in preparing a department budget request is the 4._____

   A. amounts in previous budget requests
   B. cost of material
   C. cost of personnel
   D. goals of the agency

5. The type of budget which provides the MOST flexibility in the use of appropriate funds is the _____ budget. 5._____

   A. accrual   B. item   C. line   D. program

6. A WEAKNESS of many budgetary systems today is that they 6._____

   A. are subjectively determined by those most directly involved
   B. focus on management weakness rather than management strength
   C. only show variable costs
   D. show in detail why losses are occurring

7. Standards on which budgets are developed should be based PRIMARILY on   7._____

   A. a general consensus   B. agency wishes
   C. analytical studies   D. historical performance

8. The income, cost, and expense goals making up a budget are aimed at achieving a pre-   8._____
   determined objective but do not necessarily measure the lowest possible costs.
   This is PRIMARILY so because

   A. budget committees are accounting-oriented and are not sympathetic with the
      supervisor's personnel problems
   B. budget committees fail to recognize the difference between direct and indirect
      costs
   C. the level of expenditures provided for in a budget by budget committees is fre-
      quently an arbitrary rather than a scientifically determined amount
   D. budget committees spend considerable time evaluating data to the point that the
      material gathered is not representative or current

9. You, as a unit head, have been asked to submit budget estimates of staff, equipment,   9._____
   and supplies in terms of programs for your unit for the coming fiscal year.
   In addition to their use in planning, such unit budget estimates can be BEST used to

   A. reveal excessive costs in operations
   B. justify increases in the debt limit
   C. analyze employee salary adjustments
   D. predict the success of future programs

10. Which of the following is the BEST reason for budgeting a new calculating machine for   10._____
    an office?

    A. The clerks in the office often make mistakes in adding.
    B. The machine would save time and money.
    C. It was budgeted last year but never received.
    D. All the other offices have calculating machines.

11. As an aspect of the managerial function, a budget is described BEST as a   11._____

    A. set of qualitative management controls over productivity
    B. tool based on historical accounting reports
    C. type of management plan expressed in quantitative terms
    D. precise estimate of future quantitative and qualitative contingencies

12. Which one of the following is *generally* accepted as the MAJOR immediate advantage of   12._____
    installing a system of program budgeting? It

    A. encourages managers to relate their decisions to the agency's long-range goals
    B. is a replacement for the financial or fiscal budget
    C. decreases the need for managers to make trade-offs in the decision-making pro-
       cess
    D. helps to adjust budget figures to provide for unexpected developments

13. Of the following, the BEST means for assuring necessary responsiveness of a budgetary   13.____
program to changing conditions is by

    A. overestimating budgetary expenditures by 15% and assigning the excess to
unforeseen problem areas

    B. underestimating budgetary expenditures by at least 20% and setting aside a
reserve account in the same amount

    C. reviewing and revising the budget at regular intervals so that it retains its character
as a current document

    D. establishing *budget by exception* policies for each division in the agency

14. According to expert thought in the area of budgeting, participation in the preparation of a   14.____
government agency's budget should GENERALLY involve

    A. only top management
    B. only lower levels of management
    C. all levels of the organization
    D. only a central budget office or bureau

15. Of the following, the MOST useful guide to analysis of budget estimates for the coming   15.____
fiscal year is a comparison with

    A. appropriations as amended for the current fiscal year
    B. manpower requirements for the previous two years
    C. initial appropriations for the current fiscal year
    D. budget estimates for the preceding five years,

16. Line managers often request more funds for their units than are actually required to   16.____
attain their current objectives.
Which one of the following is the MOST important reason for such inflated budget
requests? The

    A. expectation that budget examiners will exercise their prerogative of budget cutting
    B. line manager's interest in improving the performance of his unit is thereby indicated
to top management
    C. expectation that such requests will make it easier to obtain additional funds in
future years
    D. opinion that it makes sense to obtain additional funds and decide later how to use
them

17. Integrating budgeting with program planning and evaluation in a city agency is GENER-   17.____
ALLY considered to be

    A. *undesirable*; budgeting must focus on the fiscal year at hand, whereas planning
must concern itself with developments over a period of years
    B. *desirable*; budgeting facilitates the choice-making process by evaluating the finan-
cial implications of agency programs and forcing cost comparisons among them
    C. *undesirable*; accountants and statisticians with the required budgetary skills have
little familiarity with the substantive programs that the agency is conducting
    D. *desirable*; such a partnership increases the budgetary skills of planners, thus pro-
moting more effective use of public resources

18. In government budgeting, the problem of relating financial transactions to the fiscal year   18._____
    in which they are budgeted is BEST met by

    A. determining the cash balance by comparing how much money has been received
       and how much has been paid out
    B. applying net revenue to the fiscal year in which they are collected as offset by rele-
       vant expenses
    C. adopting a system whereby appropriations are entered when they are received
       and expenditures are entered when they are paid out
    D. entering expenditures on the books when the obligation to make the expenditure is
       made

19. If the agency's bookkeeping system records income when it is received and expenditures   19._____
    when the money is paid out, this system is USUALLY known as a _____ system.

    A. cash   B. flow-payment
    C. deferred   D. fiscal year income

20. An audit, as the term applies to budget execution, is MOST NEARLY a   20._____

    A. procedure based on the budget estimates
    B. control exercised by the executive on the legislature in the establishment of pro-
       gram priorities
    C. check on the legality of expenditures and is based on the appropriations act
    D. requirement which must be met before funds can be spent

21. In government budgeting, there is a procedure known as *allotment.*   21._____
    Of the following statements which relate to allotment, select the one that is MOST gen-
    erally considered to be correct. Allotment

    A. increases the practice of budget units coming back to the legislative branch for
       supplemental appropriations
    B. is simply an example of red tape
    C. eliminates the requirement of timing of expenditures
    D. is designed to prevent waste

22. In government budgeting, the establishment of the schedules of allotments is MOST   22._____
    generally the responsibility of the

    A. budget unit and the legislature
    B. budget unit and the executive
    C. budget unit only
    D. executive and the legislature

23. Of the following statements relating to preparation of an organization's budget request,   23._____
    which is the MOST generally valid precaution?

    A. Give specific instructions on the format of budget requests and required supporting
       data.
    B. Because of the complexity of preparing a budget request, avoid argumentation to
       support the requests
    C. Put requests in whatever format is desirable.
    D. Consider that final approval will be given to initial estimates.

Question 24.

DIRECTIONS: Answer Question 24 on the basis of the following information.

<u>Sample Budget</u>

<u>Environmental Safety</u>
   Air Pollution Protection

Personal Services	$20,000,000	
Contractual Services	4,000,000	
Supplies and Materials	4,000,000	
Capital Outlay	2,000,000	
Total Air Pollution Protection		$30,000,000

   Water Pollution Protection

Personal Services	$23,000,000	
Supplies and Materials	4,500,000	
Capital Outlay	20,500,000	
Total Water Pollution Protection		$48,000,000
Total Environmental Safety		$78,000,000

24.   Based on the above budget, which is the MOST valid statement?   24._____

   A.   Environmental Safety, Air Pollution Protection, and Water Pollution Protection could all be considered program elements.
   B.   The object listings included water pollution protection and capital outlay.
   C.   Examples of the program element listings in the above are personal services and supplies and materials.
   D.   Contractual Services and Environmental Safety were the program element listings.

25.   Which of the following is NOT an advantage of a program budget over a line-item bud-   25._____
get?
A program budget

   A.   allows us to set up priority lists in deciding what activities we will spend our money on
   B.   gives us more control over expenditures than a line-item budget
   C.   is more informative in that we know the broad purposes of spending money
   D.   enables us to see if one program is getting much less money than the others

26.   Of the following statements which relate to the budget process in a well-organized gov-   26._____
ernment, select the one that is MOST NEARLY correct.

   A.   The budget cycle is the step-by-step process which is repeated each and every fiscal year.
   B.   Securing approval of the budget does not take place within the budget cycle.
   C.   The development of a new budget and putting it into effect is a two-step process known as the budget cycle.
   D.   The fiscal period, usually a fiscal year, has no relation to the budget cycle.

27. If a manager were asked what PPBS stands for, he would be right if he said 27._____

    A. public planning budgeting system
    B. planning programming budgeting system
    C. planning projections budgeting system
    D. programming procedures budgeting system

Questions 28-29

DIRECTIONS: Answer Questions 28 and 29 on the basis of the following information.

Sample Budget

	Amount
Refuse Collection	
Personal Services	$ 30,000
Contractual Services	5,000
Supplies and Materials	5,000
Capital Outlay	10,000
	$ 50,000
Residential Collections	
Dwellings—1 pickup per week	1,000
Tons of refuse collected per year	375
Cost of collections per ton	$ 8
Cost per dwelling pickup per year	$ 3
Total annual cost	$ 3,000

28. The sample budget shown is a simplified example of a _____ budget. 28._____

    A. factorial   B. performance
    C. qualitative   D. rational

29. The budget shown in the sample differs CHIEFLY from line-item and program budgets in that it includes 29._____

    A. objects of expenditure but not activities or functions
    B. only activities, functions, and controls
    C. activities and functions, but not objects of expenditure
    D. levels of service

30. Performance budgeting focuses PRIMARY attention upon which one of the following? The 30._____

    A. things to be acquired, such as supplies and equipment
    B. general character and relative importance of the work to be done or the service to be rendered
    C. list of personnel to be employed, by specific title
    D. separation of employee performance evaluations from employee compensation

KEY (CORRECT ANSWERS)

1.	A		16.	A
2.	B		17.	B
3.	C		18.	D
4.	A		19.	A
5.	D		20.	C
6.	A		21.	D
7.	C		22.	C
8.	C		23.	A
9.	A		24.	A
10.	B		25.	B
11.	C		26.	A
12.	A		27.	B
13.	C		28.	B
14.	C		29.	D
15.	A		30.	B

———

TEST 2

DIRECTIONS: Each question or incomplete statement is followed by several suggested answers or completions. Select the one that BEST answers the question or completes the statement. *PRINT THE LETTER OF THE CORRECT ANSWER IN THE SPACE AT THE RIGHT.*

1. Of the following, the FIRST step in the installation and operation of a performance budgeting system generally should be the   1.____

    A. identification of program costs in relationship to the accounting system and operating structure
    B. identification of the specific end results of past programs in other jurisdictions
    C. identification of work programs that are meaningful for management purposes
    D. establishment of organizational structures each containing only one work program

2. Of the following, the MOST important purpose of a system of quarterly allotments of appropriated funds generally is to enable the   2.____

    A. head of the judicial branch to determine the legality of agency requests for budget increases
    B. operating agencies of government to upgrade the quality of their services without increasing costs
    C. head of the executive branch to control the rate at which the operating agencies obligate and expend funds
    D. operating agencies of government to avoid payment for services which have not been properly rendered by employees

3. In the preparation of the agency's budget, the agency's central budget office has two responsibilities: program review and management improvement.   3.____
Which one of the following questions concerning an operating agency's program is MOST closely related to the agency budget officer's program review responsibility?

    A. Can expenditures for supplies, materials, or equipment be reduced?
    B. Will improved work methods contribute to a more effective program?
    C. What is the relative importance of this program as compared with other programs?
    D. Will a realignment of responsibilities contribute to a higher level of program performance?

Questions 4-9.

DIRECTIONS: Questions 4 through 9 are to be answered only on the basis of the information contained in the charts below which relate to the budget allocations of City X, a small suburban community. The charts depict the annual budget allocations by Department and by Expenditures over a five-year period.

CITY X BUDGET IN MILLIONS OF DOLLARS

TABLE I.   Budget Allocations by Department

Department	1997	1998	1999	2000	2001
Public Safety	30	45	50	40	50
Health and Welfare	50	75	90	60	70
Engineering	5	8	10	5	8
Human Resources	10	12	20	10	22
Conservation and Environment	10	15	20	20	15
Education and Development	15	25	35	15	15
TOTAL BUDGET	120	180	225	150	180

TABLE II.   Budget Allocations by Expenditures

Category	1997	1998	1999	2000	2001
Raw Materials and Machinery	36	63	68	30	98
Capital Outlay	12	27	56	15	18
Personal Services	72	90	101	105	64
TOTAL BUDGET	120	180	225	150	160

4. The year in which the SMALLEST percentage of the total annual budget was allocated to   4.____
the Department of Education and Development is

    A. 1997   B. 1998   C. 2000   D. 2001

5. Assume that in 2000 the Department of Conservation and Environment divided its   5.____
annual budget into the three categories of expenditures and in exactly the same proportion as the budget shown in Table II for the year 2000. The amount allocated for capital outlay in the Department of Conservation and Environment's 2000 budget was MOST
NEARLY _____ million.

    A. $2   B. $4   C. $6   D. $10

6. From the year 1998 to the year 2000, the sum of the annual budgets for the Departments   6.____
of Public Safety and Engineering showed an overall _____ million.

    A. decline of $8   B. increase of $7
    C. decline of $15   D. increase of $22

7. The LARGEST dollar increase in departmental budget allocations from one year to the   7.____
next was in

    A. Public Safety from 1997 to 1998
    B. Health and Welfare from 1997 to 1998
    C. Education and Development from 1999 to 2000
    D. Human Resources from 1999 to 2000

8. During the five-year period, the annual budget of the Department of Human Resources   8.____
was greater than the annual budget for the Department of Conservation and Environment in _____ of the years.

    A. none   B. one   C. two   D. three

9. If the total City X budget increases at the same rate from 2001 to 2002 as it did from 2000 to 2001, the total City X budget for 2002 will be MOST NEARLY _____ million.

    A. $180   B. $200   C. $210   D. $215

9.____

10. The one of the following which is LEAST important in developing a budget for the next fiscal year for project maintenance is the

    A. adequacy of the current year's budget
    B. changes in workload that can be anticipated
    C. budget restrictions indicated in a memorandum covering budget preparations
    D. staff reassignments which are expected during the next fiscal year

10.____

11. The performance budget used by the department places MOST emphasis on

    A. building facilities   B. equipment costs
    C. personnel costs   D. services rendered

11.____

12. The LARGEST part of the expenditures of the department is for

    A. equipment   B. maintenance
    C. operating materials   D. personnel services

12.____

13. The department function which requires the GREATEST expenditure of funds is

    A. refuse collection   B. refuse disposal
    C. snow removal   D. street cleaning

13.____

14. A FIRST step in budget preparation is *usually*

    A. a realistic attempt to satisfy all unit requests
    B. forecasting the amount of various kinds of work to be done during the coming budget year
    C. an effort to increase work output
    D. appraising the quality of work done in the previous year

14.____

15. There are various types of budgets which are used to measure different government activities.
The type of budget which *particularly* measures input of resource as compared with output of service is the _____ budget.

    A. capital   B. traditional   C. performance   D. program

15.____

16. The budget for a given cost during a given period was $100,000. The actual cost for the period was $90,000. Based upon these facts, one should say that the responsible manager has done a better than expected job in controlling the cost if the cost is

    A. variable and actual production equaled budgeted production
    B. a discretionary fixed cost and actual production equaled budgeted production
    C. variable and actual production was 90% of budgeted production
    D. variable and actual production was 80% of budgeted production

16.____

17. In most municipal budgeting systems involving capital and operating budgets, the leasing   17.____
or renting of facilities is usually shown in

    A. the operating budget   B. the capital budget
    C. a separate schedule   D. either budget

18. New York City's budgeting procedure is unusual in that budget appropriations are consid-   18.____
ered in two parts, as follows: _____ budget and _____ budget.

    A. capital; income   B. expense; income
    C. revenue; expense   D. expense; capital

19. Budget planning is MOST useful when it achieves   19.____

    A. cost control   B. forecast of receipts
    C. performance review   D. personnel reduction

20. After a budget has been developed, it serves to   20.____

    A. assist the accounting department in posting expenditures
    B. measure the effectiveness of department managers
    C. provide a yardstick against which actual costs are measured
    D. provide the operating department with total expenditures to date

21. A budget is a plan whereby a goal is set for future operations. It affords a medium for   21.____
comparing actual expenditures with planned expenditures.
The one of the following which is the MOST accurate statement on the basis of this
statement is that

    A. the budget serves as an accurate measure of past as well as future expenditures
    B. the budget presents an estimate of expenditures to be made in the future
    C. budget estimates should be based upon past budget requirements
    D. planned expenditures usually fall short of actual expenditures

22. If one attempts to list the advantages of the management-by-exception principle as it is   22.____
used in connection with the budgeting process, several distinct advantages could be
cited.
Which of the following is NOT an advantage of this principle as it applies to the budgeting process? Management-by-exception

    A. saves time
    B. identifies critical problem areas
    C. focuses attention and concentrates effort
    D. escalates the frequency and importance of budget-related decisions

23. Of the following statements that relate to a budget, select the one that is MOST accurate.   23.____

    A. A budget is made up by an organization to plan its future activities.
    B. A budget specifies how much the organization to which it relates estimates it will
        spend over a certain period of time.
    C. A budget specifies in dollars and cents how much is spent in a particular time
        period.
    D. All plans dealing with money are budgets.

24. Of the following, the one which is NOT a contribution that a budget makes to organizational programming is that a budget   24.____

    A. enables a comparison of what actually happened with what was expected
    B. stresses the need to forecast specific goals and eliminates the need to focus on tasks needed to accomplish goals
    C. may illustrate duplication of effort between interdependent activities
    D. shows the relationship between various organizational segments

25. A line-item budget is a GOOD control budget because   25.____

    A. it clearly specifies how the items being purchased will be used
    B. expenditures can be shown primarily for contractual services
    C. it clearly specifies what the money is buying
    D. it clearly specifies the services to be provide

———

KEY (CORRECT ANSWERS)

1.	C		11.	D
2.	C		12.	D
3.	C		13.	A
4.	D		14.	B
5.	A		15.	C
6.	A		16.	A
7.	B		17.	A
8.	B		18.	D
9.	D		19.	A
10.	D		20.	C

21. B
22. D
23. B
24. B
25. C

———

EXAMINATION SECTION

TEST 1

DIRECTIONS: Each question or incomplete statement is followed by several suggested answers or completions. Select the one that BEST answers the question or completes the statement. *PRINT THE LETTER OF THE CORRECT ANSWER IN THE SPACE AT THE RIGHT.*

1. A woman in her mid-30s comes up to your desk and asks you how she can apply to work at your office. You do not know the immediate answer to that question. Which of the following would be the BEST way to respond to her request?
   A. Tell her what sounds like the right answer
   B. Tell her to talk to your boss and show her how to do that
   C. Explain you are not allowed to give out confidential information to the public
   D. Inform her that you do not know right now, but you will find out

1.____

2. A person approaches the customer service desk and asks you to do something that you are ultimately unable to do. Which of the following should you avoid doing next?
   A. Opening your policy handbook and reading from it verbatim
   B. Clarifying why you cannot do what he or she is asking of you
   C. Crafting detailed and precise statements
   D. Giving the person alternative options

2.____

3. When talking to someone from the public, which of the following statements would be least frustrating for the customer to hear?
   A. "You'll have to..."
   B. "Mr. X will be back at any moment..."
   C. "Let me see what I can do..."
   D. "I'll do my best..."

3.____

4. Your office recently received a letter from an individual expressing extreme frustration and disappointment at how it was handling the customer's problems. You have written an apology letter and are reviewing it before sending it to the customer. You should ensure the letter is NOT
   A. sincere   B. official
   C. personal   D. sent immediately

4.____

5. If you are unable to provide a certain service or product with dependability and accuracy, it would be defined as a lack of
   A. courtesy   B. reliability
   C. assurance   D. responsiveness

5.____

6.   As most civil service employees know, customer feedback can be, and usually   6.____
is, an integral part of customer service. Which of the following feedback
scenarios would be MOST useful to your organization?
   A. When it is an ongoing feedback system
   B. When centered on internal customers
   C. When it is focused on only a few indicators
   D. When every employee can see the feedback coming in

7.   Which of the following is the LEAST important factor in making sure a   7.____
customer survey is a valuable tool for your company?
   A. Taking every precaution to ensure the survey input is maintained in a
      confidential manner
   B. Making sure the customers believe in the confidentiality of the survey
   C. Ensuring confidentiality by having an outside company administer the
      survey
   D. Making sure the employees buy in an promote the survey to customers

8.   Which of the following would NOT be considered part of the resolution process   8.____
when identifying and dealing with a customer's problems?
   A. Following up with the customer after resolving the issue
   B. Listening and responding to each complaint the customer registers
   C. Giving the customer what they originally requested
   D. Promising the customer whatever you need to

9.   A customer approaches you with a complaint. You want to arrive at a fair   9.____
solution to the problem. What is the FIRST step you should take in this
situation?
   A. Immediately defend your company from any customer criticisms
   B. Listen to the customer describe their problem
   C. Ask the customer questions to confirm the type of problem they are
      having
   D. Determine a solution to the customer's problem(s)

10.   If you are dealing with a customer in a prompt manner when addressing   10.____
their complaints or issues, which of the following are you demonstrating?
   A. Assurance   B. Empathy
   C. Responsiveness   D. Reliability

11.   Steve has recently been hired to work at the postal office in town. A   11.____
customer comes into the office to complain about the number of packages of
his they have lost over the past year. When Steve attempts to help the upset
customer, what should he make sure to do FIRST? He should
   A. check into how legitimate the customer's complaints are and see if he can
      do anything about the missing packages
   B. just let the customer blow off some steam and chalk it up to an emotional
      outburst
   C. ask for help from his boss to see how to handle the situation
   D. assume the complaints are accurate and immediately attempt to correct
      them

12. How should a service representative react when a customer first presents them with a request?
  A. Apologize
  B. Greet them in a friendly manner
  C. Read from the employee handbook about the request
  D. Ask the customer to clarify information

12.____

13. In order to assuage a customer's frustration, which of the following should a civil service employee demonstrate?
  A. Urgency   B. Indifference   C. Surprise   D. Compassion

13.____

14. A customer comes into the office requesting that your organization do something for them that you know is not part of organization policy. Your FIRST responsibility would be to
  A. pass the customer on to higher management to deal with the issue
  B. persuade the customer to believe that the organization can grant their request
  C. mold expectations so they more closely resemble what the organization can do for the customer
  D. tell the customer there is no way you can comply with their request

14.____

15. Of the following potential distractors, which one MOST prevents a civil service employee from displaying good listening skills while a customer is speaking?
  A. Cell phones or checking e-mail
  B. Asking superfluous questions
  C. Background office noise
  D. Interrupting the customer to speak with colleagues

15.____

16. If you are in a situation where you have to deliver a negative response to a customer, it is often better to say _____ instead of just saying "no"?
  A. "I will try to..."   B. "You can..."
  C. "Our policy does not allow..."   D. "I do not believe..."

16.____

17. You are working one-on-one with a customer. Which of the following would be the MOST appropriate body language to display?
  A. Make frowning faces
  B. Stare at a spot over the customer's shoulder
  C. Lean in toward the customer
  D. Cross your arms while they speak

17.____

18. The majority of communication in face-to-face meetings with customers is shown through
  A. word choice   B. tone
  C. clothing choice   D. body language

18.____

19. A customer angrily approaches you at your service desk and starts expressing his frustration with recent actions by your department. Which of the following should be your FIRST responses to the customer?
    A. Listen to the person, then express understanding and apologize for how they have been negatively affected by your department's actions
    B. Interrupt them while they are speaking and tell them to calm down or you will not help them
    C. Give them an explanation of why your department took the actions they did
    D. None of the above

19.____

20. Of the following services, which one is NOT customized to a specific individual's needs?
    A. Hair salon
    B. Elementary education
    C. Computer counseling
    D. Dental care

20.____

21. Which of the following civil service employees demonstrates excellent customer service?
    A. A park ranger who minimizes public interaction and contact
    B. The Postal Service employee who sees the customer as a commodity
    C. The office clerk who spends a lot of time with customers sharing personal stories and anecdotes
    D. A DMV employee with open body language and direct communication

21.____

22. It is important to have excellent knowledge of services and products, if applicable, when interacting with consumers because
    A. you can demonstrate your knowledge and impress the customer
    B. your organization can have a higher margin of profit regardless of customer benefit
    C. the customer's needs can best be matched with appropriate services/products
    D. you can look good to your superiors and keep your job

22.____

23. A park ranger has recently been coming to a kids' camp dirty and unkempt. Even though her job requires her to be outside at times, why should she still care about her personal appearance?
    A. To speed up her service to the public
    B. So she is seen as a professional in her field
    C. It would help her organizational skills
    D. To show her level of expertise as a park ranger

23.____

24. How could guided conversation be a positive with interacting with the public?
    A. It allows you to anticipate a person's needs and expectations
    B. Most people know what they want even before they show up to your office
    C. It creates the impression of friendliness
    D. It helps time move faster

24.____

25. In the event a conflict or crisis arises, which of the following would be considered a POOR action to take when interacting with the public?
    A. Provide a constant flow of information
    B. Put the public's needs first
    C. Avoid saying "No Comment" as much as possible
    D. Assign multiple spokespeople so media calls can be dealt with efficiently

25.____

———————

KEY (CORRECT ANSWERS)

1.	D		11.	A
2.	A		12.	D
3.	C		13.	A
4.	B		14.	C
5.	B		15.	D
6.	A		16.	B
7.	C		17.	C
8.	D		18.	D
9.	B		19.	A
10.	C		20.	B

21.	D
22.	C
23.	B
24.	A
25.	D

———————

TEST 2

DIRECTIONS: Each question or incomplete statement is followed by several suggested answers or completions. Select the one that BEST answers the question or completes the statement. *PRINT THE LETTER OF THE CORRECT ANSWER IN THE SPACE AT THE RIGHT.*

1. John Smith answers a caller who struggles to understand a convoluted policy of your agency. How should he handle the customer's question?
   A. Tell the caller to go to the agency's website
   B. He should be honest and say he does not know the answer to the question
   C. John should explain the policy in general terms and refer them to a written version of the policy
   D. Tell the caller to talk to his supervisor and then give the caller the supervisor's extension

1.____

2. While meeting with a group of young campers at the local parks and recreation office, you conduct a lecture on the importance of avoiding dangerous plants near the forest. What can you do to make sure your inexperienced audience remembers the main points of your presentation?
   A. Use flashy visuals that catch the eye
   B. Repeat and emphasize your points
   C. Make jokes so the presentation is livelier
   D. Allow the campers to ask questions at the end of the presentation

2.____

3. A park ranger is about to deliver a speech at a public conservation meeting. Which of the following is the MOST important thing to keep in mind as he preps for the presentation?
   A. How large the audience is
   B. Whether or not he will be able to use visual aids
   C. If he will have time to use charts and graphs
   D. Audience interests

3.____

4. Jerry receives a letter from a customer and is about to shred it without reading. When you stop him, he says that there is no reason to read it because you cannot learn very much from letters you receive from the public. Which of the following should you tell him in order to convince him that reading letters sent from the public is beneficial and necessary?
   A. These public letters can give us a feel for how we are meeting customer needs.
   B. Letters from the public tell us how well our informational efforts are working.
   C. These letters can inform us of what additional training we may need.
   D. The letters can tell us whether public information processes need to be changed or not.

4.____

5. Mary Jane is a volunteer with the Parks and Recreation Department and her
    children also attend various summer programs through the district. She comes
    to you today to complain that one of her children was not allowed to join a
    program because they missed the sign-up by one day. She calls your staff a
    bunch of "morons" and complains that your department's actions are creating
    serious issues for her. How should you handle this situation?
    A. Let Ms. Johnson rant until she gets it out of her system
    B. Tell her you cannot help her and will ask her to leave if she cannot stop
        referring to your colleagues as "morons"
    C. Refer Ms. Johnson to your boss
    D. Try to alter the tone of the conversation to a more objective and less
        emotional discussion of Ms. Johnson's problems

    5.____

6. A civil service employee is tasked with moderating a town hall meeting
    regarding child safety, but he knows that residents will be attending the
    meeting with different motives. How can the employee make sure the town hall
    meeting is as beneficial and informational as possible?
    A. Ask attendees to be open to changing their opinions and preferences
    B. Start out by recognizing the various motives but also stress the common
        objectives and interests
    C. Call out individuals who you know have specific reasons for attending and
        put them on the spot
    D. Cancel the meeting and avoid rescheduling it until you can be sure
        everyone is on the same page

    6.____

7. During the question-and-answer session at the end of a presentation, a member
    of the public makes a suggestion that you deem not only practical but worthy of
    further discussion. How should you react to this?
    A. Tell them you will let the appropriate people know of the suggestion
    B. Tell the person you concur with them wholeheartedly
    C. Let the person know you think it is a good idea but you cannot make
        decisions based on suggestions during Q and A
    D. Even though the suggestion is good, tell the person that someone in your
        organization has probably already thought of the idea

    7.____

8. When in a conversation with a group of local residents, what is the BIGGEST
    problem with one or two people dominating the conversation?
    A. Your interaction could take longer than it should
    B. Some people will become distracted and not focus on the meeting
        anymore
    C. The other members of the group may not have an opportunity to share
        their opinions
    D. None of the above

    8.____

9. You receive a phone call at the village hall, but the information being requested would need to come from the police station. How should you respond to the caller?
    A. Give them the police station's website and wish them well
    B. Tell them you are not responsible for their request
    C. Refer them to the police station's number and information
    D. Provide them with the information as best as you can

9._____

10. Which of the following should almost always be avoided when interacting with a member of the community?
    A. Contentious matters   B. Topics about financial material
    C. Rules and regulations   D. Technical lingo or jargon

10._____

11. When people use inflammatory language laced with obscenities, a town employee should
    A. refuse to continue the dialogue if the person cannot stop using the offensive language
    B. tell the person to talk to your supervisor
    C. allow the person to finish "venting" before attempting to find a solution to the problem
    D. hang up if on the phone; if in person, leave the area and ask the individual to leave as well

11._____

12. A member of the public has sent your agency a letter. Which of the following will help you figure out how much explaining you need to do when writing a response?
    A. Go to the agency website and search for how much explanation is provided there
    B. Take out the original customer letter and study it
    C. Presume the person who wrote the letter already has a working knowledge of the subject and thus will not require a lot of background explanation
    D. Look at past letters sent by your agency

12._____

13. During an informational meeting with local townspeople, a man makes a suggestion for a new town measure that is based on incorrect information and is impractical. What is the BEST way to handle a situation such as this?
    A. Ask if anyone else in attendance would like to respond to the suggestion
    B. Tell the person it is a great idea even though you are aware of its folly
    C. Thank the man for coming and tell everyone you always welcome their suggestions
    D. Inform the person that his/her comment clearly reflects an inferior knowledge about the subject

13._____

14. A member from the public calls your office about negative comments he has
    heard about one of your programs. You believe the comments were made by
    someone who had inaccurate material, but you are not completely certain of
    that because you are not directly involved with the program. What is the BEST
    way to handle this situation?
    A. Tell the caller you will analyze the situation in depth and then call them
       back
    B. Tell the caller the evidence on which they have based their judgment is
       not supported
    C. Explain that your office has a "No Comment" policy regarding negative
       comments
    D. Let the caller know you are not involved with the program directly, and tell
       them to call the person who is

14.____

15. Which of the following quotes reflects the BEST way to handle an angry
    resident that keeps interrupting during a village meeting?
    A. "I am here as a volunteer and I do not need this."
    B. "I understand your anger, but we have quite a bit of information to cover
       tonight, so in fairness to everyone else, please let me continue."
    C. "Every crowd has one black sheep in it."
    D. "Sir, (or Ma'am) if you cannot stop interjecting, I will have security escort
       you from the premises."

15.____

16. Of the following, which is an example of nonverbal communication?
    A. Frowning   B. Hand signs
    C. A "21 Gun Salute"   D. All of the above

16.____

17. Residents of Masterton, Georgia, were recently made aware that the main
    road into and out of town will be under construction for the next four years. The
    construction will make travel times much more difficult for the citizens and they
    have demanded a meeting with your department. You are tasked with creating
    a presentation to explain to them why the construction is necessary. At the
    start of the presentation, you should
    A. make a joke to lighten the mood
    B. state the purpose of your presentation
    C. provide a detailed account of the history behind the project
    D. make a call to action

17.____

18. When a member of the public asks questions that are confusing or you do not
    understand right away, what is the BEST way to handle this situation?
    A. Answer the question as you understand it
    B. Stick to generalizations dealing with the subject of the question
    C. Rephrase the question and ask the person if you understood what they
       were asking
    D. Ask the person to repeat the question

18.____

19. When preparing for a public interaction, which of the following situations would be MOST appropriate to include handouts?
    A. If you want to help the attendees remember important information after the interaction is over
    B. If you want to keep the interaction short
    C. When you want to remember key points to talk about
    D. When you do not want attendees to have to pay attention during the interaction

19.____

20. John is in the process of handling a phone call when a local citizen approaches his desk to ask a question. Neither the caller nor the visitor seem to be in a crisis. What should John do in this scenario?
    A. Keep talking with the caller until he is finished. Then tell the visitor he is sorry for making them wait.
    B. Remain on the phone with the caller but look up at the visitor every once and awhile so they know he has not forgotten about them.
    C. Tell the caller he has a visitor, so the conversation needs to end.
    D. Tell the visitor he will be with them as soon as he finishes the phone call

20.____

21. When engaged in conversation with another person, which communication technique is MOST likely to ensure you comprehend fully what the other person is trying to communicate to you?
    A. Repeat back to the person what you think they are communicating
    B. Continual eye contact
    C. Making sure the person speaks slowly
    D. Nodding your head while they speak

21.____

22. You encounter someone who is frustrated about a situation and needs to vent by talking it out before they can move onto a productive conversation. When a situation is like this, it is often BEST to
    A. Recommend various strategies for calming down
    B. Ask to be excused from the conversation without offering why
    C. Explain to the person that it is unproductive to behave the way they are currently behaving
    D. Acknowledge that venting is a crucial step to moving past the emotions and allow the person to express his or her feelings

22.____

23. Which of the following is NOT an example of active listening?
    A. Taking notes
    B. Referring the customer to the manager after they are done speaking
    C. Using phrases like "I see" or "Go on"
    D. Repeating back to the customer what you've heard

23.____

24. Which of the following questions would be classified as a clarification question?   24.____
    A. "How long have you sold spoiled meat?"
    B. "Do you like our brand?"
    C. "You mentioned you liked this merchandise. How would you feel about this?"
    D. None of the above

25. When interacting with a member of the public, which of the following words should you avoid using as it is not positive as perceived by most people?   25.____
    A. "Absolutely"   B. "You are welcome"
    C. "Here's what I can do"   D. "I'll do my best"

KEY (CORRECT ANSWERS)

1.	C		11.	A
2.	B		12.	B
3.	D		13.	C
4.	A		14.	A
5.	D		15.	B
6.	B		16.	D
7.	A		17.	B
8.	C		18.	C
9.	C		19.	A
10.	D		20.	D

21.	A
22.	D
23.	B
24.	C
25.	D

EXAMINATION SECTION
TEST 1

Each question or incomplete statement is followed by several suggested answers or completions. Select the one that BEST answers the question or completes the statement. *PRINT THE LETTER OF THE CORRECT ANSWER IN THE SPACE AT THE RIGHT.*

1. Files are used to store   1.____

    A. data   B. programs
    C. operating systems   D. source programs
    E. all of the above

2. MOST hard disks hold _____ bytes.   2.____

    A. 1-100 trillion   B. 1-100 billion   C. 1-100 million
    D. 1-1000   E. less than 1000

3. MOST floppy disks can store _____ bytes.   3.____

    A. 1-100 trillion   B. 1-100 billion   C. 1-100 million
    D. 1-1 million   E. less than 1000

4. A master file stores   4.____

    A. data about particular events
    B. relatively permanent data
    C. source copies of programs
    D. copies of other files
    E. data extracted from another file and held for a short term

5. A transaction file stores   5.____

    A. data about particular events
    B. relatively permanent data
    C. source copies of programs
    D. copies of other files
    E. data extracted from another file and held for a short term

6. A program file stores   6.____

    A. data about particular events
    B. relatively permanent data
    C. source copies of programs
    D. copies of other files
    E. data extracted from another file and held for a short term

7. A backup file stores   7.____

    A. data about particular events
    B. relatively permanent data
    C. source copies of programs
    D. copies of other files
    E. data extracted from another file and held for a short term

8. Which of the following is NOT a type of storage method?   8.____

    A. EBCDIC   B. Packed hexadecimal
    C. Packed decimal   D. True binary
    E. ASCII

9. Which of the following is the storage method commonly used by IBM?   9.____

    A. EBCDIC   B. Packed hexadecimal
    C. Packed decimal   D. True binary
    E. ASCII

10. Which of the following is a very efficient numerical storage method?   10.____

    A. EBCDIC   B. Packed hexadecimal
    C. Packed decimal   D. True binary
    E. ASCII

11. Which of the following is the type of storage method commonly found on home or per-sonal computers, as well as many mini-computers?   11.____

    A. EBCDIC   B. Packed hexadecimal
    C. Packed decimal   D. True binary
    E. ASCII

12. In the EBCDIC storage method,   12.____

    A. numbers follow letters
    B. letters follow numbers
    C. numbers are intermixed with letters
    D. numbers cannot be stored
    E. letters cannot be stored

13. In the ASCII storage method,   13.____

    A. numbers follow letters
    B. letters follow numbers
    C. numbers are intermixed with letters
    D. numbers cannot be stored
    E. letters cannot be stored

14. The collating sequence refers to   14.____

    A. the order of the letters in the alphabet
    B. the order of the digits 0 through 9
    C. the order of manufacturers of computers
    D. the order of numbers and letters relative to each other
    E. none of the above

15. A two-letter state abbreviation takes how many bytes of computer memory when stored in ASCII?   15.____

    A. 0   B. 1   C. 2
    D. 5   E. None of the above

16. A two-letter state abbreviation takes how many bytes of computer memory when stored   16.____
    in EBCDIC?

    A. 0   B. 1   C. 2
    D. 5   E. None of the above

17. An alternative to storing numeric data in EBCDIC is to store it in   17.____

    A. ZIP format   B. true trinary   C. true hexabinary
    D. true binary   E. all of the above

18. Packed decimal means each decimal digit is stored in   18.____

    A. one nibble   B. one byte   C. ASCII format
    D. EBCDIC format   E. all of the above

19. Generally speaking, alphanumeric data should be stored in   19.____

    A. nibbles   B. straight binary   C. EBCDIC
    D. packed decimal   E. all of the above

20. Which statement below BEST describes a capability associated with virtual storage?   20.____

    A. It is possible to program as if more core is available than exists in the system
    B. All computers are now automatically compatible
    C. Only tapes and disks can be used for storage
    D. The programmer can write efficient programs while completely ignoring the nature
       of the computer system being used
    E. None of the above

————

KEY (CORRECT ANSWERS)

1.	A	11.	E
2.	C	12.	A
3.	D	13.	B
4.	B	14.	D
5.	A	15.	C
6.	C	16.	C
7.	D	17.	D
8.	B	18.	A
9.	A	19.	C
10.	D	20.	A

————

TEST 2

DIRECTIONS: Each question or incomplete statement is followed by several suggested answers or completions. Select the one that BEST answers the question or completes the statement. *PRINT THE LETTER OF THE CORRECT ANSWER IN THE SPACE AT THE RIGHT.*

1. Which of the following is NOT a common tape density?   1.____

    A. 800   B. 1600   C. 2400   D. 6250
    E. All are common densities

2. Which of the following is a common tape length?   2.____

    A. 800   B. 1600   C. 2400   D. 6250
    E. All are common densities

3. Blocking refers to the   3.____

    A. number of physical records in a logical record
    B. number of bytes in a record
    C. number of bytes per inch of tape
    D. number of logical records in a physical record
    E. the space between physical records

4. The inter block gap refers to the   4.____

    A. number of physical records in a logical record
    B. number of bytes in a record
    C. number of bytes per inch of tape
    D. number of logical records in a physical record
    E. the space between physical records

5. Density refers to the   5.____

    A. number of physical records in a logical record
    B. number of bytes in a record
    C. number of bytes per inch of tape
    D. number of logical records in a physical record
    E. the space between physical records

6. The record length refers to the   6.____

    A. number of physical records in a logical record
    B. number of bytes in a record
    C. number of bytes per inch of tape
    D. number of logical records in a physical record
    E. the space between physical records

7. Disks are BEST used in situations where   7.____

    A. we need to store ineexpensively
    B. we need to store historical data
    C. we want to process data sequentially
    D. we need to store data for on-line applications
    E. All of the above

8. Tape is BEST used in situations where   8._____

    A. we need to store data inexpensively
    B. we need to store historical data
    C. we want to process data sequentially
    D. we do not need to store data for on-line applications
    E. All of the above

9. Which of the following is NOT a direct access method?   9._____

    A. VSAM
    B. Sequential
    C. KSAM
    D. ISAM
    E. All of the above are direct access methods

10. A basing algorithm calculates a records location in a file using a(n)   10._____

    A. record address
    B. social security number
    C. key field like a social security number
    D. using the binary search strategy
    E. all of the above

11. The soundex algorithm converts   11._____

    A. numeric keys to disk addresses
    B. disk addresses to numeric keys
    C. disk addresses to alphanumeric keys
    D. alphanumeric keys to disk addresses
    E. disk addresses to collisions

12. A collision occurs if two records have the   12._____

    A. same record key
    B. hash to the same disk address
    C. same length
    D. same blocking factor
    E. same density

13. In designing a tape file, an analyst should consider which of the following factors?   13._____

    A. Record fields
    B. Sequential order of records
    C. Estimate the number of records in the file
    D. Calculate the record length
    E. All of the above

14. In designing a tape file, an analyst should consider which of the following factors?   14.____

    A.   Order of fields in a record
    B.   Placement of fields in a record
    C.   An expansion area for future use
    D.   Data storage method, EBCDIC or packed decimal
    E.   All of the above

15. A record count tallies the number of   15.____

    A.   records in the file
    B.   number of fields in each record
    C.   number of bytes in a record
    D.   files in the database
    E.   All of the above

16. The term backup means   16.____

    A.   copying each record to a new record
    B.   copying a file to tape
    C.   copying a disk to memory
    D.   deleting a file from disk
    E.   deleting a file from a tape

17. The interblock gap is typically _____ inch(es).   17.____

    A. .05   B. .005   C. .5   D. 5   E. 50

18. In writing the schema, the analyst defines   18.____

    A.   data sets
    B.   data elements
    C.   data type, numeric or alphanumeric
    D.   slave data sets
    E.   All of the above

19. Which of the following is a typical data manipulation language command?   19.____

    A. QUERY   B. LOCK   C. DML
    D. DDL   E. None of the above

20. Which of the following statements concerning index files and backup programs is TRUE?   20.____

    A.   Index files may not be backed up.
    B.   All appropriate index files are automatically backed up whenever a database file backup is created.
    C.   Index files are often not backed up because they are so easily rebuilt.
    D.   Index files must be backed up whenever their database files are backed up.
    E.   None of the above

KEY (CORRECT ANSWERS)

1.	B	11.	D
2.	C	12.	B
3.	D	13.	E
4.	E	14.	E
5.	C	15.	A
6.	B	16.	B
7.	D	17.	C
8.	E	18.	E
9.	B	19.	B
10.	C	20.	C

INTERPRETING STATISTICAL DATA
GRAPHS, CHARTS AND TABLES
TEST 1

DIRECTIONS: Each question or incomplete statement is followed by several suggested answers or completions. Select the one that BEST answers the question or completes the statement. *PRINT THE LETTER OF THE CORRECT ANSWER IN THE SPACE AT THE RIGHT.*

1. The following chart shows the number of persons employed in a certain industry for each year from 2007 through 2012.   1.____

	Thousands of Employees
2007	5.7
2008	6.8
2009	7.0
2010	7.1
2011	7.4
2012	6.4

In making a forecast of future trends, the one of the following steps which should be taken FIRST is to
   A. take the six-year average
   B. fit a curvilinear trend to the data
   C. fit a straight line, omitting 2012 as an *outlier,* i.e., as an unusually low reading
   D. check on what happened to the industry in 2012

2. Of the following concepts, the one which CANNOT be represented suitably by a pie chart is   2.____

   A. percent shares
   B. shares in absolute units
   C. time trends
   D. successive totals over time, with their shares

3. A pictogram is ESSENTIALLY another version of a(n)_____ chart.   3.____

   A. plain bar   B. component bar
   C. pie   D. area

4. A time series for a certain cost is presented in a graph. It is drawn so that the vertical (cost) axis starts at a point well above zero.   4.____
This is a legitimate method of presentation for some purposes, but it may have the effect of

   A. hiding fixed components of the cost
   B. exaggerating changes which, in actual amounts, may be insignificant
   C. magnifying fixed components of the cost
   D. impairing correlation analysis

5. Certain budgetary data may be represented by bar, area or volume charts.   5._____
    Which one of the following BEST expresses the most appropriate order of usefulness?

    A. Descends from bar to volume and area charts, the last two being about the same
    B. Descends from volume to area to bar charts
    C. Depends on the nature of the data presented
    D. Descends from bar to area to volume charts

Questions 6-7.

DIRECTIONS: Questions 6 and 7 are to be answered on the basis of the layout below.

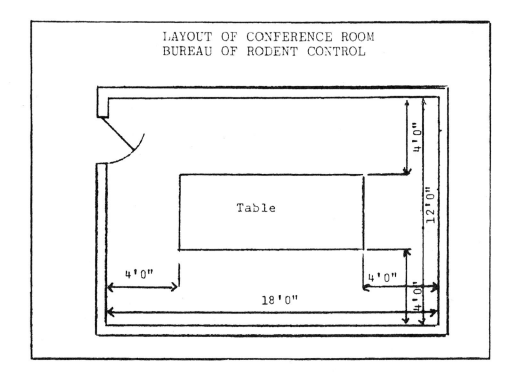

6. The LARGEST number of persons that can be accommodated in the area shown in the   6._____
    layout is

    A. 16   B. 10   C. 8   D. 6

7. Assume that the Bureau's programs undergo expansion and the Director indicates that   7._____
    the feasibility of increasing the size of the conference room should be explored.
    For every two additional persons that are to be accommodated, the analyst should rec-
    ommend that _____ be added to table length and _____ be added to room length.

    A. 2'-6"; 2'-6"   B. 5'-0"; 5'-0"
    C. 2'-6"; 5'-0"   D. 5'-0"; 2'-6"

Questions 8-9.

DIRECTIONS: Questions 8 and 9 are to be answered on the basis of the following groups, both of which depict the same information in different ways. The x and y axes in graphs A and B are not necessarily drawn in the same scale. The points along the curves on both graphs represent corresponding points and are the upper limits of class intervals.

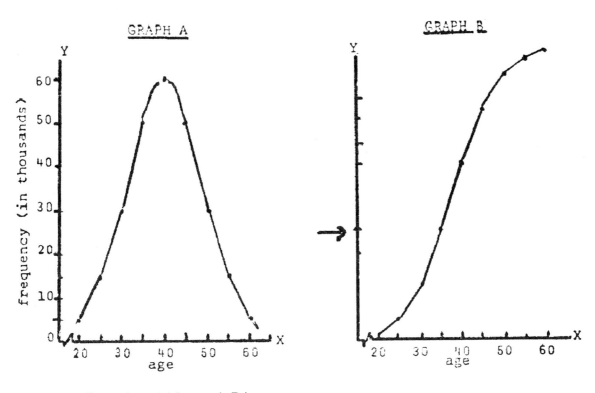

8. The ordinate (y-axis) in graph B is 8._____

   A. frequency   B. cumulative frequency
   C. average frequency   D. log frequency

9. The arrow on the y-axis in graph B indicates a particular number. 9._____
   That number is MOST NEARLY

   A. 100   B. 50,000   C. 100,000   D. 150,000

Questions 10-11.

DIRECTIONS: Questions 10 and 11 are to be answered on the basis of the graphs below.

ROAD REPAIR COSTS IF PERFORMED BY
CITY STAFF OR AN OUTSIDE CONTRACTOR

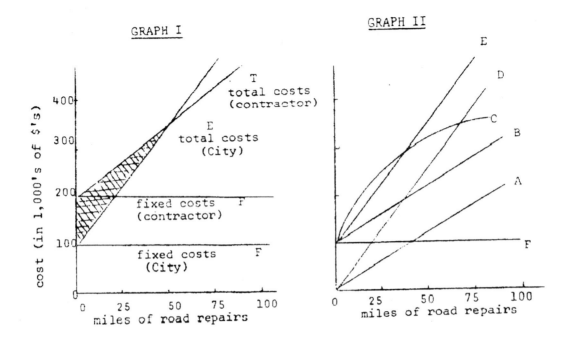

10. In Graph I, the vertical distance between lines E and T within the crosshatched area rep-   10.____
    resents the _____ than 50 miles is performed by the city.

    A. savings to the city if work of less
    B. loss to the city if work of less
    C. savings to the city if work of more
    D. loss to the city if work of more

11. Graph II is identical to Graph I except that contractor costs have been eliminated. Total   11.____
    costs (line E) are the sum of fixed costs (line F) a.nd variable costs. Variable costs are
    represented by line

    A. A   B. B   C. C   D. D

Questions 12-13.

DIRECTIONS: Questions 12 and 13 are to be answered on the basis of the following chart. In
             a hypothetical problem involving four criteria and four alternatives, the follow-
             ing data have been assembled.

Cost Criterion	Effectiveness Criterion	Timing Criterion	Feasibility Criterion
Alternative A $500,000	50 units	3 months	probably feasible
Alternative B $300,000	100 units	6 months	probably feasible
Alternative C $400,000	50 units	12 months	probably infeasible
Alternative D $200,000	75 units	3 months	probably infeasible

12. On the basis of the above data, it appears that the one alternative which is dominated by another alternative is Alternative   12.____

    A. A   B. B   C. C   D. D

13. If the feasibility constraint is absolute and fixed, then the critical trade-off is between lower cost _____ on the other.   13.____

    A.   on the one hand and faster timing and higher effectiveness
    B.   and higher effectiveness on one hand and faster timing
    C.   and faster timing on the one hand and higher effectiveness
    D.   on the one hand and higher effectiveness

14. The following illustration depicts the structure of a municipal agency.   14.____

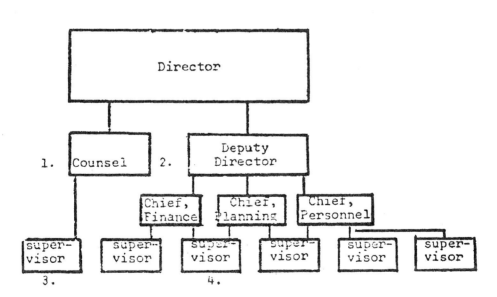

In the above illustration, which individual would generally be expected to encounter the MOST difficulty in carrying out his organizational functions?
    A. 1   B. 2   C. 3   D. 4

Questions 15-16.

DIRECTIONS: Questions 15 and 16 are to be answered on the basis of the information given on the report forms pictured below and on the following page.

Chart I and Chart II are parts of the Field Patrol Sheets of two Parking Enforcement Agents. They show the number of violations issued on a particular day. Chart III is the Tally Sheet for that day prepared by the Senior Parking Enforcement Agent from the Field Patrol Sheets of the entire squad.

CHART I

Area or Post	TYPE OF VIOLATION											Total
	Mtrs	B/S	D/P	Hyd	N/S	N/Sp	Taxi	Curb	N/P	Alt	Other	
19	2	3	2	2	3	3	0	1	1	5	1	23
21	4	0	2	0	1	2	2	0	5	9	1	26
Totals	6	3	4	2	4	5	2	1	6	14	2	49

2/4 — Date   100 — Badge   PEA Browne — Signature

TCB-61   Checked by _____ Date _____

CHART II

Area or Post	TYPE OF VIOLATION											Total
	Mtrs	B/S	D/P	Hyd	N/S	N/Sp	Taxi	Curb	N/P	Alt	Other	
31	8	2	0	0	3	2	2	0	4	5	0	26
33	7	0	1	2	3	1	2	0	6	3	0	25
Totals	15	2	1	2	6	3	4	0	10	8	0	51

2/4 — Date   101 — Badge   PEA Grey — Signature

TCB-61   Checked by _____ Date _____

TRAFFIC CONTROL BUREAU
SENIORS TALLY SHEET   Enf. 23A

Name	Mtrs Ptld	Mtrs	Bus Stop	Dble Park	Hyd	No Stand	No Stop	Taxi Stand	Curb	No Park	Alt Park	Other	Total
Green		18	2	3	1	6	0	0	0	4	10	1	45
Browne		6	3	4	2	4	5	2	1	6	14	2	49
White		12	0	0	0	2	1	1	0	8	8	1	33
Black		20	5	2	3	8	7	5	1	5	4	0	60
Grey		15	2	1	2	9	3	4	0	10	8	0	51
Redding		17	0	1	3	7	5	3	0	8	6	0	50
TOTAL		88	12	11	11	36	21	15	2	41	50	4	288

15. The Senior Parking Enforcement Agent who prepared Chart III made an error in transfer- 15.____
ring the violation totals from the Field Patrol Sheets to the Seniors Tally Sheet. Which
one of the following PROPERLY describes the Tally Sheet entry if this error were corrected? Parking Enforcement Agent

    A. Browne's overall total of summonses issued would be 50
    B. Browne's total of summonses issued for Double-Parking violations would be 3
    C. Grey's total number of summonses issued for meter violations would be 6
    D. Grey's total number of summonses issued for No Standing violations would be 6

16. The parking enforcement agent who issued the MOST summonses for bus stop and taxi 16.____
stand violations is

    A. Black   B. Redding   C. White   D. Browne

17. During a period of probation in which records were kept for 360 children fourteen to eigh- 17.____
teen years of age, probation officers found that the group committed certain offenses, as
shown in the following table:

I.Q.	No. of Offenders	No. of Offenses	Offenses Per Offender
61-80	125	338	2.7
81-100	160	448	2.8
101 & over	75	217	2.9

According to the foregoing data,
    A. the more intelligent offenders are no more law-abiding than, and perhaps not so
       law-abiding as, the dull offenders
    B. brighter offenders present no more difficult problems than less intelligent offenders
    C. the majority of this probation group is found to be above the average in intelligence
       of a normal group of young persons within this age range
    D. the relationship between the effectiveness of probation work and the number of
       offenders is in inverse ratio

18.   18.____

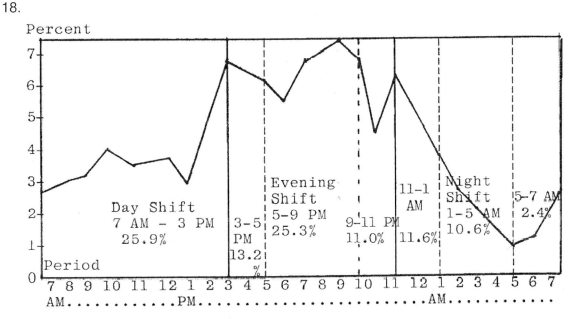

The percent for each hour is charted at the beginning of the hour. For example, 2.6% at the extreme left is for 7:00 A.M. to 7:59 A.M.

A certain police department has analyzed its need for police service and has computed the percentage distributions as shown on the chart on the preceding page. Despite good supervisory effort, there is a significant decrease in the amount of police service provided during the half-hour surrounding shift changes. The police commander wishes to minimize this effect.

To accomplish its objective, taking into account the distribution of need for police services, which one of the following is the BEST time for this department to schedule its three principal shift changes? (Assume 8-hour shifts.)

- A. A. 4:00 A.M., Noon, 8:00 P.M.
- B. 4:00 A.M., 1:00 P.M., 9:00 P.M.
- C. 6:00 A.M., 2:00 P.M., 10:00 P.M.
- D. 7:00 A.M., 3:00 P.M., 11:00 P.M.

19. An inspector on a painting contract has to keep records on the progress of the work completed by a painting contractor .   19._____

The following is the progress of the work completed by a contractor at the end of 8 months.

Apartment Size	Estimated Number of Apartments	Number of Apartments Painted
3 rooms	120	100
4 rooms	160	140
5 rooms	120	40

The percentage of work completed on a room basis is MOST NEARLY

A.	62%	B.	66%	C.	70%	D.	74%

20. Assume that an officer reported the following amounts of toll monies collected during each day of a five-day period: 20._____

Tuesday	$3,247.50
Wednesday	$2,992.50
Thursday	$3,917.50
Friday	$4,862.50
Saturday	$1,675.00

The TOTAL amount of toll money collected during this period was

- A. $15,702.50
- B. $16,485.00
- C. $16,695.00
- D. $16,997.50

21. Suppose that during a two-hour period in a toll booth an officer collected the following: 21._____

Type of Money	Number of Bills
$20 bills	2
$10 bills	5
$5 bills	23
$1 bills	269

The TOTAL amount of money the officer collected was

A.	$299	B.	$464	C.	$474	D.	$501

Questions 22-23.

DIRECTIONS: Questions 22 and 23 are to be answered SOLELY on the basis of the information shown below which indicates the charges for hospital services and physician services given in a hospital and a patient's annual income for each of four
consecutive years.

Year	Patient's Annual Income	Charges for Hospital Services and Physician Services Given in a Hospital
2009	$45,000	$11,100
2010	$46,500	$11,970
2011	$64,500	$16,230
2012	$70,500	$17,325

22. A hospitalized patient may qualify for Medicaid benefits when the charges for hospital   22.____
services and for physician services given in the hospital exceed 25 percent of the
patient's annual income.
According to the information shown above, the one of the following that indicates ONLY
those years in which the patient qualifies for Medicaid benefits is

   A.   2010, 2011   B.   2009, 2010, 2012
   C.   2010, 2012   D.   2010, 2011, 2012

23. The one of the following that is the patient's average annual income for the entire four-   23.____
year period shown above is MOST NEARLY

   A. $48,375   B. $49,125   C. $56,025   D. $56,625

Questions 24-25.

DIRECTIONS: Questions 24 and 25 are to be answered SOLELY on the basis of the information shown below, which gives the hospital bill and the amount paid by an
Insurance Plan for each of four patients.

Patient's Name	Hospital Bill	Amount Paid by the Insurance Plan Toward Hospital Bill
Mr. Harris	$ 8,753	$5,952
Mr. W. Smith	$ 4,504	$3,285
Mr. T. Jones	$ 7,211	$5,048
Mr. M. White	$12,255	$8,712

24. According to the information given above, which patient, when compared with the other   24.____
three patients, had the HIGHEST percentage of his bill paid by the Insurance Plan?

   A.   Mr. W. Smith   B.   Mr. D. Harris
   C.   Mr. T. Jones   D.   Mr. M. White

25. The average amount paid by the Insurance Plan toward the hospital bills of the four   25.____
patients shown above is MOST NEARLY

   A. $5,269   B. $5,499   C. $5,749   D. $5,766

KEY (CORRECT ANSWERS)

1.	D		11.	D
2.	C		12.	C
3.	A		13.	B
4.	B		14.	D
5.	D		15.	D
6.	B		16.	A
7.	A		17.	A
8.	B		18.	C
9.	C		19.	B
10.	A		20.	C

21. C
22. A
23. D
24. A
25. C

———

TEST 2

DIRECTIONS: Each question or incomplete statement is followed by several suggested
answers or completions. Select the one that BEST answers the question or
completes the statement. *PRINT THE LETTER OF THE CORRECT ANSWER
IN THE SPACE AT THE RIGHT.*

Questions 1-2.

DIRECTIONS: Questions 1 and 2 are to be answered on the basis of the information contained in the chart below.

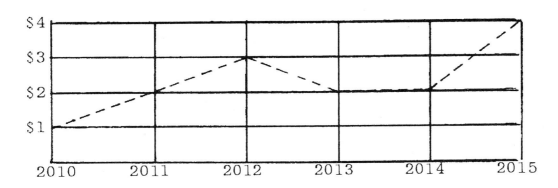

1. According to the above chart, the increase in the average price of the commodity from   1.____
    2012 to 2015 was APPROXIMATELY

    A. 25%   B. 33 1/3%   C. *50%*   D. 75%

2. According to the above chart, the increase in the average price of the commodity from   2.____
    2010 to 2012 was APPROXIMATELY

    A. 20%   B. 30%   C. 200%   D. 300%

Questions 3-4.

DIRECTIONS: Questions 3 and 4 are to be answered SOLELY on the basis of the information
contained in the chart below, which shows supply and demand of a commodity
from January 1, 2011 to January 1, 2015.

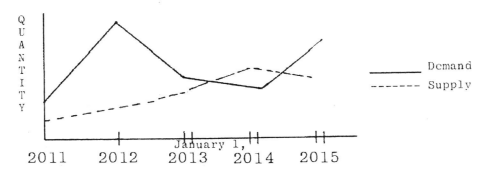

3. The above chart indicates that there was a seller's market during most of each of the following years EXCEPT

    A. 2011   B. 2012   C. 2013   D. 2014

3.____

4. According to the above chart, in the absence of price controls or other artificial or unusual circumstances, when would the price of the commodity have been the HIGHEST?
January 1,

    A. 2011   B. 2012   C. 2013   D. 2014

4.____

5. In order to pay its employees, the Convex Company obtained bills and coins in the following denominations:

5.____

Denomination	$20	$10	$5	$1	$.50	$.25	$.10	$.05	$.01
Number	317	122	38	73	69	47	39	25	36

What was the TOTAL amount of cash obtained?
    A. $7,874.76   B. $7,878.00
    C. $7,889.25   D. $7,924.35

6. Suppose that a business you are investigating presents the following figures:

6.____

Year	Net Income	Tax Rate On Net Income
2014	$55,000	20%
2015	$55,000	30%
2016	$65,000	20%
2017	$52,000	25%
2018	$62,000	30%
2019	$68,000	25%

According to these figures, it is MOST accurate to say that
    A. less tax was due in 2018 than in 2019
    B. more tax was due in 2014 than in 2017
    C. the same amount of tax was due in 2014 and 2015
    D. the same amount of tax was due in 2016 and 2017

7. The table below shows the total amount of money owed on the bills sent to each of four different accounts and the total amount of money which has been received from each of these accounts.

7.____

Name of Account	Amount Owed	Amount Received
Arnold	$55,989	$37,898
Barry	$97,276	$79,457
Carter	$62,736	$47,769
Daley	$77,463	$59,534

The balance of an account is determined by subtracting the amount received from the amount owed.
Based on this method of determining a balance, the account with the LARGEST balance is
    A. Arnold   B. Barry   C. Carter   D. Daley

8. A work sheet for a booth audit has the readings shown below for four turnstiles: 8.____

Turnstile No.	Opening Readings	Readings For Audit
1	26178	26291
2	65489	65752
3	72267	72312
4	45965	46199

With a fare of $1.00, what is the cash value of the TOTAL difference between the Opening Readings and the Readings for Audit for the four turnstiles?

A. $635   B. $653   C. $654   D. $675

Questions 9-10.

DIRECTIONS: Questions 9 and 10 are to be answered SOLELY on the basis of the information contained in the following table.

COMPARISON OF CUNY ATTRITION RATES FOR FALL 2010 DAY FRESHMEN
THROUGH FALL 2011

Colleges	Open Admissions (a)	Regular (b)	Overall
Senior	30%	14%	21%
Community	40%	34%	39%
Total	36%	20%	29%

a. Represents senior college students admitted with high school averages below 80 and community college students admitted with high school averages below 75
b. Represents senior college students admitted with averages of 80 and above and community college students admitted with averages of 75 and above

9. The category of students who remained in the City University in the GREATEST proportion were   9.____

A. regular students in community colleges
B. open admissions students in community colleges
C. regular students in senior colleges
D. open admissions students in senior colleges

10. Regular admission to a senior college was on the basis of an academic average   10.____

A. above 70   B. of 80 or above
C. above 75   D. above 85

Questions 11-12.

DIRECTIONS: Questions 11 and 12 are to be answered SOLELY on the basis of the information given below.

Time Scores

Maximum qualifying time	15 minutes
Minimum qualifying time (subtract)	5 minutes
Range in qualifying time	10 minutes

Weighted Point Scores (Weight = 10)
Maximum weighted score   10 points
Minimum qualifying score (subtract   7 points
        Range in weighted scores   3 points

From the foregoing, it is apparent that a simple conversion table can be prepared by giving the maximum qualifying time a minimum qualifying weighted score of 7 points and
crediting three-tenths additional weighted points for each minute less than 15.

11. On the basis of the above paragraph, it is apparent that if the maximum *time* taken by   11.____
    any candidate on the task was 15 minutes,

    A. the test was too easy
    B. too much weight was given to the *time* portion
    C. less time should have been given for the task
    D. no one failed the *time* portion of the test

12. The BEST of the following interpretations of the above paragraph is that any candidate   12.____
    completing the task in 8 minutes would have received a weighted score for *time* of
    _____ points.

    A. 9.1   B. 8.5   C. 8.2   D. 7.9

Questions 13-14.

DIRECTIONS: Questions 13 and 14 are to be answered on the basis of the following illustra-
              tion. Assume that the figures in the chart are cubes.

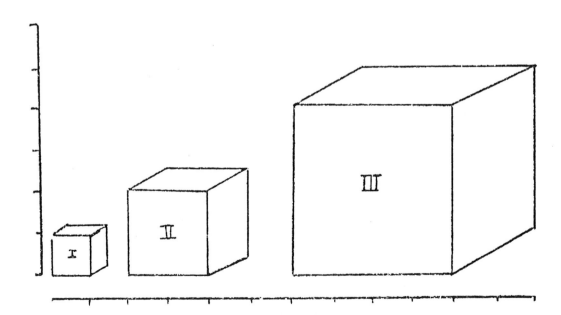

13. In the illustration above, how many times GREATER is the quantity represented by Fig-   13.____
    ure III than the quantity represented by Figure II?

    A. 2   B. 4   C. 8   D. 16

14. The illustration above illustrates a progression in quantity BEST described as   14._____

    A. arithmetic   B. geometric
    C. discrete   D. linear

Questions 15-16.

DIRECTIONS: Questions 15 and 16 are to be answered SOLELY on the basis of the following summary of salary increases applicable to a group of employees in a college office.

Hourly Rate 6/30/12	Increase 7/1/12	Increase 7/1/13
$10.20	$1.40/hr.	$1.40/hr.
$11.20	$1.20/hr.	$1.20/hr.
$12.20	$1.20/hr.	$1.20/hr.

Hourly Rate 6/30/12	Increase 7/1/12	Increase 7/1/13
$13.20	$1.00/hr.	$1.00/hr.
$14.20	$1.00/hr.	$1.00/hr.
$15.20	$1.00/hr.	$1.00/hr.

15. A college office employee with an hourly salary of $14.20 as of June 30, 2012 worked for   15._____
32 hours during the week of April 16, 2013.
Her GROSS salary for that week was

    A. $422.40   B. $454.40   C. $486.40   D. $518.40

16. A college office employee was earning an hourly salary of $12.20 in June of 2012.   16._____
The percentage increase in her hourly salary as of July 2, 2013 will be MOST NEARLY
_____ percent.

    A. 10   B. 15   C. 20   D. 25

17. An experiment was conducted to measure the error rate of typists. The results follow: 17._____

Typists	Percent of Total Output	Error Rate (in percent)
A	30	1.00
B	30	1.50
C	40	0.50

The error rate (in percent) for the three typists combined
    A. is 0.95
    B. is 1.00
    C. is 3.00
    D. cannot be calculated from the given data

Question 18.

DIRECTIONS: Question 18 is to be answered on the basis of the information given below.

At midnight on January 31, the following bodies were remaining:

Adults	Infants	Stillbirths	Amputations
37	23	40	21

On February 1st, from 12:01 A.M. to 12:00 midnight, the following bodies were received:

Adults	Infants	Stillbirths	Amputations
24	13	18	8

In addition, the following bodies were claimed:

Adults	Infants	Stillbirths	Amputations
33	9	4	2

18.   What is the number of cases remaining at midnight on February 1?   18._____

	Adults	Infants	Stillbirths	Amputations
A.	31	26	41	23
B.	28	27	54	27
C.	29	28	48	25
D.	27	29	62	28

Questions 19-25.

DIRECTIONS: Questions 19 through 25 are to be answered SOLELY on the basis of the following information.

ACCIDENTS

During one month, a certain division reported the number of accidents from various causes as follows:

Falls	6
Flying objects..................................	5
Handling objects	4
Striking objects	3
Assaults	2
Stepping on objects	1

19.   The GREATEST cause of accidents was   19._____

    A.   striking objects   B.   handling objects
    C.   flying objects   D.   falls

20.   The accidents over which the injured person had LEAST control were those due to   20._____

    A.   handling objects   B.   falls
    C.   assaults   D.   flying objects

21. The accidents due to flying objects exceeded those due to striking objects by   21.____

    A. 8   B. 6   C. 3   D. 2

22. The TOTAL number of accidents as shown was   22.____

    A. 19   B. 20   C. 21   D. 22

23. The MOST likely cause for an accident to a station porter is   23.____

    A. stepping on objects   B. falls
    C. striking objects   D. assaults

24. The accidents which would MOST likely result in disciplinary action are those due to   24.____

    A. stepping on objects   B. assaults
    C. striking objects   D. falls

25. The TOTAL number of accidents involving objects was   25.____

    A. 8   B. 12   C. 13   D. 21

KEY (CORRECT ANSWERS)

1.	B		11.	D
2.	C		12.	A
3.	C		13.	C
4.	B		14.	B
5.	A		15.	C
6.	D		16.	C
7.	A		17.	A
8.	C		18.	B
9.	C		19.	D
10.	B		20.	D

21.	D
22.	C
23.	B
24.	B
25.	C

READING COMPREHENSION
UNDERSTANDING AND INTERPRETING WRITTEN MATERIAL
EXAMINATION SECTION
TEST 1

DIRECTIONS: Each question or incomplete statement is followed by several suggested answers or completions. Select the one that BEST answers the question or completes the statement. *PRINT THE LETTER OF THE CORRECT ANSWER IN THE SPACE AT THE RIGHT.*

Questions 1-5.

DIRECTIONS: Questions 1 through 5 are to be answered SOLELY on the basis of the following passage.

The most effective control mechanism to prevent gross incompetence on the part of public employees is a good personnel program. The personnel officer in the line departments and the central personnel agency should exert positive leadership to raise levels of performance. Although the key factor is the quality of the personnel recruited, staff members other than personnel officers can make important contributions to efficiency. Administrative analysts, now employed in many agencies, make detailed studies of organization and procedures, with the purpose of eliminating delays, waste, and other inefficiencies. Efficiency is, however, more than a question of good organization and procedures; it is also the product of the attitudes and values of the public employees. Personal motivation can provide the will to be efficient. The best management studies will not result in substantial improvement of the performance of those employees who feel no great urge to work up to their abilities.

1. The above passage indicates that the KEY factor in preventing gross incompetence of public employees is the

    A. hiring of administrative analysts to assist personnel people
    B. utilization of effective management studies
    C. overlapping of responsibility
    D. quality of the employees hired

1.____

2. According to the above passage, the central personnel agency staff SHOULD

    A. work more closely with administrative analysts in the line departments than with personnel officers
    B. make a serious effort to avoid jurisdictional conflicts with personnel officers in line departments
    C. contribute to improving the quality of work of public employees
    D. engage in a comprehensive program to change the public's negative image of public employees

2.____

3. The above passage indicates that efficiency in an organization can BEST be brought about by

    A. eliminating ineffective control mechanisms
    B. instituting sound organizational procedures

3.____

C. promoting competent personnel
D. recruiting people with desire to do good work

4. According to the above passage, the purpose of administrative analysis in a public agency is to

    4.____

A. prevent injustice to the public employee
B. promote the efficiency of the agency
C. protect the interests of the public
D. ensure the observance of procedural due process

5. The above passage implies that a considerable rise in the quality of work of public employees can be brought about by

    5.____

A. encouraging positive employee attitudes toward work
B. controlling personnel officers who exceed their powers
C. creating warm personal associations among public employees in an agency
D. closing loopholes in personnel organization and procedures

Questions 6-8.

DIRECTIONS: Questions 6 through 8 are to be answered SOLELY on the basis of the following passage on Employee Needs.

EMPLOYEE NEEDS

The greatest waste in industry and in government may be that of human resources. This waste usually derives not from employees' unwillingness or inability, but from management's ineptness to meet the maintenance and motivational needs of employees. Maintenance needs refer to such needs as providing employees with safe places to work, written work rules, job security, adequate salary, employer-sponsored social activities, and with knowledge of their role in the overall framework of the organization. However, of greatest significance to employees are the motivational needs of job growth, achievement, responsibility, and recognition.

Although employee dissatisfaction may stem from either poor maintenance or poor motivation factors, the outward manifestation of the dissatisfaction may be very much alike, i.e., negativism, complaints, deterioration of performance, and so forth. The improvement in the lighting of an employee's work area or raising his level of pay won't do much good if the source of the dissatisfaction is the absence of a meaningful assignment. By the same token, if an employee is dissatisfied with what he considers inequitable pay, the introduction of additional challenge in his work may simply make matters worse.

It is relatively easy for an employee to express frustration by complaining about pay, washroom conditions, fringe benefits, and so forth; but most people cannot easily express resentment in terms of the more abstract concepts concerning job growth, responsibility, and achievement.

It would be wrong to assume that there is no interaction between maintenance and motivational needs of employees. For example, conditions of high motivation often overshadow poor maintenance conditions. If an organization is in a period of strong growth and expansion, opportunities for job growth, responsibility, recognition, and achievement are usually abundant, but the rapid growth may have outrun the upkeep of maintenance factors. In this situation, motivation may be high, but only if employees recognize the poor maintenance conditions as unavoidable and temporary. The subordination of maintenance factors cannot go on indefinitely, even with the highest motivation.

Both maintenance and motivation factors influence the behavior of all employees, but employees are not identical and, furthermore, the needs of any individual do not remain constant. However, a broad distinction can be made between employees who have a basic orientation toward maintenance factors and those with greater sensitivity toward motivation factors.

A highly maintenance-oriented individual, preoccupied with the factors peripheral to his job rather than the job itself, is more concerned with comfort than challenge. He does not get deeply involved with his work but does with the condition of his work area, toilet facilities, and his time for going to lunch. By contrast, a strongly motivation-oriented employee is usually relatively indifferent to his surroundings and is caught up in the pursuit of work goals.

Fortunately, there are few people who are either exclusively maintenance-oriented or purely motivation-oriented. The former would be deadwood in an organization, while the latter might trample on those around him in his pursuit to achieve his goals.

6. With respect to employee motivational and maintenance needs, the management policies of an organization which is growing rapidly will probably result   6.____

   A. more in meeting motivational needs rather than maintenance needs
   B. more in meeting maintenance needs rather than motivational needs
   C. in meeting both of these needs equally
   D. in increased effort to define the motivational and maintenance needs of its employees

7. In accordance with the above passage, which of the following CANNOT be considered as an example of an employee maintenance need for railroad clerks?   7.____

   A. Providing more relief periods
   B. Providing fair salary increases at periodic intervals
   C. Increasing job responsibilities
   D. Increasing health insurance benefits

8. Most employees in an organization may be categorized as being interested in   8.____

   A. maintenance needs *only*
   B. motivational needs *only*
   C. both motivational and maintenance needs
   D. money only, to the exclusion of all other needs

Questions 9-11.

DIRECTIONS: Questions 9 through 11 are to be answered SOLELY on the basis of the following passage on Good Employee Practices.

GOOD EMPLOYEE PRACTICES

As a city employee, you will be expected to take an interest in your work and perform the duties of your job to the best of your ability and in a spirit of cooperation. Nothing shows an interest in your work more than coming to work on time, not only at the start of the day but also when returning from lunch. If it is necessary for you to keep a personal appointment at lunch hour which might cause a delay in getting back to work on time, you should explain the situation to your supervisor and get his approval to come back a little late before you leave for lunch.

You should do everything that is asked of you willingly and consider important even the small jobs that your supervisor gives you. Although these jobs may seem unimportant, if you forget to do them or if you don't do them right, trouble may develop later.

Getting along well with your fellow workers will add much to the enjoyment of your work. You should respect your fellow workers and try to see their side when a disagreement arises. The better you get along with your fellow workers and your supervisor, the better you will like your job and the better you will be able to do it.

9. According to the above passage, in your job as a city employee, you are expected to   9.____

    A. show a willingness to cooperate on the job
    B. get your supervisor's approval before keeping any personal appointments at lunch hour
    C. avoid doing small jobs that seem unimportant
    D. do the easier jobs at the start of the day and the more difficult ones later on

10. According to the above passage, getting to work on time shows that you   10.____

    A. need the job
    B. have an interest in your work
    C. get along well with your fellow workers
    D. like your supervisor

11. According to the above passage, the one of the following statements that is NOT true is   11.____

    A. if you do a small job wrong, trouble may develop
    B. you should respect your fellow workers
    C. if you disagree with a fellow worker, you should try to see his side of the story
    D. the less you get along with your supervisor, the better you will be able to do your job

Questions 12-15.

DIRECTIONS: Questions 12 through 15 are to be answered SOLELY on the basis of the following passage on Employee Suggestions.

EMPLOYEE SUGGESTIONS

To increase the effectiveness of the city government, the city asks its employees to offer suggestions when they feel an improvement could be made in some government operation. The Employees' Suggestions Program was started to encourage city employees to do this.

Through this Program, which is only for city employees, cash awards may be given to those whose suggestions are submitted and approved. Suggestions are looked for not only from supervisors but from all city employees as any city employee may get an idea which might be approved and contribute greatly to the solution of some problem of city government

Therefore, all suggestions for improvement are welcome, whether they be suggestions on how to improve working conditions, or on how to increase the speed with which work is done, or on how to reduce or eliminate such things as waste, time losses, accidents or fire hazards. There are, however, a few types of suggestions for which cash awards cannot be given. An example of this type would be a suggestion to increase salaries or a suggestion to change the regulations about annual leave or about sick leave. The number of suggestions sent in has increased sharply during the past few years. It is hoped that it will keep increasing in the future in order to meet the city's needs for more ideas for improved ways of doing things.

12. According to the above passage, the MAIN reason why the city asks its employees for suggestions about government operations is to   12.____

    A. increase the effectiveness of the city government
    B. show that the Employees' Suggestion Program is working well
    C. show that everybody helps run the city government
    D. have the employee win a prize

13. According to the above passage, the Employees' Suggestion Program can approve awards ONLY for those suggestions that come from   13.____

    A. city employees
    B. city employees who are supervisors
    C. city employees who are not supervisors
    D. experienced employees of the city

14. According to the above passage, a cash award cannot be given through the Employees' Suggestion Program for a suggestion about   14.____

    A. getting work done faster
    B. helping prevent accidents on the job
    C. increasing the amount of annual leave for city employees
    D. reducing the chance of fire where city employees work

15. According to the above passage, the suggestions sent in during the past few years have   15.____

    A. all been approved
    B. generally been well written
    C. been mostly about reducing or eliminating waste
    D. been greater in number than before

Questions 16-18.

DIRECTIONS: Questions 16 through 18 are to be answered SOLELY on the basis of the following passage.

The supervisor will gain the respect of the members of his staff and increase his influence over them by controlling his temper and avoiding criticizing anyone publicly. When a mistake is made, the good supervisor will talk it over with the employee quietly and privately. The supervisor will listen to the employee's story, suggest the better way of doing the job, and offer help so the mistake won't happen again. Before closing the discussion, the supervisor should try to find something good to say about other parts of the employee's work. Some praise and appreciation, along with instruction, is more likely to encourage an employee to improve in those areas where he is weakest.

16. A good title that would show the meaning of the above passage would be   16.____

    A. HOW TO CORRECT EMPLOYEE ERRORS
    B. HOW TO PRAISE EMPLOYEES
    C. MISTAKES ARE PREVENTABLE
    D. THE WEAK EMPLOYEE

17. According to the above passage, the work of an employee who has made a mistake is   17.____
more likely to improve if the supervisor

    A. avoids criticizing him
    B. gives him a chance to suggest a better way of doing the work
    C. listens to the employee's excuses to see if he is right
    D. praises good work at the same time he corrects the mistake

18. According to the above passage, when a supervisor needs to correct an employee's mis-   18.____
take, it is important that he

    A. allow some time to go by after the mistake is made
    B. do so when other employees are not present
    C. show his influence with his tone of voice
    D. tell other employees to avoid the same mistake

Questions 19-23.

DIRECTIONS: Questions 19 through 23 are to be answered SOLELY on the basis of the following passage.

In studying the relationships of people to the organizational structure, it is absolutely necessary to identify and recognize the informal organizational structure. These relationships are
necessary when coordination of a plan is attempted. They may be with *the boss,* line supervisors, staff personnel, or other representatives of the formal organization's hierarchy, and they
may include the *liaison men* who serve as the leaders of the informal organization. An
acquaintanceship with the people serving in these roles in the organization, and its formal
counterpart, permits a supervisor to recognize sensitive areas in which it is simple to get a
conflict reaction. Avoidance of such areas, plus conscious efforts to inform other people of his
own objectives for various plans, will usually enlist their aid and support. Planning *without
people* can lead to disaster because the individuals who must act together to make any plan
a success are more important than the plans themselves.

19. Of the following titles, the one that MOST clearly describes the above passage is   19.____

    A. COORDINATION OF A FUNCTION
    B. AVOIDANCE OF CONFLICT
    C. PLANNING WITH PEOPLE
    D. PLANNING OBJECTIVES

20. According to the above passage, attempts at coordinating plans may fail unless   20._____

    A. the plan's objectives are clearly set forth
    B. conflict between groups is resolved
    C. the plans themselves are worthwhile
    D. informal relationships are recognized

21. According to the above passage, conflict   21._____

    A. may, in some cases, be desirable to secure results
    B. produces more heat than light
    C. should be avoided at all costs
    D. possibilities can be predicted by a sensitive supervisor

22. The above passage implies that   22._____

    A. informal relationships are more important than formal structure
    B. the weakness of a formal structure depends upon informal relationships
    C. liaison men are the key people to consult when taking formal and informal structures into account
    D. individuals in a group are at least as important as the plans for the group

23. The above passage suggests that   23._____

    A. some planning can be disastrous
    B. certain people in sensitive areas should be avoided
    C. the supervisor should discourage acquaintanceships in the organization
    D. organizational relationships should be consciously limited

Questions 24-25.

DIRECTIONS: Questions 24 and 25 are to be answered SOLELY on the basis of the following passage.

    Good personnel relations of an organization depend upon mutual confidence, trust, and good will. The basis of confidence is understanding. Most troubles start with people who do not understand each other. When the organization's intentions or motives are misunderstood, or when reasons for actions, practices, or policies are misconstrued, complete cooperation from individuals is not forthcoming. If management expects full cooperation from employees, it has a responsibility of sharing with them the information which is the foundation of proper understanding, confidence, and trust. Personnel management has long since outgrown the days when it was the vogue to *treat them rough and tell them nothing.* Up-to-date personnel management provides all possible information about the activities, aims, and purposes of the organization. It seems altogether creditable that a desire should exist among employees for such information which the best-intentioned executive might think would not interest them and which the worst-intentioned would think was none of their business.

24. The above passage implies that one of the causes of the difficulty which an organization   24._____
might have with its personnel relations is that its employees

    A. have not expressed interest in the activities, aims, and purposes of the organization
    B. do not believe in the good faith of the organization

C. have not been able to give full cooperation to the organization
D. do not recommend improvements in the practices and policies of the organization

25. According to the above passage, in order for an organization to have good personnel   25._____
relations, it is NOT essential that

A. employees have confidence in the organization
B. the purposes of the organization be understood by the employees
C. employees have a desire for information about the organization
D. information about the organization be communicated to employees

———

KEY (CORRECT ANSWERS)

1. D	11. D
2. C	12. A
3. D	13. A
4. B	14. C
5. A	15. D
6. A	16. A
7. C	17. D
8. C	18. B
9. A	19. C
10. B	20. D

21.	D
22.	D
23.	A
24.	B
25.	C

———

TEST 2

Questions 1-8.

DIRECTIONS: Questions 1 through 8 are to be answered SOLELY on the basis of the following passage.

Important figures in education and in public affairs have recommended development of a private organization sponsored in part by various private foundations which would offer installment payment plans to full-time matriculated students in accredited colleges and universities in the United States and Canada. Contracts would be drawn to cover either tuition and fees, or tuition, fees, room and board in college facilities, from one year up to and including six years. A special charge, which would vary with the length of the contract, would be added to the gross repayable amount. This would be in addition to interest at a rate which would vary with the income of the parents. There would be a 3% annual interest charge for families with total income, before income taxes, of $50,000 or less. The rate would increase by 1/10 of 1% for every $1,000 of additional net income in excess of $50,000 up to a maximum of 10% interest. Contracts would carry an insurance provision on the life of the parent or guardian who signs the contract; all contracts must have the signature of a parent or guardian. Payment would be scheduled in equal monthly installments.

1. Which of the following students would be eligible for the payment plan described in the above passage? A

    A. matriculated student taking six semester hours toward a graduate degree
    B. matriculated student taking seventeen semester hours toward an undergraduate degree
    C. graduate matriculated at the University of Mexico taking eighteen semester hours toward a graduate degree
    D. student taking eighteen semester hours in a special pre-matriculation program

1.____

2. According to the above passage, the organization described would be sponsored in part by

    A. private foundations
    B. colleges and universities
    C. persons in the field of education
    D. persons in public life

2.____

3. Which of the following expenses could NOT be covered by a contract with the organization described in the above passage?

    A. Tuition amounting to $20,000 per year
    B. Registration and laboratory fees
    C. Meals at restaurants near the college
    D. Rent for an apartment in a college dormitory

3.____

4. The total amount to be paid would include ONLY the

    A. principal
    B. principal and interest
    C. principal, interest, and special charge
    D. principal, interest, special charge, and fee

4.____

5. The contract would carry insurance on the　　　　　　　　　　　　　5.___

    A. life of the student
    B. life of the student's parents
    C. income of the parents of the student
    D. life of the parent who signed the contract

6. The interest rate for an annual loan of $25,000 from the organization described in the　　6.___
above passage for a student whose family's net income was $55,000 should be

    A. 3%　　　　　B. 3.5%　　　　　C. 4%　　　　　D. 4.5%

7. The interest rate for an annual loan of $35,000 from the organization described in the　　7.___
above passage for a student whose family's net income was $100,000 should be

    A. 5%　　　　　B. 8%　　　　　C. 9%　　　　　D. 10%

8. John Lee has submitted an application for the installment payment plan described in the　　8.___
above passage. John's mother and father have a store which grossed $500,000 last
year, but the income which the family received from the store was $90,000 before taxes.
They also had $5,000 income from stock dividends. They paid $10,000 in income taxes.
The amount of income upon which the interest should be based is

    A. $85,000　　　　B. $90,000　　　　C. $95,000　　　　D. $105,000

Questions 9-13.

DIRECTIONS: Questions 9 through 13 are to be answered SOLELY on the basis of the following passage.

Since an organization chart is pictorial in nature, there is a tendency for it to be drawn in
an artistically balanced and appealing fashion, regardless of the realities of actual organizational structure. In addition to being subject to this distortion, there is the difficulty of communicating in any organization chart the relative importance or the relative size of various
component parts of an organizational structure. Furthermore, because of the need for sim-
plicity of design, an organization chart can never indicate the full extent of the interrelationships among the component parts of an organization.

These interrelationships are often just as vital as the specifications which an organization
chart endeavors to indicate. Yet, if an organization chart were to be drawn with all the wide
variety of criss-crossing communication and cooperation networks existent within a typical
organization, the chart would probably be much more confusing than informative. It is also
obvious that no organization chart as such can prove or disprove that the organizational
structure it represents is effective in realizing the objectives of the organization. At best, an
organization chart can only illustrate some of the various factors to be taken into consideration in understanding, devising, or altering organizational arrangements.

9. According to the above passage, an organization chart can be expected to portray the　　9.___

    A. structure of the organization along somewhat ideal lines
    B. relative size of the organizational units quite accurately
    C. channels of information distribution within the organization graphically
    D. extent of the obligation of each unit to meet the organizational objectives

10. According to the above passage, those aspects of internal functioning which are NOT shown on an organization chart   10.____

    A. can be considered to have little practical application in the operations of the organization
    B. might well be considered to be as important as the structural relationships which a chart does present
    C. could be the cause of considerable confusion in the operations of an organization which is quite large
    D. would be most likely to provide the information needed to determine the overall effectiveness of an organization

11. In the above passage, the one of the following conditions which is NOT implied as being a defect of an organization chart is that an organization chart may   11.____

    A. present a picture of the organizational structure which is different from the structure that actually exists
    B. fail to indicate the comparative size of various organizational units
    C. be limited in its ability to convey some of the meaningful aspects of organizational relationships
    D. become less useful over a period of time during which the organizational facts which it illustrated have changed

12. The one of the following which is the MOST suitable title for the above passage is   12.____

    A. THE DESIGN AND CONSTRUCTION OF AN ORGANIZATION CHART
    B. THE INFORMAL ASPECTS OF AN ORGANIZATION CHART
    C. THE INHERENT DEFICIENCIES OF AN ORGANIZATION CHART
    D. THE UTILIZATION OF A TYPICAL ORGANIZATION CHART

13. It can be INFERRED from the above passage that the function of an organization chart is to   13.____

    A. contribute to the comprehension of the organization form and arrangements
    B. establish the capabilities of the organization to operate effectively
    C. provide a balanced picture of the operations of the organization
    D. eliminate the need for complexity in the organization's structure

Questions 14-16.

DIRECTIONS: Questions 14 through 16 are to be answered SOLELY on the basis of the following passage.

In dealing with visitors to the school office, the school secretary must use initiative, tact, and good judgment. All visitors should be greeted promptly and courteously. The nature of their business should be determined quickly and handled expeditiously. Frequently, the secretary should be able to handle requests, receipts, deliveries, or passes herself. Her judgment should determine when a visitor should see members of the staff or the principal. Serious problems or doubtful cases should be referred to a supervisor.

14. In general, visitors should be handled by the

    A. school secretary   B. principal
    C. appropriate supervisor   D. person who is free

14.____

15. It is wise to obtain the following information from visitors:

    A. Name   B. Nature of business
    C. Address   D. Problems they have

15.____

16. All visitors who wish to see members of the staff should

    A. be permitted to do so
    B. produce identification
    C. do so for valid reasons only
    D. be processed by a supervisor

16.____

Questions 17-19.

DIRECTIONS: Questions 17 through 19 are to be answered SOLELY on the basis of the following passage.

Information regarding payroll status, salary differentials, promotional salary increments, deductions, and pension payments should be given to all members of the staff who have questions regarding these items. On occasion, if the secretary is uncertain regarding the information, the staff member should be referred to the principal or the appropriate agency. No question by a staff member regarding payroll status should be brushed aside as immaterial or irrelevant. The school secretary must always try to handle the question or pass it on to the person who can handle it.

17. If a teacher is dissatisfied with information regarding her salary status, as given by the school secretary, the matter should be

    A. dropped
    B. passed on to the principal
    C. passed on by the secretary to proper agency or the principal
    D. made a basis for grievance procedures

17.____

18. The following is an adequate summary of the above passage:

    A. The secretary must handle all payroll matters
    B. The secretary must handle all payroll matters or know who can handle them
    C. The secretary or the principal must handle all payroll matters
    D. Payroll matters too difficult to handle must be followed up until they are solved

18.____

19. The above passage implies that

    A. many teachers ask immaterial questions regarding payroll status
    B. few teachers ask irrelevant pension questions
    C. no teachers ask immaterial salary questions
    D. no question regarding salary should be considered irrelevant

19.____

Questions 20-22.

DIRECTIONS: Questions 20 through 22 are to be answered SOLELY on the basis of the following passage.

The necessity for good speech on the part of the school secretary cannot be overstated. The school secretary must deal with the general public, the pupils, the members of the staff, and the school supervisors. In every situation which involves the general public, the secretary serves as a representative of the school. In dealing with pupils, the secretary's speech must serve as a model from which students may guide themselves. Slang, colloquialisms, malapropisms, and local dialects must be avoided.

20. The above passage implies that the speech pattern of the secretary must be 20._____

    A. perfect
    B. very good
    C. average
    D. on a level with that of the pupils

21. The last sentence indicates that slang 21._____

    A. is acceptable
    B. occurs in all speech
    C. might be used occasionally
    D. should be shunned

22. The above passage implies that the speech of pupils 22._____

    A. may be influenced   B. does not change readily
    C. is generally good   D. is generally poor

Questions 23-25.

DIRECTIONS: Questions 23 through 25 are to be answered SOLELY on the basis of the following passage.

The school secretary who is engaged in the task of filing records and correspondence should follow a general set of rules. Items which are filed should be available to other secretaries or to supervisors quickly and easily by means of the application of a modicum of common sense and good judgment. Items which, by their nature, may be difficult to find should be cross-indexed. Folders and drawers should be neatly and accurately labeled. There should never be a large accumulation of papers which have not been filed.

23. A good general rule to follow in filing is that materials should be 23._____

    A. placed in folders quickly
    B. neatly stored
    C. readily available
    D. cross-indexed

24. Items that are filed should be available to 24._____

    A. the secretary charged with the task of filing
    B. secretaries and supervisors
    C. school personnel
    D. the principal

25. A modicum of common sense means _____ common sense.

    A.   an average amount of   B.   a great deal of
    C.   a little   D.   no

25.___

KEY (CORRECT ANSWERS)

1.	B		11.	D
2.	A		12.	C
3.	C		13.	A
4.	C		14.	A
5.	D		15.	B
6.	B		16.	C
7.	B		17.	C
8.	C		18.	B
9.	A		19.	D
10.	B		20.	B

21. D
22. A
23. C
24. B
25. C

TEST 3

Questions 1-4.

DIRECTIONS: Questions 1 through 4 are to be answered SOLELY on the basis of the following passage.

The proposition that administrative activity is essentially the same in all organizations appears to underlie some of the practices in the administration of private higher education. Although the practice is unusual in public education, there are numerous instances of indus-trial, governmental, or military administrators being assigned to private institutions of higher education and, to a lesser extent, of college and university presidents assuming administra-tive positions in other types of organizations. To test this theory that administrators are inter-changeable, there is a need for systematic observation and classification. The myth that an educational administrator must first have experience in the teaching profession is firmly rooted in a long tradition that has historical prestige. The myth is bound up in the expectations of the public and personnel surrounding the administrator. Since administrative success depends significantly on how well an administrator meets the expectations others have of him, the myth may be more powerful than the special experience in helping the administrator attain organizational and educational objectives. Educational administrators who have risen through the teaching profession have often expressed nostalgia for the life of a teacher or scholar, but there is no evidence that this nostalgia contributes to administrative success

1. Which of the following statements as completed is MOST consistent with the above pas-sage? The greatest number of administrators has moved from   1.____

    A. industry and the military to government and universities
    B. government and universities to industry and the military
    C. government, the armed forces, and industry to colleges and universities
    D. colleges and universities to government, the armed forces, and industry

2. Of the following, the MOST reasonable inference from the above passage is that a spe-cific area requiring further research is the   2.____

    A. place of myth in the tradition and history of the educational profession
    B. relative effectiveness of educational administrators from inside and outside the teaching profession
    C. performance of administrators in the administration of public colleges
    D. degree of reality behind the nostalgia for scholarly pursuits often expressed by educational administrators

3. According to the above passage, the value to an educational administrator of experience in the teaching profession   3.____

    A. lies in the firsthand knowledge he has acquired of immediate educational problems
    B. may lie in the belief of his colleagues, subordinates, and the public that such expe-rience is necessary
    C. has been supported by evidence that the experience contributes to administrative success in educational fields
    D. would be greater if the administrator were able to free himself from nostalgia for his former duties

4. Of the following, the MOST suitable title for the above passage is   4._____

    A. EDUCATIONAL ADMINISTRATION, ITS PROBLEMS
    B. THE EXPERIENCE NEEDED FOR EDUCATIONAL ADMINISTRATION
    C. ADMINISTRATION IN HIGHER EDUCATION
    D. EVALUATING ADMINISTRATIVE EXPERIENCE

Questions 5-6.

DIRECTIONS: Questions 5 and 6 are to be answered SOLELY on the basis of the following passage.

Management by objectives (MBO) may be defined as the process by which the superior and the subordinate managers of an organization jointly define its common goals, define each individual's major areas of responsibility in terms of the results expected of him and use these measures as guides for operating the unit and assessing the contribution of each of its members.

The MBO approach requires that after organizational goals are established and communicated, targets must be set for each individual position which are congruent with organizational goals. Periodic performance reviews and a final review using the objectives set as criteria are also basic to this approach.

Recent studies have shown that MBO programs are influenced by attitudes and perceptions of the boss, the company, the reward-punishment system, and the program itself. In addition, the manner in which the MBO program is carried out can influence the success of the program. A study done in the late sixties indicates that the best results are obtained when the manager sets goals which deal with significant problem areas in the organizational unit, or with the subordinate's personal deficiencies. These goals must be clear with regard to what is expected of the subordinate. The frequency of feedback is also important in the success of a management-by-objectives program. Generally, the greater the amount of feedback, the more successful the MBO program.

5. According to the above passage, the expected output for individual employees should be   5._____
determined

    A. after a number of reviews of work performance
    B. after common organizational goals are defined
    C. before common organizational goals are defined
    D. on the basis of an employee's personal qualities

6. According to the above passage, the management-by-objectives approach requires   6._____

    A. less feedback than other types of management programs
    B. little review of on-the-job performance after the initial setting of goals
    C. general conformance between individual goals and organizational goals
    D. the setting of goals which deal with minor problem areas in the organization

Questions 7-10.

DIRECTIONS: Questions 7 through 10 are to be answered SOLELY on the basis of the following passage.

Management, which is the function of executive leadership, has as its principal phases the planning, organizing, and controlling of the activities of subordinate groups in the accomplishment of organizational objectives. Planning specifies the kind and extent of the factors, forces, and effects, and the relationships among them, that will be required for satisfactory accomplishment. The nature of the objectives and their requirements must be known before determinations can be made as to what must be done, how it must be done and why, where actions should take place, who should be responsible, and similar problems pertaining to the formulation of a plan. Organizing, which creates the conditions that must be present before the execution of the plan can be undertaken successfully, cannot be done intelligently without knowledge of the organizational objectives. Control, which has to do with the constraint and regulation of activities entering into the execution of the plan, must be exercised in accordance with the characteristics and requirements of the activities demanded by the plan.

7. The one of the following which is the MOST suitable title for the above passage is   7.____

   A. THE NATURE OF SUCCESSFUL ORGANIZATION
   B. THE PLANNING OF MANAGEMENT FUNCTIONS
   C. THE IMPORTANCE OF ORGANIZATIONAL FUNCTIONS
   D. THE PRINCIPLE ASPECTS OF MANAGEMENT

8. It can be inferred from the above passage that the one of the following functions whose   8.____
   existence is essential to the existence of the other three is the

   A. regulation of the work needed to carry out a plan
   B. understanding of what the organization intends to accomplish
   C. securing of information of the factors necessary for accomplishment of objectives
   D. establishment of the conditions required for successful action

9. The one of the following which would NOT be included within any of the principal phases   9.____
   of the function of executive leadership as defined in the above passage is

   A. determination of manpower requirements
   B. procurement of required material
   C. establishment of organizational objectives
   D. scheduling of production

10. The conclusion which can MOST reasonably be drawn from the above passage is that   10.____
    the control phase of managing is most directly concerned with the

    A. influencing of policy determinations
    B. administering of suggestion systems
    C. acquisition of staff for the organization
    D. implementation of performance standards

Questions 11-12.

DIRECTIONS: Questions 11 and 12 are to be answered SOLELY on the basis of the following
              passage.

Under an open-and-above-board policy, it is to be expected that some supervisors will gloss over known shortcomings of subordinates rather than face the task of discussing them face-to-face. It is also to be expected that at least some employees whose job performance is below par will reject the supervisor's appraisal as biased and unfair. Be that as it may, these are inescapable aspects of any performance appraisal system in which human beings are involved. The supervisor who shies away from calling a spade a spade, as well as the employee with a chip on his shoulder, will each in his own way eventually be revealed in his true light--to the benefit of the organization as a whole.

11. The BEST of the following interpretations of the above passage is that   11._____

    A. the method of rating employee performance requires immediate revision to improve employee acceptance
    B. substandard performance ratings should be discussed with employees even if satisfactory ratings are not
    C. supervisors run the risk of being called unfair by their subordinates even though their appraisals are accurate
    D. any system of employee performance rating is satisfactory if used properly

12. The BEST of the following interpretations of the above passage is that   12._____

    A. supervisors generally are not open-and-above-board with their subordinates
    B. it is necessary for supervisors to tell employees objectively how they are performing
    C. employees complain when their supervisor does not keep them informed
    D. supervisors are afraid to tell subordinates their weaknesses

Questions 13-15.

DIRECTIONS: Questions 13 through 15 are to be answered SOLELY on the basis of the following passage.

During the last decade, a great deal of interest has been generated around the phenomenon of *organizational development,* or the process of developing human resources through conscious organization effort. Organizational development (OD) stresses improving interpersonal relationships and organizational skills, such as communication, to a much greater degree than individual training ever did. The kind of training that an organization should emphasize depends upon the present and future structure of the organization. If future organizations are to be unstable, shifting coalitions, then individual skills and abilities, particularly those emphasizing innovativeness, creativity, flexibility, and the latest technological knowledge, are crucial and individual training is most appropriate.

But if there is to be little change in organizational structure, then the main thrust of training should be group-oriented or organizational development. This approach seems better designed for overcoming hierarchical barriers, for developing a degree of interpersonal relationships which make communication along the chain of command possible, and for retaining a modicum of innovation and/or flexibility.

13. According to the above passage, group-oriented training is MOST useful in   13._____

    A. developing a communications system that will facilitate understanding through the chain of command
    B. highly flexible and mobile organizations
    C. preventing the crossing of hierarchical barriers within an organization
    D. saving energy otherwise wasted on developing methods of dealing with rigid hierarchies

14. The one of the following conclusions which can be drawn MOST appropriately from the   14.____
above passage is that

    A. behavioral research supports the use of organizational development training methods rather than individualized training
    B. it is easier to provide individualized training in specific skills than to set up sensitivity training programs
    C. organizational development eliminates innovative or flexible activity
    D. the nature of an organization greatly influences which training methods will be most effective

15. According to the above passage, the one of the following which is LEAST important for   15.____
large-scale organizations geared to rapid and abrupt change is

    A. current technological information
    B. development of a high degree of interpersonal relationships
    C. development of individual skills and abilities
    D. emphasis on creativity

Questions 16-18.

DIRECTIONS: Questions 16 through 18 are to be answered SOLELY on the basis of the following passage.

    The increase in the extent to which each individual is personally responsible to others is most noticeable in a large bureaucracy. No one person *decides* anything; each decision of any importance, is the product of an intricate process of brokerage involving individuals inside and outside the organization who feel some reason to be affected by the decision, or who have special knowledge to contribute to it. The more varied the organization's constituency, the more outside *veto-groups* will need to be taken into account. But even if no outside consultations were involved, sheer size would produce a complex process of decision. For a large organization is a deliberately created system of tensions into which each individual is expected to bring work-ways, viewpoints, and outside relationships markedly different from those of his colleagues. It is the administrator's task to draw from these disparate forces the elements of wise action from day to day, consistent with the purposes of the organization as a whole.

16. The above passage is essentially a description of decision making as   16.____

    A. an organization process
    B. the key responsibility of the administrator
    C. the one best position among many
    D. a complex of individual decisions

17. Which one of the following statements BEST describes the responsibilities of an adminis-   17.____
trator?

    A. He modifies decisions and goals in accordance with pressures from within and outside the organization.
    B. He creates problem-solving mechanisms that rely on the varied interests of his staff and *veto-groups.*
    C. He makes determinations that will lead to attainment of his agency's objectives.
    D. He obtains agreement among varying viewpoints and interests.

18. In the context of the operations of a central public personnel agency, a *veto group* would   18.____
    LEAST likely consist of

    A. employee organizations
    B. professional personnel societies
    C. using agencies
    D. civil service newspapers

Questions 19-25.

DIRECTIONS: Questions 19 through 25 are to be answered SOLELY on the basis of the fol-
              lowing passage, which is an extract from a report prepared for Department X,
              which outlines the procedure to be followed in the case of transfers of employ-
              ees.

Every transfer, regardless of the reason therefore, requires completion of the record of
transfer, Form DT 411. To denote consent to the transfer, DT 411 should contain the signatures of the transferee and the personnel officer(s) concerned, except that, in the case of an
involuntary transfer, the signatures of the transferee's present and prospective supervisors
shall be entered in Boxes 8A and 8B, respectively, since the transferee does not consent.
Only a permanent employee may request a transfer; in such cases, the employee's attendance record shall be duly considered with regard to absences, latenesses, and accrued
overtime balances. In the case of an inter-district transfer, the employee's attendance record
must be included in Section 8A of the transfer request, Form DT 410, by the personnel officer
of the district from which the transfer is requested. The personnel officer of the district to
which the employee requested transfer may refuse to accept accrued overtime balances in
excess of ten days.

An employee on probation shall be eligible for transfer. If such employee is involuntarily
transferred, he shall be credited for the period of time already served on probation. However,
if such transfer is voluntary, the employee shall be required to serve the entire period of his
probation in the new position. An employee who has occurred a disability which prevents him
from performing his normal duties may be transferred during the period of such disability to
other appropriate duties. A disability transfer requires the completion of either Form DT 414 if
the disability is job-connected, or Form DT 415 if it is not a job-connected disability. In either
case, the personnel officer of the district from which the transfer is made signs in Box 6A of
the first two copies and the personnel officer of the district to which the transfer is made signs
in Box 6B of the last two copies, or, in the case of an intra-district disability transfer, the personnel officer must sign in Box 6A of the first two copies and Box 6B of the last two copies.

19. When a personnel officer consents to an employee's request for transfer from his district,   19.___
    this procedure requires that the personnel officer sign Form(s)

    A. DT 411
    B. DT 410 and DT 411
    C. DT 411 and either Form DT 414 or DT 415
    D. DT 410 and DT 411, and either Form DT 414 or DT 415

20. With respect to the time record of an employee transferred against his wishes during his   20.____
    probationary period, this procedure requires that

    A. he serve the entire period of his probation in his present office
    B. he lose his accrued overtime balance

C. his attendance record be considered with regard to absences and latenesses
D. he be given credit for the period of time he has already served on probation

21. Assume you are a supervisor and an employee must be transferred into your office against his wishes. According to the this procedure, the box you must sign on the record of transfer is

21.____

    A. 6A   B. 8A   C. 6B   D. 8B

22. Under this procedure, in the case of a disability transfer, when must Box 6A on Forms DT 414 and DT 415 be signed by the personnel officer of the district to which the transfer is being made?

22.____

A. In all cases when either Form DT 414 or Form DT 415 is used
B. In all cases when Form DT 414 is used and only under certain circumstances when Form DT 415 is used
C. In all cases when Form DT 415 is used and only under certain circumstances when Form DT 414 is used
D. Only under certain circumstances when either Form DT 414 or Form DT 415 is used

23. From the above passage, it may be inferred MOST correctly that the number of copies of Form DT 414 is

23.____

A. no more than 2
B. at least 3
C. at least 5
D. more than the number of copies of Form DT 415

24. A change in punctuation and capitalization only which would change one sentence into two and possibly contribute to somewhat greater ease of reading this report extract would be MOST appropriate in the

24.____

A. 2nd sentence, 1st paragraph
B. 3rd sentence, 1st paragraph
C. next to he last sentence, 2nd paragraph
D. 2nd sentence, 2nd paragraph

25. In the second paragraph, a word that is INCORRECTLY used is

25.____

A. *shall* in the 1st sentence
B. *voluntary* in the 3rd sentence
C. *occurred* in the 4th sentence
D. *intra-district* in the last sentence

KEY (CORRECT ANSWERS)

1.	C		11.	C
2.	B		12.	B
3.	B		13.	A
4.	B		14.	D
5.	B		15.	B
6.	C		16.	A
7.	D		17.	C
8.	B		18.	B
9.	C		19.	A
10.	D		20.	D

21.	D
22.	D
23.	B
24.	B
25.	C

WRITTEN ENGLISH EXPRESSION

EXAMINATION SECTION
TEST 1

DIRECTIONS: In each of the sentences below, four portions are underlined and lettered.
Read each sentence and decide whether any of the UNDERLINED parts contains an error in spelling, punctuation, or capitalization, or employs grammatical usage which would be inappropriate for carefully written English. If so, note
the letter printed under the unacceptable form and indicate this choice in the
space at the right. If all four of the underlined portions are acceptable as they
stand, select the answer E.
(No sentence contains more than ONE unacceptable form.)

1. The revised <u>procedure</u> was <u>quite</u> different <u>than</u> the one which <u>was</u> employed
          A   B   C   D

   up to that time. <u>No error</u>
                      E

1.____

2. <u>Blinded</u> by the storm that <u>surrounded</u> him, his plane <u>kept going</u> in <u>circles.</u>
     A   B   C   D

   <u>No error</u>
     E

2.____

3. They <u>should</u> give the book to <u>whoever</u> <u>they</u> think deserves <u>it</u> . <u>No error</u>
            A   B   C   D   E

3.____

4. The <u>government</u> will not consent to your <u>firm</u> <u>sending</u> that package as
          A   B   C

   <u>second class</u> matter. <u>No error</u>
        D   E

4.____

5. She <u>would have</u> avoided all the trouble <u>that</u> followed if she <u>would have</u> waited
          A   B   C

   ten minutes <u>longer</u> . <u>No error</u>
                  D   E

5.____

6. <u>His</u> poetry, <u>when</u> it was carefully examined, showed <u>characteristics</u> not unlike
     A   B   C

   <u>Wordsworth</u> . <u>No error</u>
        D   E

6.____

7. <u>In my opinion,</u> based upon long years of research, <u>I think</u> the plan offered by my
       A   B

   opponent is <u>unsound,</u> because it is not <u>founded</u> on true facts. <u>No error</u>
             C   D   E

8. The soldiers of <u>Washington's</u> army at Valley Forge <u>were</u> men ragged in
                 A   B

   <u>appearance</u> but <u>who were</u> noble in character. <u>No error</u>
         C   D   E

9. Rabbits <u>have a distrust</u> of man <u>due to</u> the fact <u>that</u> they are <u>so often</u> shot.
              A   B   C   D

   <u>No error</u>
    E

10. <u>This</u> is the man <u>who</u> I believe <u>is</u> best <u>qualified</u> for the position. <u>No error</u>
    A   B   C   D   E

11. Her voice was <u>not only</u> <u>good,</u> but <u>she</u> also very clearly <u>enunciated.</u>
                A   B   C   D

   <u>No error</u>
    E

12. <u>Today he</u> is wearing a <u>different</u> suit <u>than</u> the <u>one</u> he wore yesterday. <u>No error</u>
    A   B   C   D   E

13. Our work <u>is</u> to improve the club; if anybody <u>must</u> resign, let it <u>not</u> be you or
          A   B   C

   <u>I</u> . <u>No error</u>
   D   E

7._____

8._____

9._____

10._____

11._____

12._____

13._____

14. There was so much talking <u>in back of</u> me <u>as</u> I <u>could</u> not <u>enjoy</u> the music.
      A   B   C   D

      <u>No error</u>
      E

14.____

15. <u>Being that</u> he is that <u>kind of</u> <u>boy</u> , he cannot be blamed <u>for</u> the mistake. <u>No error</u>
      A   B   C   D   E

15.____

16. <u>The king, having read</u> the speech, <u>he</u> and the <u>queen</u> <u>departed</u> . <u>No error</u>
              A   B   C   D   E

16.____

17. I <u>am</u> <u>so tired</u> I <u>can't</u> <u>scarcely</u> stand. <u>No error</u>
      A   B   C   D   E

17.____

18. We are <u>mailing bills</u> to our customers <u>in Canada</u> , and, <u>being</u> eager to clear our
              A   B   C

books before the new season opens, it is <u>to be hoped</u> they will send their remittances
                                              D

promptly. <u>No error</u>
              E

18.____

19. <u>I</u> <u>reluctantly</u> <u>acquiesced</u> to the <u>proposal</u> . <u>No error</u>
      A   B   C   D   E

19.____

20. <u>It</u> <u>had lain</u> <u>out</u> in the rain <u>all night</u> . <u>No error</u>
      A   B   C   D   E

20.____

21. <u>If he would have</u> <u>gone</u> there, he <u>would have</u> seen a <u>marvelous</u> sight. <u>No error</u>
              A   B   C   D   E

21.____

22. The climate <u>of</u> Asia Minor <u>is</u> <u>somewhat</u> like <u>Utah</u> . <u>No error</u>
                  A   B   C   D   E

22.____

23. If <u>everybody</u> <u>did</u> <u>unto others</u> as they <u>would wish</u> others to do unto them,
     A   B   C   D

this world would be a paradise. <u>No error</u>
                            E

23.____

24. <u>This</u> was the jockey <u>whom</u> I saw <u>was</u> most likely <u>to win</u> the race. <u>No error</u>
  A   B   C   D   E

24.____

25. The <u>only</u> food the general <u>demanded</u> <u>was</u> <u>potatoes</u> . <u>No error</u>
     A   B   C   D   E

25.____

KEY (CORRECT ANSWERS)

1.	C		11.	C
2.	A		12.	C
3.	B		13.	D
4.	B		14.	B
5.	C		15.	A
6.	D		16.	A
7.	B		17.	C
8.	D		18.	C
9.	B		19.	E
10.	E		20.	E

21.	A
22.	D
23.	D
24.	B
25.	E

TEST 2

DIRECTIONS: In each of the sentences below, four portions are underlined and lettered. Read each sentence and decide whether any of the UNDERLINED parts contains an error in spelling, punctuation, or capitalization, or employs grammatical usage which would be inappropriate for carefully written English. If so, note the letter printed under the unacceptable form and indicate this choice in the space at the right. If all four of the underlined portions are acceptable as they stand, select the answer E. (No sentence contains more than ONE unacceptable form.)

1. A party <u>like</u> <u>that</u> <u>only</u> <u>comes</u> once a year. <u>No error</u>
           A   B   C   D   E

                          1._____

2. <u>Our's</u> <u>is</u> <u>a</u> <u>swift moving</u> age. <u>No error</u>
       A   B C   D   E

                          2._____

3. The <u>healthy</u> climate soon <u>restored</u> him <u>to</u> his <u>accustomed</u> vigor.
         A   B   C   D

    <u>No error</u>
     E

                          3._____

4. <u>They</u> needed six typists and hoped that <u>only</u> that <u>many</u> <u>would</u> apply for the posi-
     A   B   C   D

    tion. <u>No error</u>
          E

                          5._____

5. He <u>interviewed</u> people <u>whom</u> he thought had <u>something</u> <u>to impart.</u>
           A   B   C   D

    <u>No error</u>
     E

                          6._____

6. <u>Neither</u> of his three sisters <u>is</u> older <u>than</u> <u>he.</u> <u>No error</u>
       A   B   C   D   E

                          7._____

7. <u>Since</u> he is <u>that</u> <u>kind</u> of <u>a</u> boy, he cannot be expected to cooperate with us.
      A   B   C   D
    <u>No error</u>
     E

8. When passing   through   the tunnel, the air pressure affected   our ears. No error
         A   B   C   D   E

9. The story having   a sad ending,   it   never   achieved   popularity   among   the
              A   B   C   D

    students.   No error
                   E

10. Since   we are both hungry,   shall   we go   somewhere   for lunch ?   No error
      A   B   C   D   E

11. Will   you please   bring   this book   down to   the library and give it to my friend ⸱_   who
      A   B   C   D
    is waiting for it?   No error
                            E

12. You may   have   the book; I am   finished   with it.   No error
          A   B   C   D   E

13. I   don't   know   if   I   should   mention   it   to her or not.   No error
        A   B   C   D   E

14. Philosophy is not   a subject   which   has to do   with philosophers and mathemat-
                           A   B   C

    ics   only.   No error
           D   E

15. The thoughts of the scholar in his library are little different than the old woman who
                                      A   B
    first said, "It's   no use crying over spilt milk ."   No error
                   C   D   E

16. A complete   system of philosophical ideas   are   implied   in many simple   utterances.
                    A   B   C   D
    No error
       E

17. Even <u>if</u> one has never put <u>them</u> into words, <u>his</u> ideas <u>compose</u> a kind of a
         A   B   C   D

philosophy. <u>No error</u>
            E

17.____

18. Perhaps it <u>is</u> <u>well enough</u> that most <u>people</u> do not attempt this <u>formulation.</u>
          A   B   C   D

<u>No error</u>
  E

18.____

19. <u>Leading their</u> ordered lives, this <u>confused</u> <u>body</u> of ideas and feelings <u>is</u>
         A   B   C   D

sufficient. <u>No error</u>
        E

19.____

20. Why <u>should</u> we <u>insist upon</u> <u>them</u> <u>formulating</u> it? <u>No error</u>
       A   B   C   D   E

20.____

21. <u>Since</u> it includes <u>something</u> of the wisdom of the ages, it is <u>adequate</u> for the
    A   B   C

<u>purposes</u> of ordinary life. <u>No error</u>
  D   E

21.____

22. Therefore, I <u>have sought</u> to make a pattern <u>of mine,</u> <u>and so</u> there were, early
              A   B   C

moments of <u>my trying</u> to find out what were the elements with which I had to deal;
            D

<u>No error</u>
  E

22.____

23. I <u>wanted</u> <u>to get</u> <u>what</u> knowledge I <u>could</u> about the general structure of the
     A   B   C   D

universe. <u>No error</u>
       E

23.____

24. I wanted to <u>know</u> <u>if</u> life <u>per se</u> had any meaning or <u>whether</u> I must strive to
               A   B   C   D

give it one. <u>No error</u>
              E

24._____

25. <u>So,</u> in a <u>desultory</u> way, I <u>began</u> <u>to read.</u> <u>No error</u>
    A   B   C   D   E

25._____

KEY (CORRECT ANSWERS)

1.	C		11.	B
2.	A		12.	C
3.	A		13.	B
4.	C		14.	D
5.	B		15.	B
6.	A		16.	B
7.	D		17.	A
8.	A		18.	C
9.	A		19.	A
10.	E		20.	C

21.	E
22.	C
23.	C
24.	B
25.	E

WRITTEN ENGLISH EXPRESSION
EXAMINATION SECTION
TEST 1

DIRECTIONS: The following questions are designed to test your knowledge of grammar, sentence structure, correct usage, and punctuation. In each group there is one sentence that contains no errors. Select the letter of the CORRECT sentence. *PRINT THE LETTER OF THE CORRECT ANSWER IN THE SPACE AT THE RIGHT.*

1.   A. A low ceiling is when the atmospheric conditions make flying inadvisable.
    B. They couldn't tell who the card was from.
    C. No one but you and I are to help him.
    D. What kind of a teacher would you like to be?
    E. To him fall the duties of foster parent.
       1.____

2.   A. They couldn't tell whom the cable was from.
    B. We like these better than those kind.
    C. It is a test of you more than I.
    D. The person in charge being him, there can be no change in policy.
    E. Chicago is larger than any city in Illinois.
       2.____

3.   A. Do as we do for the celebration.
    B. Do either of you care to join us?
    C. A child's food requirements differ from the adult.
    D. A large family including two uncles and four grandparents live at the hotel.
    E. Due to bad weather, the game was postponed.
       3.____

4.   A. If they would have done that they might have succeeded.
    B. Neither the hot days or the humid nights annoy our Southern visitor.
    C. Some people do not gain favor because they are kind of tactless.
    D. No sooner had the turning point come than a new issue arose.
    E. I wish that I was in Florida now.
       4.____

5.   A. We haven't hardly enough tine.
    B. Immigration is when people come into a foreign country to live.
    C. After each side gave their version, the affair was over with.
    D. Every one of the cars were tagged by the police.
    E. He either will fail in his attempt or will seek other employment.
       5.____

6.   A. They can't seem to see it when I explain the theory.
    B. It is difficult to find the genuine signature between all those submitted.
    C. She can't understand why they don't remember who to give the letter to
    D. Every man and woman in America is interested in his tax bill.
    E. Honor as well as profit are to be gained by these studies.
       6.____

7.   A. He arrived safe.
     B. I do not have any faith in John running for office.
     C. The musicians began to play tunefully and keeping the proper tempo indicated
         for the selection.
     D. Mary's maid of honor bought the kind of an outfit suitable for an afternoon wed-
         ding.
     E. If you would have studied the problem carefully you would have found the solu-
         tion more quickly.

7.____

8.   A. The new plant is to be electric lighted.
     B. The reason the speaker was offended was that the audience was inattentive.
     C. There appears to be conditions that govern his behavior.
     D. Either of the men are influential enough to control the situation.
     E. The gallery with all its pictures were destroyed.

8.____

9.   A. If you would have listened more carefully, you would have heard your name called.
     B. Did you inquire if your brother were returning soon?
     C. We are likely to have rain before nightfall.
     D. Let's you and I plan next summer's vacation together.
     E. The man whom I thought was my friend deceived me.

9.____

10. A. There's a man and his wife waiting for the doctor since early this morning.
     B. The owner of the market with his assistants is applying the most modern princi-
         ples of merchandise display.
     C. Every one of the players on both of the competing teams were awarded a gold
         watch.
     D. The records of the trial indicated that, even before attaining manhood, the mur-
         derer's parents were both dead.
     E. We had no sooner entered the room when the bell rang.

10.____

11. A. Why don't you start the play like I told you?
     B. I didn't find the construction of the second house much different from that of the
         first one I saw.
     C. "When", inquired the child, "Will we begin celebrating my birthday?"
     D. There isn't nothing left to do but not to see him anymore.
     E. There goes the last piece of cake and the last spoonful of ice cream.

11.____

12. A. The child could find neither the shoe or the stocking.
     B. The musicians began to play tunefully and keeping the proper tempo indicated
         for the selection.
     C. The amount of curious people who turned out for Opening Night was beyond cal-
         culation.
     D. I fully expected that the children would be at their desks and to find them ready
         to begin work,
     E. "Indeed," mused the poll-taker, "the winning candidate is much happier than I."

12.____

13. A. Just as you said, I find myself gaining weight.   13.____
     B. A teacher should leave the capable pupils engage in creative activities.
     C. The teacher spoke continually during the entire lesson, which, of course, was poor procedure.
     D. We saw him steal into the room, pick up the letter, and tear it's contents to shreds.
     E. It is so dark that I can't hardly see.

14. A. The new schedule of working hours and rates was satis factory to both employees   14.____
        and employer.
     B. Many common people feel keenly about the injustices of Power Politics.
     C. Mr. and Mrs. Burns felt that their grandchild was awfully cute when he waved good-bye.
     D. The tallest of the twins was also the most intelligent,
     E. Please come here and try and help me finish this piece of work.

15. A. My younger brother insists that he is as tall as me.   15.____
     B. Suffering from a severe headache all day, one dose of the prescribed medicine relieved me,
     C. "Please let my brothers and I help you with your packages," said Frank to Mrs. Powers.
     D. Every one of the rooms we visited had displays of pupils' work in them.
     E. Do you intend bringing most of the refreshments yourself?

16. A. The telephone linesmen, working steadily at their task during the severe storm, the   16.____
        telephones soon began to ring again.
     B. Meat, as well as fruits and vegetables, is considered essential to a proper diet.
     C. He looked like a real good boxer that night in the ring.
     D. The man has worked steadily for fifteen years before he decided to open his own business.
     E. The winters were hard and dreary, nothing could live without shelter.

17. A. No one can foretell when I will have another opportunity like that one again.   17.____
     B. The last group of paintings shown appear really to have captured the most modern techniques,
     C. We searched high and low, both in the attic and cellar, but were unsuccessful in locating mementos.
     D. None of the guests was able to give the rules of the game accurately.
     E. When you go to the library tomorrow, please bring this book to the librarian in the reference room.

18. A. After the debate, every one of the speakers realized that, given another chance, he   18.____
        could have done better.
     B. The reason given by the physician for the patient's trouble was because of his poor eating habits.
     C. The fog was so thick that the driver couldn't hardly see more than ten feet ahead.
     D. I suggest that you present the medal to who you think best.
     E. I don't approve of him going along.

19. A. A decision made by a man without much deliberation is sometimes no different than a slow one.
    B. By the time Mr. Brown's son will graduate Dental School, he will be twenty-six years of age.
    C. Who did you predict would win the election?
    D. The auctioneer had less stamps to sell this year than last year.
    E. Being that he is occupied, I shall not disturb him.

19.____

20. A. Having pranced into the arena with little grace and unsteady hoof for the jumps ahead, the driver reined his horse.
    B. Once the dog wagged it's tail, you knew it was a friendly animal.
    C. Like a great many artists, his life was a tragedy.
    D. When asked to choose corn, cabbage, or potatoes, the diner selected the latter.
    E. The record of the winning team was among the most noteworthy of the season.

20.____

21. A. The maid wasn't so small that she couldn't reach the top window for cleaning.
    B. Many people feel that powdered coffee produces a really good flavor.
    C. Would you mind me trying that coat on for size?
    D. This chair looks much different than the chair we selected in the store.
    E. I wish that he would have talked to me about the lesson before he presented it.

21.____

22. A. After trying unsuccessfully to land a job in the city, Will located in the country on a farm.
    B. On the last attempt, the pole-vaulter came nearly to getting hurt.
    C. The observance of Armistice Day throughout the world offers an opportunity to reflect on the horrors of war.
    D. Outside of the mistakes in spelling, the child's letter was a very good one.
    E. The annual income of New York is far greater than Florida.

22.____

23. A. Scissors is always dangerous for a child to handle.
    B. I assure you that I will not yield to pressure to sell my interest.
    C. Ask him if he has recall of the incident which took place at our first meeting.
    D. The manager felt like as not to order his usher-captain to surrender his uniform,
    E. Everyone on the boat said their prayers when the storm grew worse.

23.____

24. A. The mother of the bride climaxed the occasion by exclaiming, "I want my children should be happy forever."
    B. We read in the papers where the prospects for peace are improving.
    C. "Can I share the cab with you?" was frequently heard during the period of gas rationing.
    D. The man was enamored with his friend"s sister.
    E. Had the police suspected the ruse, they would have taken proper precautions.

24.____

25. A. The teacher admonished the other students neither to speak to John, nor should they annoy him.
    B. Fortunately we had been told that there was but one service station in that area.
    C. An usher seldom rises above a theatre manager.
    D. The epic, "Gone With the Wind," is supposed to have taken place during the Civil War Era.
    E. Now that she has been graduated she should be encouraged to make her own choice as to the career she is to follow.

25.____

KEY (CORRECT ANSWERS)

1.	E	11.	B
2.	A	12.	E
3.	A	13.	A
4.	D	14.	A
5.	E	15.	E
6.	D	16.	B
7.	A	17.	D
8.	B	18.	A
9.	C	19.	C
10.	B	20.	E

21.	B
22.	C
23.	B
24.	E
25.	B

TEST 2

DIRECTIONS: The following questions are designed to test your knowledge of grammar, sentence structure, correct usage, and punctuation. In each group, there is one sentence that contains no errors. Select the letter of the CORRECT sentence. *PRINT THE LETTER OF THE CORRECT ANSWER IN THE SPACE AT THE RIGHT.*

1.　A. Shall you be at home, let us say, on Sunday at two o'clock?　　　　　1._____
　　B. We see Mr. Lewis take his car out of the garage daily, newly polished always.
　　C. We have no place to keep our rubbers, only in the hall closet.
　　D. Isn't it true what you told me about the best way to prepare for an examination?
　　E. Mathematics is among my favorite subjects.

2.　A. The host thought the guests were of the hungry kinds so he prepared much food.　2._____
　　B. The museum is often visited by students who are fond of early inventions, and especially patent attorneys.
　　C. I rose to nominate the man who most of us felt was the most diligent worker in the group.
　　D. The child was sent to the store to purchase a bottle of milk, and brought home fresh rolls, too.
　　E. Hidden away in the closet, I found the long-lost purse.

3.　A. The garden tool was sent to be sharpened, and a new handle to be put on.　　3._____
　　B. At the end of her vacation, Joan came home with little money, but which systematic thrift soon overcame.
　　C. We people have opportunities to show the rest of the world how real democracy functions.
　　D. The guide paddled along, then fell in a reverie which he related the history of the region.
　　E. No sooner had the curtain dropped when the audience shouted its approval in chorus.

4.　A. The data you need is to be made available shortly.　　　　　　　　　　4._____
　　B. The first few strokes of the brush were enough to convince me that Tom could paint much better than me.
　　C. We inquired if we could see the owner of the store, after we waited for one hour.
　　D. The highly-strung parent was aggravated by the slightest noise that the baby made.
　　E. We should have investigated the cause of the noise by bringing the car to a halt.

5.　A. The police, investigating the crime, were successful in discovering only one possibly valuable clue.　　5._____
　　B. Due to an unexpected change in plans, the violin soloist did not perform.
　　C. Besides being awarded a Bachelor's degree at college, the scientist has since received many honorary degrees.
　　D. The data offered in advance of the recent Presidential election seems to have possessed elements of inaccuracy.
　　E. I don't believe your the only one who has been asked to come here.

6.   A. I don't quite see that I will be able to completely finish the job in time.   6.____
       B. By my statement, I infer that you are guilty of the offense as charged.
       C. Wasn't it strange that they wouldn't let no one see the body?
       D. I hope that this is the kind of rolls you requested me to buy.
       E. The storekeeper distributed cigars as bonuses between his many customers.

7.   A. He said he preferred the climate of Florida to California.   7.____
       B. Because of the excessive heat, a great amount of fruit juice was drunk by the guests.
       C. This week's dramatic presentation was neither as lively nor as entertaining as last week.
       D. The fashion expert believed that no one could develop new creations more successfully than him.
       E. A collection of Dicken's works is a "must" for every library.

8.   A. There was such a large amount of books on the floor that I couldn't find a place for my rocking chair.   8.____
       B. Walking up the rickety stairs, the bottle slipped from his hands and smashed.
       C. The reason they granted his request was because he had a good record.
       D. Little Tommy was proud that the teacher always asked him to bring messages to the office.
       E. That kind of orange is grown only in Florida.

9.   A. The new mayor is a resident of this city for thirty years.   9.____
       B. Do you mean to imply that had he not missed that shot he would have won?
       C. Next term I shall be studying French and history.
       D. I read in last night's paper where the sales tax is going to be abolished.
       E. In order to prevent breakage, she placed a sheet of paper between each of the plates when she packed them.

10.   A. To have children vie against one another is psychologically unsound.   10.____
       B. Would anyone else care to discuss his baby?
       C. He was interested and aware of the problem.
       D. I sure would like to discover if he is motivating the lesson properly.
       E. The cloth was first lain on a flat surface; then it was pressed with a hot iron.

11.   A. She graduated Barnard College twenty-five years ago.   11.____
       B. He studied the violin since he was seven.
       C. She is not so diligent a researcher as her classmate.
       D. He discovered that the new data corresponds with the facts disclosed by Werner.
       E. How could he enjoy the television program; the dog was barking and the baby was crying.

12.   A. You have three alternatives: law, dentistry, or teaching.   12.____
       B. If I would have worked harder, I would have accomplished my purpose.
       C. He affected a rapid change of pace and his opponents were outdistanced.
       D. He looked prosperous, although he had been unemployed for a year.
       E. The engine not only furnishes power but light and heat as well.

13. A. The children shared one anothers toys and seemed quite happy.   13.____
    B. They lay in the sun for many hours, getting tanned.
    C. The reproduction arrived, and had been hung in the living room.
    D. First begin by calling the roll.
    E. Tell me where you hid it; no one shall ever find it.

14. A. Deliver these things to whomever arrives first.   14.____
    B. Everybody but she and me is going to the conference.
    C. If the number of patrons is small, we can serve them.
    D. When each of the contestants find their book, the debate may begin.
    E. Some people, farmers in particular, lament the substitution of butter by margarine.

15. A. After his illness, he stood in the country three weeks.   15.____
    B. If you wish to effect a change, submit your suggestions.
    C. It is silly to leave children play with knives.
    D. Play a trick on her by spilling water down her neck.
    E. There was such a crowd of people at the crossing we couldn't hardly get on the bus.

16. A. This is a time when all of us must show our faith and devotion to our country.   16.____
    B. Either you or I are certain to be elected president of the new club.
    C. The interpellation of the Minister of Finance forced him to explain his policies.
    D. After hoisting the anchor and removing the binnacle, the ship was ready to set sail.
    E. Please bring me a drink of cold water from the refrigerator.

17. A. Mistakes in English, when due to carelessness or haste, can easily be rectified.   17.____
    B. Mr. Jones is one of those persons who will try to keep a promise and usually does.
    C. Being very disturbed by what he had heard, Fred decided to postpone his decision.
    D. There is a telephone at the other end of the corridor which is constantly in use.
    E. In his teaching, he always kept the childrens' interests and needs in mind.

18. A. The lazy pupil, of course, will tend to write the minimum amount of words acceptable.   18.____
    B. His success as a political leader consisted mainly of his ability to utter platitudes in a firm and convincing manner.
    C. To be cognizant of current affairs, a person must not only read newspapers and magazines but also recent books by recognized authorities.
    D. Although we intended to have gone fishing, the sudden outbreak of a storm caused us to change our plans.
    E. It is the colleges that must take the responsibility for encouraging greater flexibility in the high-school curriculum.

19. A. "I am sorry," he said, "but John's answer was 'No'."   19.____
     B. A spirited argument followed between those who favored and opposed Marie's
        expulsion from the club.
     C. Whether a forward child should be humored or punished often depends upon the
        circumstances.
     D. Excessive alcoholism is certainly not conducive with efficient performance of
        one's work.
     E. Stroking his beard thoughtfully, an idea suddenly came to him.

20. A. "Take care, my children," he said sadly, "lest you not be deceived."   20.____
     B. Those continuous telephone calls are preventing Betty from completing her
        homework.
     C. They dug deep into the earth at the spot indicated on the map, but they found
        nothing.
     D. We petted and cozened the little girl until she finally stopped weeping.
     E. There was, in the mail, an inquiry for a house by a young couple with two or
        three bedrooms.

21. A. Please fill in the required information on the application form and return same by   21.____
        April 15.
     B. Tom was sitting there idly, watching the clouds scud across the sky.
     C. We started for home so that our parents would not suspect that anything out of
        the ordinary took place.
     D. The sudden abatement from the storm enabled the ladies to resume their jour-
        ney.
     E. Each of the twelve members were agreed that the accused man was innocent.

22. A. The number of gifted students not continuing their education beyond secondary   22.____
        school present a nationwide problem.
     B. A man's animadversions against those he considers his enemies are usually
        reflections of his own inadequacies.
     C. The alembic of his fevered imagination produced some of the greatest romantic
        poetry of his era.
     D. The first case of smallpox dates back more than 3000 years and has gone
        unchecked until recently.
     E. He promised to go irregardless of the rain or snow.

23. A. The child picked up several of the coracles, which he had seen glittering in the   23.____
        sand, and brought them to his mother.
     B. He muttered in dejected tones – and no one contradicted him – "We have failed."
     C. A girl whom I believed to be she waved cheerily to me from a passing automo-
        bile.
     D. We discovered that she was a former resident of our own neighborhood who
        eloped some years ago with a milkman.
     E. It looks now like he will not be promoted after all.

24.   A.   Mary is the kind of a person on whom you can depend in any emergency.   24._____
      B.   I am sure that either applicant can fill the job you offer competently and effi-
          ciently.
      C.   Although we searched the entire room, the scissors was not to be found.
      D.   Being that you are here, we can proceed with the discussion.
      E.   In spite of our warning whistle, the huge ship continued to sail athwart our
          course.

25.   A.   The salaries earned by college graduates vary as much if not more than those   25._____
          earned by high school graduates.
      B.   The apothegms that he felt to be so witty were all too often either trite or platitu-
          dinous.
      C.   She read the letter carefully, took out one of the pages, and tore it into small
          pieces.
      D.   A young man, who hopes to succeed, must be diligent in his work and alert to his
          opportunities.
      E.   No one should plan a long journey for pleasure in these days.

KEY (CORRECT ANSWERS)

1.	A	11.	C
2.	C	12.	D
3.	C	13.	E
4.	E	14.	C
5.	A	15.	B
6.	D	16.	C
7.	B	17.	A
8.	E	18.	E
9.	B	19.	C
10.	B	20.	C

21.	B
22.	C
23.	B
24.	E
25.	B

———

EXAMINATION SECTION
TEST 1

DIRECTIONS: The questions that follow the paragraph below are designed to test your appreciation of correctness and effectiveness of expression in English. The paragraph is presented first in full so that you may read it through for sense. Disregard the errors you find as you will be asked to correct them in the questions that follow. The paragraph is then presented sentence by sentence with portions underlined and numbered. At the end of this material, you will find numbers corresponding to those below the underlined portions, each followed by five alternatives lettered A, B, C, D, and E. In every case, the usage in the alternative lettered A is the same as that in the original paragraph and is followed by four other possible usages. Choose the usage that you consider BEST in each case. *PRINT THE LETTER OF THE CORRECT ANSWER IN THE SPACE AT THE RIGHT.*

The use of the machine produced up to the present time outstanding changes in our modern world. One of the most significant of these changes have been the marked decreases in the length of the working day and the working week. The fourteen-hour day not only has been reduced to one of ten hours but also, in some lines of work, to one of eight or even six. The trend toward a decrease is further evidenced in the longer weekend already given to employees in many business establishments. There seems also to be a trend toward shorter working weeks and longer summer vacations. An important feature of this development is that leisure is no longer the privilege of the wealthy few, - it has become the common right of most people. Using it wisely, leisure promotes health, efficiency and happiness, for there is time for each individual to live their own "more abundant life" and having opportunities for needed recreation.

Recreation, like the name implies, is a process of revitalization. In giving expression to the play instincts of the human race, new vigor and effectiveness are afforded by recreation to the body and to the mind. Of course not all forms of amusement, by no means constitute recreation. Furthermore, an activity that provides recreation for one person may prove exhausting for another. Today, however, play among adults, as well as children, is regarded as a vital necessity of modern life. Play being recognized as an important factor in improving mental and physical health and thereby reducing human misery and poverty.

Among the most important forms of amusement available at the present time are the automobile, the moving picture, the radio, television, and organized sports. The automobile, especially, has been a boon to the American people, since it has been the chief means of them getting out into the open. The motion picture, the radio and television have tremendous opportunities to supply whole-some recreation and to promote cultural advancement. A criticism often leveled against organized sports as a means of recreation is because they make passive spectators of too many people. It has been said "that the American public is afflicted with "spectatoritis," but there is some recreational advantages to be gained even from being a spectator at organized games. Such sports afford a release from the monotony of daily toil, get people outdoors and also provide an exhilaration that is tonic in its effect.

The chief concern, of course, should be to eliminate those forms of amusement that are socially undesirable. There are, however, far too many people who, we know, do not use their leisure to the best advantage. Sometimes leisure leads to idleness, and idleness may lead to demoralization. The value of leisure both to the individual and to society will depend on the uses made of it.

The use of the machine produced up to the
                       1

1.   A. produced   B. produces   1.____
       C. has produced   D. had produced
       E. will have produced

present time many outstanding changes in our modern world. One of the most significant of these changes have been the marked
                              2

2.   A. have been   B. was   C. were   2.____
       D. has been   E. will be

decreases in the length of the working day and the working week.

The fourteen-hour day not only has been reduced to one of ten hours but also, in some
                            3

lines of work, to one of eight or even six.

3.   A. The fourteen-hour day not only has been reduced   3.____
       B. Not only the fourteen-hour day has been reduced
       C. Not the fourteen-hour day only has been reduced
       D. The fourteen-hour day has not only been reduced

The trend toward a decrease is further evidenced in the longer week-end already given
                                             4

4.   A. already   B. all ready   C. allready   4.____
       D. ready   E. all in all

to employees in many business establishments. There seems also to be a trend toward shorter working weeks and longer summer vacations. An important feature of this development is that leisure is no longer the privilege of the wealthy few ,-it has become the
                                                     5

common right of most people.

5.   A. ,-it   B. : it   C. ; it   5.____
       D. ... it   E. omit punctuation

Using it wisely, leisure promotes health, efficiency, and happiness, for there is time for
            6

each individual to live their own "more abundant life" and having opportunities for
                       7   8

needed recreation.

6.   A. Using it wisely   B. If used wisely   6.____
       C. Having used it wisely   D. Because of its wise use
       E. Because of usefulness

7.   A. their   B. his   C. its   D. our   E. your   7.____

8.   A. having   B. having had   C. to have   8.____
      D. to have had   E. had

Recreation, <u>like</u> the name implies, is a
        9

9.   A. like   B. since   C. through   D. for   E. as   9.____

process of revitalization. In giving expression to the play instincts of the human race,

<u>new vigor and effectiveness are afforded by recreation to the body and to the mind.</u>
                             10

10.   A. new vigor and effectiveness are afforded by recreation to the body and to the mind   10.____
      B. recreation affords new vigor and effectiveness to the body and to the mind
      C. there are afforded new vigor and effectiveness to the body and to the mind
      D. by recreation the body and mind are afforded new vigor and effectiveness
      E. the body and the mind afford new vigor and effectiveness to themselves by rec-
         reation

Of course not all forms of amusement, <u>by no means,</u> constitute recreation. Furthermore, an
                                    11

activity that provides recreation for one person may prove exhausting for another. Today, however, play among adults, as well as children is regarded as a vital necessity of modern life.

11.   A. by no means   B. by those means   11.____
      C. by some means   D. by every means
      E. by any means

<u>Play being recognized</u> as an important factor in improving mental and physical health and
           12
thereby reducing human misery and poverty.

12.   A. . Play being recognized as   12.____
      B. , by their recognizing play as
      C. . They recognizing play as
      D. . Recognition of it being
      E. , for play is recognized as

Among the most important forms of amusement available at the present time are the automobile, the moving picture, the radio, television, and organized sports. The automobile, especially, has been a boon to the American people, since it has been the chief means of

<u>them</u> getting out into the open. The motion picture, the radio and television have tremen-
 13
dous opportunities to supply wholesome recreation and to promote cultural advancement. A
criticism often leveled against organized

13.   A. them   B. their   C. his   13.____
      D. our   E. the people

sports as a means of recreation is <u>because</u> they make passive spectators of too many peo-

                            14

ple.

14.   A.   because   B.   since   C.   as   D.   that   E.   why   14._____

It has been said <u>"that</u> the American public is afflicted with "spectatoritis," but there <u>is</u> some

                 15   16

recreational advantages to be gained even from being a spectator at organized games.

15.   A.   that   B.   that   C.   that   D.   that   E.   that   15._____

16.   A.   is   B.   was   C.   are   D.   were   E.   will be   16._____

Such sports afford a release from the monotony of daily toil, get people outdoors and also provide an exhilaration that is tonic in its effect. The chief concern, of course, should be to eliminate
those forms of amusement that are socially undesirable. There are, however, far too many peo-

ple <u>who,</u> we know, do not use their leisure

      17

to the best advantage. Sometimes leisure leads to idleness, and idleness may lead to demoralization. The value of leisure both to the individual and to society will depend on the uses made
of it.

17.   A.   who   B.   whom   C.   which   17._____
        D.   such as   E.   that which

KEY (CORRECT ANSWERS)

1.	C		11.	E
2.	D		12.	E
3.	E		13.	B
4.	A		14.	D
5.	C		15.	E
6.	B		16.	C
7.	B		17.	A
8.	C			
9.	E			
10.	B			

TEST 2

*When this war is over, no nation will either be isolated in war or peace. Each will be within
trading distance of all the others and will be able to strike them. Every nation will be most as
dependent on the rest for the maintainance of peace as is any of our own American states on all
the others. The world that we have known was a world made up of individual nations, each of
which had the priviledge of doing about as they pleased without being embarassed by outside
interference. The world has dissolved before the impact of an invention, the airplane has done
to our world what gunpowder did to the feudal world. Whether the coming century will be a
period of further tragedy or one of peace and progress depend very largely on the wisdom and
skill with which the present generation adjusts their thinking to the problems immediately at
hand. Examining the principal movements sweeping through the world, it can be seen that they
are being accelerated by the war. There is undoubtedly many of these whose courses will be
affected for good or ill by the settlements that will follow the war. The United States will share
the responsibility of these settlements with Russia, England and China. The influence of the
United States, however, will be great. This country is likely to emerge from the war stronger
than any other nation. Having benefitted by the absence of actual hostilities on our own soil, we
shall probably be less exhausted than our allies and better able than them to help restore the
devastated areas. However many mistakes have been made in our past, the tradition of America, not only the champion of freedom but also fair play, still lives among millions who can see
light and hope scarcely nowhere else.*

When this war is over, no nation will   <u>either be isolated in war or peace.</u>
1

1. A.   either be isolated in war or peace   1.____
   B.   be either isolated in war or peace
   C.   be isolated in neither war nor peace
   D.   be isolated either in war or in peace
   E.   be isolated neither in war or peace

<u>Each</u> will be
2

2. A.   Each   B.   It   C.   Some   2.____
   D.   They   E.   A nation

within trading distance of all others and will be able to strike them.

<u>3</u>

3. A. within trading distance of all the others and will be able to strike them   3.___
    B. near enough to trade with and strike all the others
    C. trading and striking the others
    D. within trading and striking distance of all the others
    E. able to strike and trade with all the others

Every nation will be <u>most</u> as dependent on

<u>4</u>

4. A. most   B. wholly   C. much   D. mostly   E. almost   4.___

the rest for the <u>maintainance</u> of peace as is

<u>5</u>

5. A. maintainance   B. maintainence   C. maintenence   5.___
    D. maintenance   E. maintanence

any of our own American states on all the others. The world that we have known was a world

made up of individual <u>nations, each</u>

<u>6</u>

6. A. nations, each   B. nations. Each   6.___
    C. nations: each   D. nations; each
    E. nations each

of which had the <u>priviledge</u> of doing about as

<u>7</u>

7. A. priviledge   B. priveledge   C. privelege   7.___
    D. privalege   E. privilege

<u>they</u> pleased without being

<u>8</u>

8. A. they   B. it   8.___
    C. they individually   D. he
    E. the nations

<u>embarassed</u> by outside interference. That

<u>9</u>

9. A. embarassed   B. embarrassed   C. embaressed   9.___
    D. embarrased   E. embarressed

world has dissolved before the impact of an invention, the airplane has done to our world what
                                            10
gunpowder did to the feudal world. Whether the coming century will be a period of further tragedy or one of peace and

10.   A.   invention, the   B.   invention but the   10.____
       C.   invention: the   D.   invention. The
       E.   invention and the

progress depend very largely on the wisdom and skill with which the present generation
           11

11.   A.   depend   B.   will have depended   11.____
       C.   depends   D.   depended
       E.   shall depend

adjusts their thinking to the problems immediately at hand.
     12

12.   A.   adjusts their   B.   adjusts there   12.____
       C.   adjusts its   D.   adjust our
       E.   adjust it's

Examining the principal movements sweeping through the world, it can be seen
                            13

13.   A.   Examining the principal movements sweeping through the world, it can be seen   13.____
       B.   Having examined the principal movements sweeping through the world, it can be
          seen
       C.   Examining the principal movements sweeping through the world can be seen
       D.   Examining the principal movements sweeping through the world, we can see
       E.   It can be seen examining the principal movements sweeping through the world

that they are being accelerated by the war.
              14

14.   A.   accelerated   B.   acelerated   C.   accelarated   14.____
       D.   acellerated   E.   acelerrated

There is undoubtedly many of these whose courses will be affected for good or ill by the
      15
settlements that will follow the war. The United States will share the responsibility of these
settlements with Russia, England and China. The influence of the United

15.   A.   is   B.   were   C.   was   15.____
       D.   are   E.   might be

States, <u>however,</u> will be great. This country is likely to emerge from the war stronger than
16
any other nation.

16. A. , however,   B. however,   C. , however   16.____
     D. however   E. ; however,

Having <u>benefitted</u> by the absence of actual hostilities on our own soil, we shall probably be
17
less exhausted

17. A. benefitted   B. benifitted   C. benefited   17.____
     D. benifited   E. benafitted

than our allies and better able than <u>them</u> to help restore the devastated areas. However
18
many mistakes have been made in our past, the tradition of America,

18. A. them   B. themselves   C. they   18.____
     D. the world   E. the nations

<u>not only the champion of freedom but also fair play,</u> still lives among millions who can
19

19. A. not only the champion of freedom but also fair play,   19.____
     B. the champion of not only freedom but also of fair play,
     C. the champion not only of freedom but also of fair play,
     D. not only the champion but also freedom and fair play,
     E. not the champion of freedom only, but also fair play,

see light and hope <u>scarcely nowhere else.</u>
20

20. A. scarcely nowhere else.   B. elsewhere.   20.____
     C. nowheres.   D. scarcely anywhere else.
     E. anywhere.

KEY (CORRECT ANSWERS)

1.	D	11.	C
2.	A	12.	C
3.	D	13.	D
4.	E	14.	A
5.	D	15.	D
6.	A	16.	A
7.	E	17.	C
8.	B	18.	C
9.	B	19.	C
10.	D	20.	D

PREPARING WRITTEN MATERIAL

EXAMINATION SECTION
TEST 1

DIRECTIONS : Each of the sentences in the tests that follow may be classified under one of the following four categories:

    A. *Incorrect* because of faulty grammar or sentence structure
    B. *Incorrect* because of faulty punctuation
    C. *Incorrect* because of faulty capitalization
    D. *Correct*

    Examine each sentence carefully to determine under which of the above four options it is best classified. Then, in the space on the right, print the capital letter preceding the option which is the *BEST* of the four suggested above.
    (Each incorrect sentence contains but one type of error. Consider a sentence to be correct if it contains none of the types of errors mentioned, even though there may be other correct ways of expressing the same thought.)

1. This fact, together with those brought out at the previous meeting, prove that the schedule is satisfactory to the employees.   1.____

2. Like many employees in scientific fields, the work of bookkeepers and accountants requires accuracy and neatness.   2.____

3. "What can I do for you," the secretary asked as she motioned to the visitor to take a seat.   3.____

4. Our representative, Mr. Charles will call on you next week to determine whether or not your claim has merit.   4.____

5. We expect you to return in the spring; please do not disappoint us.   5.____

6. Any supervisor, who disregards the just complaints of his subordinates, is remiss in the performance of his duty.   6.____

7. Because she took less than an hour for lunch is no reason for permitting her to leave before five o'clock.   7.____

8. "Miss Smith," said the supervisor, "Please arrange a meeting of the staff for two o'clock on Monday."   8.____

9. A private company's vacation and sick leave allowance usually differs considerably from a public agency.   9.____

10. Therefore, in order to increase the efficiency of operations in the department, a report on the recommended changes in procedures was presented to the departmental committee in charge of the program.   10.____

11. We told him to assign the work to whoever was available.   11.____

12. Since John was the most efficient of any other employee in the bureau, he received the highest service rating.   12.____

13. Only those members of the national organization who resided in the middle West   13.____
    attended the conference in Chicago.

14. The question of whether the office manager has as yet attained, or indeed can ever hope   14.____
    to secure professional status is one which has been discussed for years.

15. No one knew who to blame for the error which, we later discovered, resulted in a consid-   15.____
    erable loss of time.

KEY (CORRECT ANSWERS)

1.	A	6.	B
2.	A	7.	A
3.	B	8.	C
4.	B	9.	A
5.	D	10.	D

11.	D
12.	A
13.	C
14.	B
15.	A

TEST 2

DIRECTIONS : Each of the sentences in the tests that follow may be classified under one of the following four categories:

      A.   *Incorrect* because of faulty grammar or sentence structure
      B.   *Incorrect* because of faulty punctuation
      C.   *Incorrect* because of faulty capitalization
      D.   *Correct*

1. The National alliance of Businessmen is trying to persuade private businesses to hire youth in the summertime.

    1._____

2. The supervisor who is on vacation, is in charge of processing vouchers.

    2._____

3. The activity of the committee at its conferences is always stimulating.

    3._____

4. After checking the addresses again, the letters went to the mailroom.

    4._____

5. The director, as well as the employees, are interested in sharing the dividends.

    5._____

KEY (CORRECT ANSWERS)

1. C
2. B
3. D
4. A
5. A

———

TEST 3

DIRECTIONS: In each of the following groups of sentences, one of the four sentences is faulty in grammar, punctuation, or capitalization. Select the incorrect sentence in each case.

1. A. Sailing down the bay was a thrilling experience for me.   1.____
   B. He was not consulted about your joining the club.
   C. This story is different than the one I told you yesterday.
   D. There is no doubt about his being the best player.

2. A. He maintains there is but one road to world peace.   2.____
   B. It is common knowledge that a child sees much he is not supposed to see.
   C. Much of the bitterness might have been avoided if arbitration had been resorted to earlier in the meeting.
   D. The man decided it would be advisable to marry a girl somewhat younger than him.

3. A. In this book, the incident I liked least is where the hero tries to put out the forest fire.   3.____
   B. Learning a foreign language will undoubtedly give a person a better understanding of his mother tongue.
   C. His actions made us wonder what he planned to do next.
   D. Because of the war, we were unable to travel during the summer vacation.

4. A. The class had no sooner become interested in the lesson than the dismissal bell rang.   4.____
   B. There is little agreement about the kind of world to be planned at the peace conference.
   C. "Today," said the teacher, "we shall read 'The Wind in the Willows.' I am sure you'll like it.
   D. The terms of the legal settlement of the family quarrel handicapped both sides for many years.

5. A. I was so suprised that I was not able to say a word.   5.____
   B. She is taller than any other member of the class.
   C. It would be much more preferable if you were never seen in his company.
   D. We had no choice but to excuse her for being late.

———

KEY (CORRECT ANSWERS)

1. C
2. D
3. A
4. C
5. C

———

TEST 4

DIRECTIONS: In each of the following groups of sentences, one of the four sentences is faulty in grammar, punctuation, or capitalization. Select the incorrect sentence in each case.

1. A. Please send me these data at the earliest opportunity.
    B. The loss of their material proved to be a severe handicap.
    C. My principal objection to this plan is that it is impracticable .
    D. The doll had laid in the rain for an hour and was ruined.

    1.____

2. A. The garden scissors, left out all night in the rain, were in a badly rusted condition.
    B. The girls felt bad about the misunderstanding which had arisen.
    C. Sitting near the campfire, the old man told John and I about many exciting adventures he had had.
    D. Neither of us is in a position to undertake a task of that magnitude.

    2.____

3. A. The general concluded that one of the three roads would lead to the besieged city.
    B. The children didn't, as a rule, do hardly anything beyond what they were told to do.
    C. The reason the girl gave for her negligence was that she had acted on the spur of the moment.
    D. The daffodils and tulips look beautiful in that blue vase.

    3.____

4. A. If I was ten years older, I should be interested in this work.
    B. Give the prize to whoever has drawn the best picture.
    C. When you have finished reading the book, take it back to the library.
    D. My drawing is as good as or better than yours.

    4.____

5. A. He asked me whether the substance was animal or vegetable.
    B. An apple which is unripe should not be eaten by a child.
    C. That was an insult to me who am your friend.
    D. Some spy must of reported the matter to the enemy.

    5.____

6. A. Limited time makes quoting the entire message impossible.
    B. Who did she say was going?
    C. The girls in your class have dressed more dolls this year than we.
    D. There was such a large amount of books on the floor that I couldn't find a place for my rocking chair.

    6.____

7. A. What with his sleeplessness and his ill health, he was unable to assume any responsibility for the success of the meeting.
    B. If I had been born in February, I should be celebrating my birthday soon.
    C. In order to prevent breakage, she placed a sheet of paper between each of the plates when she packed them.
    D. After the spring shower, the violets smelled very sweet.

    7.____

8. A. He had laid the book down very reluctantly before the end of the lesson.
    B. The dog, I am sorry to say, had lain on the bed all night.
    C. The cloth was first lain on a flat surface; then it was pressed with a hot iron.
    D. While we were in Florida, we lay in the sun until we were noticeably tanned.

    8.____

9. A. If John was in New York during the recent holiday season, I have no doubt he spent   9.____
        most of his time with his parents.
    B. How could he enjoy the television program; the dog was barking and the baby
        was crying.
    C. When the problem was explained to the class, he must have been asleep.
    D. She wished that her new dress were finished so that she could go to the party.

10. A. The engine not only furnishes power but light and heat as well.   10.____
    B. You're aware that we've forgotten whose guilt was established, aren't you?
    C. Everybody knows that the woman made many sacrifices for her children.
    D. A man with his dog and gun is a familiar sight in this neighborhood.

―――

KEY (CORRECT ANSWERS)

1.	D	6.	D
2.	C	7.	B
3.	B	8.	C
4.	A	9.	B
5.	D	10.	A

―――

TEST 5

DIRECTIONS: Each of Questions 1 to 15 consists of a sentence which may be classified
appropriately under one of the following four categories:
   A. *Incorrect* because of faulty grammar
   B. *Incorrect* because of faulty punctuation
   C. *Incorrect* because of faulty spelling
   D. *Correct*
Examine each sentence carefully. Then, print, in the space on the right, the letter preceding the category which is the best of the four suggested above.
   (Note: Each incorrect sentence contains only one type of error. Consider a sentence correct if it. contains no errors, although there may be other correct ways of writing the sentence.)

1.   Of the two employees, the one in our office is the most efficient.   1._____

2.   No one can apply or even understand, the new rules and regulations.   2._____

3.   A large amount of supplies were stored in the empty office.   3._____

4.   If an employee is occassionally asked to work overtime, he should do so willingly.   4._____

5.   It is true that the new procedures are difficult to use but, we are certain that you will learn   5._____
     them quickly.

6.   The office manager said that he did not know who would be given a large allotment   6._____
     under the new plan.

7.   It was at the supervisor's request that the clerk agreed to postpone his vacation.   7._____

8.   We do not believe that it is necessary for both he and the clerk to attend the conference.   8._____

9.   All employees, who display perseverance, will be given adequate recognition.   9._____

10. He regrets that some of us employees are dissatisfied with our new assignments.   10._____

11. "Do you think that the raise was merited," asked the supervisor?   11._____

12. The new manual of procedure is a valuable supplament to our rules and regulations.   12._____

13. The typist admitted that she had attempted to pursuade the other employees to assist   13._____
     her in her work.

14. The supervisor asked that all amendments to the regulations be handled by you and I.   14._____

15. The custodian seen the boy who broke the window.   15._____

KEY (CORRECT ANSWERS)

1.	A		6.	D
2.	B		7.	D
3.	A		8.	A
4.	C		9.	B
5.	B		10.	D

11.	B
12.	C
13.	C
14.	A
15.	A

———

ARITHMETICAL REASONING
EXAMINATION SECTION
TEST 1

DIRECTIONS: Each question or incomplete statement is followed by several suggested answers or completions. Select the one that BEST answers the question or completes the statement. *PRINT THE LETTER OF THE CORRECT ANSWER IN THE SPACE AT THE RIGHT.*

1. In 2013, a public agency spent $180 to buy pencils that cost three cents each. In 2015, the agency spent $420 to buy the same number of pencils that it had bought in 2013. The price per pencil that the agency paid in 2010 was _____ cents.   1._____

   A. 6 1/3   B. 2/3   C. 7   D. 7 3/4

2. A stenographer spent her 35 hour work week on taking dictation, transcribing the dictated material, and filing.   2._____
   If she spent 20% of the work week on taking dictation and 1/2 of the remaining time on transcribing the dictated material, the number of hours of the work week that she spent on filing was

   A. 7   B. 10.5   C. 14   D. 17.5

3. A typist typed eight pages in two hours. $8 - 2hrs$ 3._____
   If she typed an average of 50 lines per page and an average of 12 words per line, what was her typing speed, in words per minute?

   A. 40   B. 50   C. 60   D. 80

4. The daily compensation to be paid to each consultant hired in a certain agency is computed by dividing his professional earnings in the previous year by 250. The maximum daily compensation they can receive is $200 each. Four consultants who were hired to work on a special project had the following professional earnings in the previous year: $37,500, $144,000, $46,500, and $61,100. What will be the TOTAL daily cost to the agency for these four consultants?   4._____

   A. $932   B. $824   C. $736   D. $712

5. In a typing and stenographic pool consisting of 30 employees, 2/5 of them are typists, 1/3 of them are senior typists and senior stenographers, and the rest are stenographers.   5._____
   If there are 5 more stenographers than senior stenographers, how many senior stenographers are in the typing and stenographic pool?

   A. 3   B. 5   C. 8   D. 10

6. There are 3,330 copies of a three-page report to be collated. One clerk starts collating at 9:00 A.M. and is joined 15 minutes later by two other clerks. It takes 15 minutes for each of these clerks to collate 90 copies of the report.   6._____
   At what time should the job be completed if all three clerks continue working at the same rate without breaks?

   A. 12:00 Noon   B. 12:15 P.M.
   C. 1:00 P.M.   D. 1:15 P.M.

7. By the end of last year, membership in the blood credit program in a certain agency had increased from the year before by 500, bringing the total to 2,500.
If the membership increased by the same percentage this year, the TOTAL number of members in the blood credit program for this agency by the end of this year should be

   A. 2,625   B. 3,000   C. 3,125   D. 3,250   7._____

8. During this year, an agency suggestion program put into practice suggestions from 24 employees, thereby saving the agency 40 times the amount of money it paid in awards. If 1/3 of the employees were awarded $50 each, 1/2 of the employees were awarded $25 each, and the rest were awarded $10 each, how much money did the agency save by using the suggestions?

   A. $18,760   B. $29,600   C. C, $32,400   D. $46,740   8._____

9. A senior stenographer earned $20,100 a year and had 4.5% state tax withheld for the year.
If she was paid every two weeks, the amount of state tax that was taken out of each of her paychecks, based on a 52-week year, was MOST NEARLY

   A. $31.38   B. $32.49   C. $34.77   D. $36.99   9._____

10. Two stenographers have been assigned to address 750 envelopes. One stenographer addresses twice as many envelopes per hour as the other stenographer.
If it takes five hours for them to complete the job, the rate of the slower stenographer is _____ envelopes per hour.

   A. 35   B. 50   C. 75   D. 100   10._____

11. Suppose that the postage rate for mailing single copies of a magazine to persons not included on a subscription list is 18 cents for the first two ounces of the single copy and 3 cents for each additional ounce.
If 19 copies of a magazine, each of which weighs eleven ounces, are mailed to 19 different people, the TOTAL postage cost of these magazines is

   A. $3.42   B. $3.99   C. $6.18   D. $8.55   11._____

12. A senior stenographer spends about 40 hours a month taking dictation. Of that time, 44% is spent taking minutes of meetings, 38% is spent taking dictation of lengthy reports, and the rest of the time is spent taking dictation of letters and memoranda.
How much MORE time is spent taking minutes of meetingsthan in taking dictation of letters and memoranda?
10 hours _____ minutes.

   A. 6   B. 16   C. 24   D. 40   12._____

13. In one week, a stenographer typed 65 letters. Forty letters had 4 copies on colored paper. The rest had 3 copies on colored paper.
If the stenographer had 500 sheets of colored paper on hand at the beginning of the week when she started typing the letters, how many sheets of colored paper did she have left at the end of the week?

   A. 190   B. 235   C. 265   D. 305   13._____

14. An agency is planning to microfilm letters and other correspondence of the last five   14.____
years. The number of letter-size documents that can be photographed on a 100-foot roll
of microfilm is 2,995. The agency estimates that it will need 240 feet of microfilm to do all
the pages of all of the letters.
How many pages of letter-size documents can be photographed on this microfilm?

    A. 5,990   B. 6,786   C. 7,188   D. 7,985

15. In an agency, 2/3 of the total number of female stenographers and 1/2 of the total number   15.____
of male stenographers attended a general staff meeting.
If there are a total of 56 stenographers in the agency and 25% of them are male, the
number of female stenographers who attended the general staff meeting is

    A. 14   B. 28   C. 36   D. 42

16. A worker is currently earning $17,140 a year and pays $350 a month for rent. He expects   16.____
to get a raise that will enable him to move into an apartment where his rent will be 25% of
his new yearly salary.
If this new apartment is going to cost him $390 a month, what is the TOTAL amount of
raise that he expects to get?

    A. $480   B. $980   C. $1,580   D. $1,840

17. The tops of five desks in an office are to be covered with a scratch-resistant material.   17.____
Each desk top measures 60 inches by 36 inches.
How many square feet of material will be needed for the five desk tops?

    A. 15   B. 75   C. 96   D. 180

18. Three grades of bond paper are used in a central transcribing unit. The cost per ream of   18.____
paper is $1.90 for Grade A, $1.70 for Grade B, and $1.60 for Grade C.
If the central transcribing unit used 6 reams of Grade A paper, 14 reams of Grade B
paper, and 20 reams of Grade C paper, the AVERAGE cost, per ream, of the bond
paper used by this unit is between

    A. $1.62 and $1.66   B. $1.66 and $1.70
    C. $1.70 and $1.74   D. $1.74 and $1.80

19. The Complaint Bureau of a city agency is composed of an investigation unit, a clerical   19.____
unit, and a central transcribing unit. The sum of $264,000 has been appropriated for the
operation of this bureau. Of this sum, $170,000 is to be allotted to the clerical unit.
Of this bureau's total appropriation, the percentage that is left for the central transcribing unit is MOST NEARLY ____ if $41,200 is allotted for investigations.

    A. 20%   B. 30%   C. 40%   D. 50%

20. Three typists were assigned to address a total of 2,655 postcards. Typist A addressed   20.____
the postcards at the rate of 170 per hour. Typist B addressed the postcards at the rate of
150 per hour. Typist C's rate is not known. After the three typists had addressed postcards for three and a half hours, Typist C was taken off this assignment. It was necessary
for Typist A and Typist B to work two and a half hours more to complete this assignment.
The rate per hour at which Typist C addressed the postcards was

A. less than 150
B. between 150 and 170
C. more than 170 but less than 200
D. more than 200

21. In 2015, a city agency bought 12,000 envelopes at $4.00 per hundred. In 2016, the price   21.____
of envelopes purchased was 40 percent higher than the 2010 price, but only 60 percent
as many envelopes were bought.
The total cost of the envelopes purchased in 2016 was MOST NEARLY

   A. $250   B. $320   C. $400   D. $480

22. A stenographer has been assigned to place entries on 500 forms. She places entries on   22.____
25 forms by the end of half an hour, when she is joined by another stenographer. The
second stenographer places entries at the rate of 45 an hour.
Assuming that both stenographers continue to work at their respective rates of speed,
the TOTAL number of hours required to carry out the entire assignment is

   A. 5   B. 54   C. 64   D. 7

23. On Monday, a stenographer took dictation without interruption for 1 1/2 hours and tran-   23.____
scribed all the dictated material in 3 1/2 hours. On Tuesday, she took dictation uninter-
ruptedly for 1 3/4 hours and transcribed all the material in 3 3/4 hours. On Wednesday,
she took dictation without interruption for 2 1/4 hours and transcribed all the material in 4
1/2 hours.
If she took dictation at the average rate of 90 words per minute during these three
days, then her average transcription rate, in words per minute, for the same three days
was MOST NEARLY

   A. 36   B. 41   C. 54   D. 58

24. In a division of clerks and stenographers, 15 people are currently employed, 20% of   24.____
whom are stenographers.
If management plans are to maintain the current number of stenographers, but to
increase the clerical staff to the point where 12% of the total staff are stenographers,
what is the MAXIMUM number of additional clerks that should be hired to meet these
plans?

   A. 3   B. 8   C. 10   D. 12

25. In the first quarter of the year, a certain operator sent out 230 quarterly reports. In the   25.____
second quarter of that year, he sent out 310 quarterly reports.
The percent increase in the number of quarterly reports he sent out in the second
quarter of the year compared to the first quarter of the year is MOST NEARLY

   A. 26%   B. 29%   C. 35%   D. 39%

KEY (CORRECT ANSWERS)

1.	C		11.	D
2.	C		12.	C
3.	A		13.	C
4.	C		14.	C
5.	A		15.	B
6.	B		16.	C
7.	C		17.	B
8.	B		18.	B
9.	C		19.	A
10.	B		20.	D

21. C
22. B
23. B
24. C
25. C

———

SOLUTIONS TO PROBLEMS

1. $180 ÷ .03 = 6000 pencils bought. In 2015, the price per pencil = $420 / 6000 = .07 = 7 cents.

2. Number of hours on filing = 35 - (.20)(35) - (1/2)(28) = 14

3. Eight pages contains (8)(50)(12) = 4800 words. She thus typed 4800 words in 120 minutes = 40 words per minute.

4. $37,500 ÷ 250 = $150; $144,000 ÷ 250 = $576; $46,500 ÷ 250 = $186; $61,100 ÷ 250 = $244.40 Since $200 = maximum compensation for any single consultant, total compensation = $150 + $200 + $186 + $200 = $736

5. Number of typists = (2/5)(30) = 12, number of senior typists and senior stenographers = (1/3)(30) = 10, number of stenographers = 30 - 12 - 10 = 8. Finally, number of senior stenographers = 8-5 = 3

6. At 9:15 AM, 90 copies have been collated. The remaining 3240 copies are being collated at the rate of (3)(90) = 270 every 15 minutes = 1080 per hour. Since 3240 ÷ 1080 = 3 hours, the clerks will finish at 9:15 AM + 3 hours = 12:15 PM.

7. During last year, the membership increased from 2000 to 2500, which represents a (500/2000)(100) = 25% increase. A 25% increase during this year means the membership = (2500)(1.25) = 3125

8. Total awards = (1/3)(24)($50) + (1/2)(24)($25) + (1/6)(24)($10) = $740. Thus, the savings = (40)($740) = $29,600

9. Her pay for 2 weeks = $20,100 ÷ 26 ≈ $773.08. Thus, her state tax for 2 weeks ≈ ($773.08)(.045) ≈ $34.79. (Nearest correct answer is $34.77 in four selections.)

10. 750 ÷ 5 hours = 150 envelopes per hour for the 2 stenographers combined. Let x = number of envelopes addressed by the slower stenographer . Then, x + 2x = 150. Solving, x = 50

11. Total cost = (19)[.18+(.03)(9)] = $8.55

12. (.44)(40) - (.18)(40) = 10.4 hrs. = 10 hrs. 24 rain.

13. 500 - (40)(4) - (25)(3) = 265

14. 2995 ÷ 100 = 29.95 documents per foot of microfilm roll. Then, (29.95)(240 ft) = 7188 documents

15. There are (.75)(56) = 42 female stenographers. Then, (2/3)(42) = 28 of them attended the meeting.

16. ($390)(12) = $4680 new rent per year. Then, ($4680)(4) = $18,720 = his new yearly salary. His raise = $18,720 - $17,140 = $1580

17. Number of sq.ft. = (5)(60)(36) ÷ 144 = 75

18. Average cost per ream = [($1.90)(6) + ($1.70) (14) + ($1.60) (20)] / 40 = $1.68, which is between $1.66 and $1.70

19. $264,000 - $170,000 - $41,200 = 52,800 = 20%

20. Let x = typist C's rate. Since typists A and B each worked 6 hrs., while typist C worked only 3.5 hrs., we have (6)(170) + (6)(150) + 3.5x = 2655. Solving, x = 210, which is nore than 200.

21. In 2016, the cost per hundred envelopes was ($4.00)(1.40) = $5.60 and (.60)(12,000) = 7200 envelopes were bought. Total cost in 2016 = (72)($5.60) = $403.20, or about $400.

22. The 1st stenographer's rate is 50 forms per hour. After 1/2 hr., there are 500 - 25 = 475 forms to be done and the combined rate of the 2 stenographers is 95 forms per hr. Thus, total hrs. required = 1/2 + (475) ÷ (95) = 5 1/2

23. Total time for dictation = 1 1/4 + 1 3/4 + 2 1/4 = 5 1/4 hrs. = 315 min. The number of words = (90)(315) = 28,350. The total transcription 3 time = 3 1/4 + 3 3/4 + 44 = 11 1/2 hrs. = 690 min. Her average transcription rate

= 28,350 ÷ 690 ≈ 41 words per min.

24. Currently, there are (.20)(15) = 3 stenographers, and thus 12 clerks. Let x = additional clerks. Then, $\frac{3}{3+12+x}$ =.12. This simplifies to 3 = (.12)(15+x). Solving, x = 10

25. Percent increase = ($\frac{80}{230}$)(100) ≈ 35%

───────

TEST 2

DIRECTIONS: Each question or incomplete statement is followed by several suggested answers or completions. Select the one that BEST answers the question or completes the statement. *PRINT THE LETTER OF THE CORRECT ANSWER IN THE SPACE AT THE RIGHT.*

1. A school has 112 homeroom classes. There were 15 school days in February. The aggregate register of the school for the month of February was 52,920; the aggregate attendance was 43,860.
   The average class size, to the NEAREST tenth, is

   A. 35.3   B. 31.5   C. 29.2   D. 26.9

   1.____

2. As the school secretary in charge of supplies, you are asked to order the following items on a supplementary requisition for general supplies:
   5 gross of red pencils at $8.90 per dozen
   5,000 manila envelopes at $2.35 per C
   36 rulers at $187.20 per gross
   6 boxes of manila paper at $307.20 per carton (24 boxes to a carton)
   180 reams of composition paper at $27.80 per carton (20 reams to a carton)
   The TOTAL amount of the order is

   A. $957.20   B. $1,025.30   C. $916.80   D. $991.30

   2.____

3. In the high school to which you have been assigned as a school secretary, the annual allotment for general supplies, textbooks, repairs, etc. for the school year 2015-16 was $37,500. A special allotment of $10,000 was granted for textbooks ordered from the State Textbook List. The original requisition for general and vocational supplies amounted to $12,514.75; for science supplies, $6,287.25; for textbooks, including the special funds, $13,785.00; monies spent for equipment repairs and science perishables through December 31, 2015, $1,389.68.
   The balance in your supply allotment account on January 1, 2016 will be

   A. $14,913.00   B. $13,523.32
   C. $17,308.32   D. $3,523.32

   3.____

4. The teacher of one of the sixth term typing classes in the high school to which you are assigned as a school secretary has agreed to have her students type attendance cards for the incoming students for the new school year, commencing in September, as a work project. There are 24 students in the class; each student can complete 8 cards during a typing period. There will be 4,032 new students in September.
   The number of typing periods required to complete the task is

   A. 31   B. 21   C. 28   D. 24

   4.____

5. As a school secretary assigned to payroll duties, you are required to prepare the extra-curricular payroll report for the coaches teams in your high school. The rate of pay for these activities was increased on November 1 from $148 per session to $174.50 per session. The pay period which you are reporting is for the months of October, November, and December. Mr. Jones, the football coach, conducted 15 practice sessions in October, 20 in November, and 30 in December.
   His TOTAL gross pay on the December extra-curricular payroll report is

   5.____

A. $10,547.50
C. $10,945.00

B. $10,415.00
D. $11,342.50

6. The comparative results on a uniform examination given in your school for the last three years follow:

	2014	2015	2016
Number taking test	501	496	485
Number passing test	441	437	436

The percentage of passing, to the nearest tenth of a percent, for the year in which the HIGHEST percent of students passed is

6.____

A. 89.3%   B. 88%   C. 89.9%   D. 90.3%

7. During his first seven terms in high school, a student compiled the following averages:

7.____

Term	Numbers of Majors Completed	Average
1	4	81.25%
2	4	83.75%
3	5	86.2%
4	5	85.8%
5	5	87.0%
6	5	83.4%
7	5	82.6%

In his eighth term, the student had the following final marks in major subjects: 90%, 95%, 80%, 90%, 85%. The student's average for all eight terms of high school, correct to the nearest tenth of a percent, is

A. 84.8%   B. 84.7%   C. 84.9%   D. 85.8%

8. A secretary is asked by her employer to order an office machine which lists at a price of $360, less trade discounts of 20% and 10%, terms 2/10, n/30. There is a delivery charge of $8 and an installation charge of $12. If the machine is paid for in 10 days, the TOTAL cost of the machine will be

8.____

A. $264.80   B. $258.40   C. $266.96   D. $274.02

9. The school to which you have been assigned as school secretary has an annual allow-ance of 5,120 hours for all teacher aides. The principal decides to employ 5 teacher aides from 8:00 A.M. to 12:00 Noon, and 5 other teacher aides from 12:00 Noon to 4:00 P.M. daily for as many days as his allowance permits.
If a teacher aide earns $17.00 an hour, and he is present every day, his TOTAL earn-ings for the school year will be more than

9.____

A. $7,000 but less than $8,000
B. $8,000 but less than $9,000
C. $9,000 but less than $10,000
D. $10,000

10. During examination week in a high school to which you have been assigned as school secretary, teachers are required to be in school at least 6 hours and 20 minutes daily although their arrival and departure times may vary each day. A teacher's time card that you have been asked to check shows the following entries for the week of June 17:

Date	Arrival	Departure
17	7:56 AM	2:18 PM
18	9:53 AM	4:22 PM
19	12:54 PM	7:03 PM
20	9:51 AM	4:15 PM
21	7:58 AM	2:11 PM

During the week of June 17 to June 21, the teacher was in school for AT LEAST the minimum required time on _____ days.

   A. 2 of the 5   B. 3 of the 5
   C. 4 of the 5   D. all 5

10.____

11. As school secretary, you are asked to find the total of the following bill received in your school:

   750 yellow envelopes at $.22 per C
   2,400 white envelopes at $2.80 per M
   30 rulers at $5.04 per gross
The TOTAL of the bill is

   A. $69.90   B. $24.27   C. $18.87   D. $9.42

11.____

12. A department in the school to which you have been assigned as school secretary has been given a textbook allowance of $5,500 for the school year. The department's textbook order is:

   75 books at $32.50 each 2437.5
   45 books at $49.50 each 2227.5
   25 books at $34.50 each 862.50
The TOTAL of the department's order is _____ the allowance.

   A. $27.50 over   B. $27.50 under
   C. $72.50 under   D. $57.50 over

12.____

13. The total receipts, including 5% city sales tax, for the G.O. store for the first week of school amounted to $489.09.
The receipts from the G.O. store for the first week of school, excluding the 5% city sales tax, amounted to

   A. $465.80   B. $464.64   C. $464.63   D. $513.54

13.____

14. Class sizes in the school to which you have been assigned as school secretary are as follows:

Number of Classes	Class Size
9	29 pupils
12	31 pupils
15	32 pupils
7	33 pupils
11	34 pupils

The average class size in this school, correct to the nearest tenth, is

   A. 30.8   B. 31.9   C. 31.8   D. 30.9

14.____

15. In 2013, the social security tax was 4.2% for the first $6,600 earned a year. In 2014, the social security tax was 4.4% on the first $6,600 earned a year.
For a teacher aide earning $19,200 in 2013 and $20,400 in 2014, the increase in social security tax deduction in 2014 over 2013 was

    A. $132.00   B. $13.20   C. $19.20   D. $20.40

15.____

16. A teacher aide earning $23,900 a year will incur automatic deductions of 3.90% for social security and .50% for medicare, based on the first $6,600 a year earnings. The TOTAL tax deduction for these two items will be

    A. $274   B. $290.40   C. $525.80   D. $300.40

16.____

17. The school store turns in receipts totaling $131.25 to the school treasurer, including 5% which has been collected for sales tax.
The amount of money which the treasurer MUST set aside for sales tax is

    A. $6.56   B. $6.25   C. $5.00   D. $5.25

17.____

18. One of the custodial assistants can wash all the windows in the main office in 3 hours. A second assistant can wash the windows in the main office in 2 hours.
If the two men work together, they should complete the task in ____ hour(s) ____ minutes.

    A. 1; 0   B. 1.5; 0   C. 1; 12   D. 1; 15

18.____

19. A school secretary is requested by the principal to order an office machine which lists at a price of $120, less discounts of 10% and 5%.
The net price of the machine to the school will be

    A. $100.50   B. $102.00   C. $102.60   D. $103.00

19.____

20. Five students are employed at school under a work-study program through which they are paid $10.00 an hour for work in school offices, but no student may earn more than $450 a month. Three days before the end of the month, you note that the student payroll totals $2,062.50.
The number of hours which each of the students may work during the remainder of the month is____ hour(s).

    A. 4   B. 2   C. 1   D. 3

20.____

21. You are asked to summarize expenditures made by the school within the budget allocation for the school year. You determine that the following expenditures have been made: educational supplies, $2,600; postage, $650; emergency repairs, $225; textbooks, $5,100; instructional equipment, $1,200.
Since $10,680 has been allocated to the school, the following sum still remains available for office supplies:

    A. $905   B. $1,005   C. $800   D. $755

21.____

22. In preparing the percentage of attendance for the period report, you note that the aggre-   22.____
gate attendance is 57,585 and the aggregate register is 62,000.
The percentage of attendance, to the nearest tenth of a percent, is

   A.   91.9%   B.   93.0%   C.   92.8%   D.   92.9%

23. You borrow $1,200 from your retirement fund which you must repay over a period of   23.____
three years, with interest of $144, each payment to be divided equally among 36 total
payments.
The monthly deduction from your paycheck will be

   A. $37.33   B. $36.00   C. $33.00   D. $37.30

24. Tickets for a school dance are printed, starting with number 401 and ending with number   24.____
1650. They are to be sold for 750 each. The tickets remaining unsold should start with
number 1569.
The amount of cash which should be collected for the sale of tickets is

   A. $876.75   B. $937.50   C. $876.00   D. $875.25

25. Stage curtains are purchased by the school and delivered on October 3 under terms of   25.____
5/10, 2/30, net/60. The curtains are paid in full by a check for $522.50 on October 12.
The invoice price was

   A. $533.16   B. $522.50   C. $540.00   D. $550.00

KEY (CORRECT ANSWERS)

1.	B		11.	D
2.	B		12.	A
3.	B		13.	A
4.	B		14.	C
5.	C		15.	B
6.	C		16.	B
7.	C		17.	B
8.	D		18.	C
9.	B		19.	C
10.	B		20.	D

21.	A
22.	D
23.	A
24.	C
25.	D

———

SOLUTIONS TO PROBLEMS

1. Average class size = 52,920 ÷ 15 ÷ 112 = 31.5

2. Total amount = (5)(12)($8.90) + (50)($2.35) + (36) ($187.20) ÷ 144 + (6)($307.20) ÷ 24 + (9)($27.80) = $1025.30

3. Balance = $37,500 + $10,000 - $12,514.75 - $6287.25 - $13,785 - $1389.68 = $13,523.32

4. (24)(8) = 192 cards completed in one period. Then, 4032 ÷ 192 = 21 typing periods required.

5. Total pay = (15)($148.00) + (20)($174.50) + (30)($174.50) = $10,945.00

6. The passing rates for 2014, 2015, 2016 were 88.0%, 88.1%, and 89.9%, respectively. So, 89.9% was the highest.

7. His 8th term average was 88.0%. His overall average for all 8 terms = [(4)(81.25%)+(4)(83.75%)+(5)(86.2%)+(5)(85.8%)+ (5)(87.0%)+(5)(83.4%)+(5)(82.6%)+(5)(88.0%)] ÷ 38 = 84.9%

8. Total cost = ($360)(.80)(.90)(.98) + $8 + $12 ≈ $274.02 (Exact amount = $274.016)

9. 5120 ÷ 4 = 1280 teacher-days. Then, 1280 ÷ 10 = 128 days per teacher. A teacher's earnings for these 128 days = ($17.00)(4)(128)= $8704, which is more than $8000 but less than $9000.

10. The number of hours present on each of the 5 days listed was 6 hrs. 22 min., 6 hrs. 29 min., 6 hrs. 9 min., 6 hrs. 24 min., and 6 hrs. 13 min. On 3 days, he met the minimum time.

11. Total cost = (7.5)(.22) + (2.4)($2.80) + (30/144)(5.04) = $9.42

12. Textbook order = (75)($32.50) + (45)($49.50) + (25)($34.50) = $5527.50, which is $27.50 over the allowance.

13. Receipts without the tax = $489.09 ÷ 1.05 = $465.80

14. Average class size = [(9)(29)+(12)(31)+(7)(33)+(11)(34)+(15)(32)] ÷ 54 ≈ 31.8

15. ($6600)(.044-.042) = $13.20

16. ($6600)(.039+.005) = $290.40

17. $131.25 = 1.05x, x = 125, $131.25 - 125.00 = 6.25

18. Let x = hours needed working together. Then, $(1/3)(x) + (1/2)(x) = 1$
    Simplifying, 2x + 3x = 6. Solving, x = 1 1/5 hrs. = 1 hr. 12 min.

19. Net price = 120 - 10% (12) = 108; 108 - 5% (5.40) = 102.60

20. ($225)(5) - $1031.25 = $93.75 remaining in the month. Since the 5 students earn
    $25 per hour combined, $93.75 ÷ $25 = 3.75, which must be rounded down to 3
    hours.

21. $10,680 - $2600 - $650 - $225 - $5100 - $1200 = $905 for office supplies.

22. 57,585 ÷ 62,000 ≈ .9288 ≈ 92.9%

23. Monthly deduction = $1344 ÷ 36 = $37.33 (Technically, 35 payments of $37.33
    and 1 payment of $37.45)

24. (1569-401)(.75) = $876.00

25. The invoice price (which reflects the 5% discount) is $522.50 ÷ .95 = $550.00

———

TEST 3

DIRECTIONS: Each question or incomplete statement is followed by several suggested answers or completions. Select the one that BEST answers the question or completes the statement. *PRINT THE LETTER OF THE CORRECT ANSWER IN THE SPACE AT THE RIGHT.*

1. If an inch on an office layout drawing equals 4 feet of actual floor dimension, then a room which actually measures 9 feet by 14 feet is represented on the drawing by measurements equaling _____ inches x _____ inches.

   A.   2 1/4; 3 1/2   B.   2 1/2; 3 1/2   C.   2 1/4;3 1/4   D.   2 1/2;3 1/4

   1.____

2. A cooperative education intern works from 1:30 P.M. to 5 P.M. on Mondays, Wednesdays, and Fridays, and from 10 A.M. to 2:30 P.M. with no lunch hour on Tuesdays and Thursdays. He earns $13.50 an hour on this job. In addition, he has a Saturday job paying $16.00 an hour at which he works from 9 A.M. to 3 P.M. with a half hour off for lunch. The gross amount that the student earns each week is MOST NEARLY

   A. $321.90   B. $355.62   C. $364.02   D. $396.30

   2.____

3. Thirty-five percent of the College Discovery students who entered community college earned an associate degree. Of these students, 89% entered senior college, of which 67% went on to earn baccalaureate degrees.
   If there were 529 College Discovery students who entered community college, then the number of those who went on to finally receive a baccalaureate degree is MOST NEARLY

   A.   354   B.   315   C.   124   D.   110

   3.____

4. It takes 5 office assistants two days to type 125 letters. Each of the assistants works at an equal rate of speed. How many days will it take 10 office assistants to type 200 letters?

   A.   1   B.   1 3/5   C.   2   D.   2 1/5

   4.____

5. The following are the grades and credits earned by Student X during the first two years in college.

   5.____

Grade	Credits	Weight	Quality Points
A	10 1/2	x4	
B	24	x3	
C	12	x2	
D	4 1/2	x1	
F, FW	5	x0	

   To compute an index number:
      I.   Multiply the number of credits of each grade by the weight to get the number of *quality points.*
      II.   Add the credits.
      III.   Add the quality points.
      IV.   Divide the total quality points by the total credits, and carry the division to two decimal places.
   On the basis of the given information, the index number for Student X is

   A.   2.54   B.   2.59   C.   2.63   D.   2.68

6. Typist X can type 20 forms per hour, and Typist Y can type 30 forms per hour. If there are   6._____
   30 forms to be typed and both typists are put to work on the job, how soon should they be
   expected to finish the work?
   _____ minutes.

   A.   32   B.   34   C.   36   D.   38

7. Assume that there were 18 working days in February and that the six clerks in your unit   7._____
   had the following number of absences:

Clerk	Absences
F	3
G	2
H	8
I	1
J	0
K	5

   The average percentage attendance for the six clerks in your unit in February was MOST
   NEARLY

   A.   80%   B.   82%   C.   84%   D.   86%

8. A certain employee is paid at the rate of $7.50 per hour, with time and a half for overtime.   8._____
   Hours in excess of 40 hours a week count as overtime. During the past week, the
   employee put in 48 working hours. The employee's gross wages for the week are MOST
   NEARLY

   A. $330   B. $350   C. $370   D. $390

9. You are making a report on the number of inside and outside calls handled by a particu-   9._____
   lar switchboard. Over a 15-day period, the total number of all inside and outside calls
   handled by the switchboard was 5,760. The average number of inside calls per day was
   234. You cannot find one day's tally of outside calls, but the total number of outside calls
   for the other fourteen days was 2,065. From this information, how many outside calls
   must have been reported on the missing tally?

   A.   175   B.   185   C.   195   D.   205

10. A floor plan has been prepared for a new building, drawn to a scale of 3/4 inch = 1 foot.   10._____
    A certain area is drawn 1 and 1/2 feet long and 6 inches wide on the floor plan. What are
    the ACTUAL dimensions of this area in the new building?
    _____ feet long and _____ feet wide.

    A.   21; 8   B.   24; 8   C.   27; 9   D.   30; 9

11. You are preparing a package of six books to mail to a professor who is on sabbatical.   11._____
    They weigh, respectively, 1 pound 11 ounces, 1 pound 6 ounces, 2 pounds 1 ounce, 2
    pounds 2 ounces, 1 pound 7 ounces, and 1 pound 8 ounces. The packaging material
    weighs 6 ounces.
    The TOTAL weight of the package will be_____ pounds _____ ounces.

    A.   10; 3   B.   10; 9   C.   11; 5   D.   12; 5

12. Part-time students are charged $70 per credit for courses at a particular college. In addi-   12._____
tion, they must pay a $24.00 student activity fee if they take six credits or more and
$14.00 lab fee for each laboratory course.
If a person takes one 3-credit course and one 4-credit course and his 4-credit course is
a laboratory course, the TOTAL cost to him will be

    A. $504   B. $528   C. $542   D. $552

13. The graduating class of a certain community college consisted of 378 majors in secre-   13._____
tarial science, 265 majors in engineering science, 57 majors in nursing, 513 majors in
accounting, and 865 majors in liberal arts.
The percent of students who major in liberal arts at this college was MOST NEARLY

    A.   24.0%   B.   41.6%   C.   52.3%   D.   71.6%

14. Donald Smith earns $12.80 an hour for forty hours a week, with time and a half for all   14._____
hours over forty. Last week, his total earnings amounted to $627.20.
He worked_____ hours.

    A.   46   B.   47   C.   48   D.   49

15. Mr. Jones desires to sell an article costing $28 at a gross profit of 30% of the selling   15._____
price, and to allow a trade discount of 20% of the list price.
The list price of the article should be

    A. $43.68   B. $45.50   C. $48.00   D. $50.00

16. The gauge of an oil storage tank in an elementary school indicates 1/5 full. After a truck   16._____
delivers 945 gallons of oil, the gauge indicates 4/5 full.
The capacity of the tank is _____ gallons.

    A.   1,260   B.   1,575   C.   1,625   D.   1,890

17. An invoice dated April 3, terms 3/10, 2/30, net/60, was paid in full with a check for   17._____
$787.92 on May 1.
The amount of the invoice was

    A. $772.16   B. $787.92   C. $804.00   D. $812.29

18. Two pipes supply the water for the swimming pool at Blenheim High School. One pipe   18._____
can fill the pool in 9 hours. The second pipe can fill the pool in 6 hours.
If both pipes were opened simultaneously, the pool could be filled in _____ hours minutes.

    A.   3; 36   B.   4; 30   C.   5; 15   D.   7; 30

19. John's father spent $24,000, which was one-fourth of his savings. He bought a car with   19._____
three-eighths of the remainder of his savings.
His bank balance now amounts to

    A. $30,000   B. $32,000   C. $45,000   D. $50,000

20. A clock that loses 4 minutes every 24 hours was set at 6 A.M. on October 1.
What time was indicated by the clock when the CORRECT time was 12:00 Noon on
October 6th?
_____ A.M.

   A.   11:36   B.   11:38   C.   11:39   D.   11:40

20.____

21. Unit S's production fluctuated substantially from one year to another. In 2009, Unit S's
production was 100% greater than in 2008. In 2010, production decreased by 25% from
2009. In 2011, Unit S's production was 10% greater than in 2010. On the basis of this
information, it is CORRECT to conclude that Unit S's production in 2011 exceeded Unit
S's production in 2008 by

   A.   65%   B.   85%   C.   95%   D.   135%

21.____

22. Agency X is moving into a new building. It has 1,500 employees presently on its staff and
does not contemplate much variance from this level. The new building contains 100
available offices, each with a maximum capacity of 30 employees. It has been decided
that only 2/3 of the maximum capacity of each office will be utilized. The TOTAL number
of offices that will be occupied by Agency X is

   A.   30   B.   66   C.   75   D.   90

22.____

23. One typist completes a form letter every 5 minutes and another typist completes one
every 6 minutes. If the two typists start together, how many minutes later will they again
start typing new letters simultaneously and how many letters will they have completed by
that time?
_____ minutes - _____ letters.

   A.   11; 30   B.   12; 24   C.   24; 12   D.   30; 1

23.____

24. During one week, a machine operator produces 10 fewer pages per hour of work than he
usually does.
If it ordinarily takes him six hours to produce a 300-page report, how many hours
LONGER will that same 300-page report take him during the week when he produces
more slowly?
_____ hours longer.

   A.   1 1/2   B.   1 2/3   C.   2   D.   2 3/4

24.____

25. A study reveals that Miss Brown files N cards in M hours, and Miss Smith files the same
number of cards in T hours. If the two employees work together, the number of hours it
will take them to file N cards is

   A. $\dfrac{N}{\dfrac{N}{M}+\dfrac{N}{N}}$ B. $\dfrac{N}{T+M}+\dfrac{2N}{MT}$

   C. $N\left(\dfrac{M}{N}+\dfrac{N}{T}\right)$ D. $\dfrac{N}{NT+MN}$

25.____

KEY (CORRECT ANSWERS)

1.	A		11.	B
2.	B		12.	B
3.	D		13.	B
4.	B		14.	A
5.	A		15.	D
6.	C		16.	B
7.	B		17.	C
8.	D		18.	A
9.	B		19.	C
10.	B		20.	C

21.	A
22.	C
23.	D
24.	A
25.	A

———

SOLUTIONS TO PROBLEMS

1. 9/4 = 2 1/4" and 14/4 = 3 1/2"

2. Gross amount = (3)($6.75)(3.5) + (2)($6.75)(4.5) + ($8.00)(5.5) = $175.625, which is closest to selection B ($177.81).

3. $(529)(.35)(.89)(.67) \approx 110$

4. 10 worker-days are needed to type 125 letters, so $(200)(10) \div 125 = 16$ worker-days are needed to type 200 letters. Finally, $16 \div 10$ workers = 1 3/5 days.

5. Index number = [(14)(10 1/2) + (3) (24) + (2) (12) + (1)(4 1/2) +
   $(0)(5)] \div 56 \approx 2.54$

6. Typist X could do 30 forms in 30/20 = 1 1/2 hours. Let x = number of hours needed when working together with typist Y.

   Then, $(\dfrac{1}{1\frac{1}{2}})(x)+(\dfrac{1}{1})x=1$. Simplifying, $2x+3x=3$, so $x=\dfrac{3}{5}$hr.= 36 min.

7. $(3+2+8+1+0+5) \div 6 = 3.1\overline{6}$. Then, $18 \sim 3.\overline{6} = 14.8\overline{3}$.
   Finally, $14.8\overline{3} \div 18 \approx 82\%$

8. Wages = ($7.50)(40) + ($11.25)(8) = $390

9. (234)(15) = 3510 inside calls. Then, 5760 - 3510 = 2250 outside calls. Finally, 2250 - 2065 = 185 outside calls on the missing day.

10. $18 \div 3/4 = 24$ feet long and $6 \div 3/4 = 8$ feet wide.

11. Total weight = 1 lb. 11 oz. + 1 lb. 6 oz. + 2 lbs. 1 oz. + 2 lbs. 2 oz + 1 lb. 7 oz. + 1 lb. 8 oz. + 6 oz. = 8 lbs. 41 oz. = 10 lbs. 9 oz.

12. Total cost = ($70)(7) + $24 + $14 = $528

13. $865 \div 2078 \approx 41.6\%$ liberal arts majors

14. ($12.80)(40)= $512, so he made $627.20 - $512 = $115.20 in overtime. His over-time rate = ($12.80)(1.5)= $19.20 per hour. Thus, he worked $115.20 \div $19.20 = 6 overtime hours. Total hours worked =46.

15. Let x = list price. Selling price = .80x. Then, .80x - (.30)(.80x) = $28. Simplifying, .56x = $28. Solving, x = $50.00

16. 945 gallons represents $\frac{4}{5} - \frac{1}{5} = \frac{3}{5}$ of the tank's capacity. Then, the capacity

    $= 945 \div \frac{3}{5} = 1575$ gallons

17. $787.92 \div .98 = \$804.00$

18. Let x = number of required hours. Then, (1/9)(x) + (1/6)(x) = 1 Simplifying, 2x + 3x = 18. Solving, x = 3.6 hours = 3 hrs. 36 min.

19. Bank balance = $96,000 - $24,000 - (3/8) ($72,000) = $45,000

20. From Oct. 1, 6 AM to Oct. 6, Noon = 5 1/2 days. The clock would show a loss of (4 min.)(5 1/2) = 21 min. Thus, the clock's time would (incorrectly) show 12:00 Noon - 21 min. = 11:39 AM

21. 2008 = x, 2009 = 200x, 2010 = 150x, 2011 = 165x
    65% more

22. (2/3)(30) = 20 employees in each office. Then, 1500 ÷ 20 = 75 offices

23. After 30 minutes, the typists will have finished a total of 6 + 5 = 11 letters.

24. When he works more slowly, he will only produce 300 - (6)(10) = 240 pages in 6 hrs. His new slower rate is 40 pages per hour, so he will need 60/40 = 1 1/2 more hours to do the remaining 60 pages.

25. Let x = required hours. Then, $(\frac{1}{M})(x)+(\frac{1}{T})(x)=1$. Simplifying, , x(T+M) = MT. Solving, x = MT/(T+M).
    Note: The N value is immaterial. Also, choice A reduces to MT/(T+M).

CLERICAL ABILITIES

EXAMINATION SECTION
TEST 1

DIRECTIONS: Each question or incomplete statement is followed by several suggested answers or completions. Select the one that BEST answers the question or completes the statement. *PRINT THE LETTER OF THE CORRECT ANSWER IN THE SPACE AT THE RIGHT.*

Questions 1-4.

DIRECTIONS: Questions 1 through 4 are to be answered on the basis of the information given below.

The most commonly used filing system and the one that is easiest to learn is alphabetical filing. This involves putting records in an A to Z order, according to the letters of the alphabet. The name of a person is filed by using the following order: first, the surname or last name; second, the first name; third, the middle name or middle initial. For example, *Henry C. Young* is filed under *Y* and thereafter under *Young, Henry C.* The name of a company is filed in the same way. For example, *Long Cabinet Co.* is filed under *L,* while *John T. Long Cabinet Co.* is filed under *L* and thereafter under *Long., John T. Cabinet Co.*

1. The one of the following which lists the names of persons in the CORRECT alphabetical order is:

   A. Mary Carrie, Helen Carrol, James Carson, John Carter
   B. James Carson, Mary Carrie, John Carter, Helen Carrol
   C. Helen Carrol, James Carson, John Carter, Mary Carrie
   D. John Carter, Helen Carrol, Mary Carrie, James Carson

   1.____

2. The one of the following which lists the names of persons in the CORRECT alphabetical order is:

   A. Jones, John C.; Jones, John A.; Jones, John P.; Jones, John K.
   B. Jones, John P.; Jones, John K.; Jones, John C.; Jones, John A.
   C. Jones, John A.; Jones, John C.; Jones, John K.; Jones, John P.
   D. Jones, John K.; Jones, John C.; Jones, John A.; Jones, John P.

   2.____

3. The one of the following which lists the names of the companies in the CORRECT alphabetical order is:

   A. Blane Co., Blake Co., Block Co., Blear Co.
   B. Blake Co., Blane Co., Blear Co., Block Co.
   C. Block Co., Blear Co., Blane Co., Blake Co.
   D. Blear Co., Blake Co., Blane Co., Block Co.

   3.____

4. You are to return to the file an index card on *Barry C. Wayne Materials and Supplies Co.* Of the following, the CORRECT alphabetical group that you should return the index card to is

   A. A to G   B. H to M   C. N to S   D. T to Z

   4.____

Questions 5-10.

DIRECTIONS: In each of Questions 5 through 10, the names of four people are given. For each question, choose as your answer the one of the four names given which should be filed FIRST according to the usual system of alphabetical filing of names, as described in the following paragraph.

In filing names, you must start with the last name. Names are filed in order of the first letter of the last name, then the second letter, etc. Therefore, BAILY would be filed before BROWN, which would be filed before COLT. A name with fewer letters of the same type comes first; i.e., Smith before Smithe. If the last names are the same, the names are filed alphabetically by the first name. If the first name is an initial, a name with an initial would come before a first name that starts with the same letter as the initial. Therefore, I. BROWN would come before IRA BROWN. Finally, if both last name and first name are the same, the name would be filed alphabetically by the middle name, once again an initial coming before a middle name which starts with the same letter as the initial. If there is no middle name at all, the name would come before those with middle initials or names.

Sample Question: A.   Lester Daniels
                              B.   William Dancer
                              C.   Nathan Danzig
                              D.   Dan Lester

The last names beginning with D are filed before the last name beginning with L. Since DANIELS, DANCER, and DANZIG all begin with the same three letters, you must look at the fourth letter of the last name to determine which name should be filed first. C comes before I or Z in the alphabet, so DANCER is filed before DANIELS or DANZIG. Therefore, the answer to the above sample question is B.

5.   A.   Scott Biala
      B.   Mary Byala
      C.   Martin Baylor
      D.   Francis Bauer

5._____

6.   A.   Howard J. Black
      B.   Howard Black
      C.   J. Howard Black
      D.   John H. Black

6._____

7.   A.   Theodora Garth Kingston
      B.   Theadore Barth Kingston
      C.   Thomas Kingston
      D.   Thomas T. Kingston

7._____

8.   A.   Paulette Mary Huerta
      B.   Paul M. Huerta
      C.   Paulette L. Huerta
      D.   Peter A. Huerta

8._____

9. A. Martha Hunt Morgan
   B. Martin Hunt Morgan
   C. Mary H. Morgan
   D. Martine H. Morgan

9.____

10. A. James T. Meerschaum
    B. James M. Mershum
    C. James F. Mearshaum
    D. James N. Meshum

10.____

Questions 11-14.

DIRECTIONS: Questions 11 through 14 are to be answered SOLELY on the basis of the following information.

You are required to file various documents in file drawers which are labeled according to the following pattern:

DOCUMENTS

MEMOS		LETTERS	
File	Subject	File	Subject
84PM1	(A-L)	84PC1	(A-L)
84PM2	(M-Z)	84PC2	(M-Z)

REPORTS		INQUIRIES	
File	Subject	File	Subject
84PR1	(A-L)	84PQ1	(A-L)
84PR2	(M-Z)	84PQ2	(M-Z)

11. A letter dealing with a burglary should be filed in the drawer labeled

    A. 84PM1   B. 84PC1   C. 84PR1   D. 84PQ2

11.____

12. A report on Statistics should be found in the drawer labeled

    A. 84PM1   B. 84PC2   C. 84PR2   D. 84PQ2

12.____

13. An inquiry is received about parade permit procedures. It should be filed in the drawer labeled

    A. 84PM2   B. 84PC1   C. 84PR1   D. 84PQ2

13.____

14. A police officer has a question about a robbery report you filed.
    You should pull this file from the drawer labeled

    A. 84PM1   B. 84PM2   C. 84PR1   D. 84PR2

14.____

Questions 15-22.

DIRECTIONS: Each of Questions 15 through 22 consists of four or six numbered names. For each question, choose the option (A, B, C, or D) which indicates the order in which the names should be filed in accordance with the following filing instructions:
- File alphabetically according to last name, then first name, then middle initial.
- File according to each successive letter within a name.

- When comparing two names in which, the letters in the longer name are identical to the corresponding letters in the shorter name, the shorter name is filed first.
- When the last names are the same, initials are always filed before names beginning with the same letter.

15.   I.   Ralph Robinson
           II.   Alfred Ross
           III.   Luis Robles
           IV.   James Roberts
The CORRECT filing sequence for the above names should be

    A.   IV, II, I, III   B.   I, IV, III, II
    C.   III, IV, I, II   D.   IV, I, III, II

15.____

16.   I.   Irwin Goodwin
           II.   Inez Gonzalez
           III.   Irene Goodman
           IV.   Ira S. Goodwin
           V.   Ruth I. Goldstein
           VI.   M.B. Goodman
The CORRECT filing sequence for the above names should be

    A.   V, II, I, IV, III, VI   B.   V, II, VI, III, IV, I
    C.   V, II, III, VI, IV, I   D.   V, II, III, VI, I, IV

16.____

17.   I.   George Allan
           II.   Gregory Allen
           III.   Gary Allen
           IV.   George Allen
The CORRECT filing sequence for the above names should be

    A.   IV, III, I, II   B.   I, IV, II, III
    C.   III, IV, I, II   D.   I, III, IV, II

17.____

18.   I.   Simon Kauffman
           II.   Leo Kaufman
           III.   Robert Kaufmann
           IV.   Paul Kauffmann
The CORRECT filing sequence for the above names should be

    A.   I, IV, II, III   B.   II, IV, III, I
    C.   III, II, IV, I   D.   I, II, III, IV

18.____

19.   I.   Roberta Williams
           II.   Robin Wilson
           III.   Roberta Wilson
           IV.   Robin Williams
The CORRECT filing sequence for the above names should be

    A.   III, II, IV, I   B.   I, IV, III, II
    C.   I, II, III, IV   D.   III, I, II, IV

19.____

20.   I.   Lawrence Shultz   20._____

         II.   Albert Schultz

       III. Theodore Schwartz

      IV. Thomas Schwarz

       V.   Alvin Schultz

      VI. Leonard Shultz

The CORRECT filing sequence for the above names should be

  A. II, V, III, IV, I, VI   B. IV, III, V, I, II, VI

  C. II, V, I, VI, III, IV   D. I, VI, II, V, III, IV

21.   I.   McArdle   21._____

         II.   Mayer

       III. Maletz

      IV. McNiff

       V.   Meyer

      VI. MacMahon

The CORRECT filing sequence for the above names should be

  A. I, IV, VI, III, II, V   B. II, I, IV, VI, III, V

  C. VI, III, II, I, IV, V   D. VI, III, II, V, I, IV

22.   I.   Jack E. Johnson   22._____

         II.   R.H. Jackson

       III. Bertha Jackson

      IV. J.T. Johnson

       V.   Ann Johns

      VI. John Jacobs

The CORRECT filing sequence for the above names should be

  A. II, III, VI, V, IV, I   B. III, II, VI, V, IV, I

  C. VI, II, III, I, V, IV   D. III, II, VI, IV, V, I

Questions 23-30.

DIRECTIONS: The code table below shows 10 letters with matching numbers. For each question, there are three sets of letters. Each set of letters is followed by a set of numbers which may or may not match their correct letter according to the code table. For each question, check all three sets of letters and numbers and mark your answer:

      A. if no pairs are correctly matched

      B. if only one pair is correctly matched

      C. if only two pairs are correctly matched

      D. if all three pairs are correctly matched

CODE TABLE

T	M	V	D	S	P	R	G	B	H
1	2	3	4	5	6	7	8	9	0

<u>Sample Question;</u>   TMVDSP - 123456

                               RGBHTM - 789011

                               DSPRGB - 256789

In the sample question above, the first set of numbers correctly matches its set of letters. But the second and third pairs contain mistakes. In the second pair, M is incorrectly matched with number 1. According to the code table, letter M should be correctly matched with number 2. In the third pair, the letter D is incorrectly matched with number 2. According to the code table, letter D should be correctly matched with number 4. Since only one of the pairs is correctly matched, the answer to this sample question is B.

23. RSBMRM 759262   23._____
    GDSRVH 845730
    VDBRTM 349713

24. TGVSDR 183247   24._____
    SMHRDP 520647
    TRMHSR 172057

25. DSPRGM 456782   25._____
    MVDBHT 234902
    HPMDBT 062491

26. BVPTRD 936184   26._____
    GDPHMB 807029
    GMRHMV 827032

27. MGVRSH 283750   27._____
    TRDMBS 174295
    SPRMGV 567283

28. SGBSDM 489542   28._____
    MGHPTM 290612
    MPBMHT 269301

29. TDPBHM 146902   29._____
    VPBMRS 369275
    GDMBHM 842902

30. MVPTBV 236194   30._____
    PDRTMB 647128
    BGTMSM 981232

KEY (CORRECT ANSWERS)

1.	A	11.	B	21.	C
2.	C	12.	C	22.	B
3.	B	13.	D	23.	B
4.	D	14.	D	24.	B
5.	D	15.	D	25.	C
6.	B	16.	C	26.	A
7.	B	17.	D	27.	D
8.	B	18.	A	28.	A
9.	A	19.	B	29.	D
10.	C	20.	A	30.	A

TEST 2

DIRECTIONS: Each question or incomplete statement is followed by several suggested answers or completions. Select the one that BEST answers the question or completes the statement. *PRINT THE LETTER OF THE CORRECT ANSWER IN THE SPACE AT THE RIGHT.*

Questions 1-10.

DIRECTIONS: Questions 1 through 10 each consists of two columns, each containing four lines of names, numbers and/or addresses. For each question, compare the lines in Column I with the lines in Column II to see if they match exactly, and mark your answer A, B, C, or D, according to the following instructions:
- A. all four lines match exactly
- B. only three lines match exactly
- C. only two lines match exactly
- D. only one line matches exactly

		COLUMN I	COLUMN II	
1.	I.	Earl Hodgson	Earl Hodgson	1.___
	II.	1409870	1408970	
	III.	Shore Ave.	Schore Ave.	
	IV.	Macon Rd.	Macon Rd.	
2.	I.	9671485	9671485	2.___
	II.	470 Astor Court	470 Astor Court	
	III.	Halprin, Phillip	Halperin, Phillip	
	IV.	Frank D. Poliseo	Frank D. Poliseo	
3.	I.	Tandem Associates	Tandom Associates	3.___
	II.	144-17 Northern Blvd.	144-17 Northern Blvd.	
	III.	Alberta Forchi	Albert Forchi	
	IV.	Kings Park, NY 10751	Kings Point, NY 10751	
4.	I.	Bertha C. McCormack	Bertha C. McCormack	4.___
	II.	Clayton, MO.	Clayton, MO.	
	III.	976-4242	976-4242	
	IV.	New City, NY 10951	New City, NY 10951	
5.	I.	George C. Morill	George C. Morrill	5.___
	II.	Columbia, SC 29201	Columbia, SD 29201	
	III.	Louis Ingham	Louis Ingham	
	IV.	3406 Forest Ave.	3406 Forest Ave.	
6.	I.	506 S. Elliott Pl.	506 S. Elliott Pl.	6.___
	II.	Herbert Hall	Hurbert Hall	
	III.	4712 Rockaway Pkway	4712 Rockaway Pkway	
	IV.	169 E. 7 St.	169 E. 7 St.	

	COLUMN I	COLUMN II	

7.
- I. 345 Park Ave.
- II. Colman Oven Corp.
- III. Robert Conte
- IV. 6179846

345 Park Pl.
Coleman Oven Corp.
Robert Conti
6179846

7.____

8.
- I. Grigori Schierber
- II. Des Moines, Iowa
- III. Gouverneur Hospital
- IV. 91-35 Cresskill Pl.

Grigori Schierber
Des Moines, Iowa
Gouverneur Hospital
91-35 Cresskill Pl.

8.____

9.
- I. Jeffery Janssen
- II. 8041071
- III. 40 Rockefeller Plaza
- IV. 407 6 St.

Jeffrey Janssen
8041071
40 Rockafeller Plaza
406 7 St.

9.____

10.
- I. 5971996
- II. 3113 Knickerbocker Ave.
- III. 8434 Boston Post Rd.
- IV. Penn Station

5871996
3113 Knickerbocker Ave.
8424 Boston Post Rd.
Penn Station

10.____

Questions 11-14.

DIRECTIONS: Questions 11 through 14 are to be answered by looking at the four groups of names and addresses listed below (I, II, III, and IV) and then finding out the number of groups that have their corresponding numbered lines exactly the same.

	GROUP I	GROUP II
Line 1.	Richmond General Hospital	Richman General Hospital
Line 2.	Geriatric Clinic	Geriatric Clinic
Line 3.	3975 Paerdegat St.	3975 Peardegat St.
Line 4	Loudonville, New York 11538	Londonville, New York 11538

	GROUP III	GROUP IV
Line 1.	Richmond General Hospital	Richmend General Hospital
Line 2.	Geriatric Clinic	Geriatric Clinic
Line 3.	3795 Paerdegat St.	3975 Paerdegat St.
Line 4.	Loudonville, New York 11358	Loudonville, New York 11538

11. In how many groups is line one exactly the same?   11.____

    A. Two   B. Three   C. Four   D. None

12. In how many groups is line two exactly the same?   12.____

    A. Two   B. Three   C. Four   D. None

13. In how many groups is line three exactly the same?   13.____

    A. Two   B. Three   C. Four   D. None

14. In how many groups is line four exactly the same?   14.____

    A. Two   B. Three   C. Four   D. None

Questions 15-18.

DIRECTIONS: Each of Questions 15 through 18 has two lists of names and addresses. Each list contains three sets of names and addresses. Check each of the three sets in the list on the right to see if they are the same as the corresponding set in the list on the left. Mark your answers:

    A.   if none of the sets in the right list are the same as those in the left list
    B.   if only one of the sets in the right list is the same as those in the left list
    C.   if only two of the sets in the right list are the same as those in the left list
    D.   if all three sets in the right list are the same as those in the left list

15.

Mary T. Berlinger 2351 Hampton St. Monsey, N.Y. 20117	Mary T. Berlinger 2351 Hampton St. Monsey, N.Y. 20117
Eduardo Benes 473 Kingston Avenue Central Islip, N.Y. 11734	Eduardo Benes 473 Kingston Avenue Central Islip, N.Y. 11734
Alan Carrington Fuchs 17 Gnarled Hollow Road Los Angeles, CA 91635	Alan Carrington Fuchs 17 Gnarled Hollow Road Los Angeles, CA 91685

15.____

16.

David John Jacobson 178 35 St. Apt. 4C New York, N.Y. 00927	David John Jacobson 178 53 St. Apt. 4C New York, N.Y. 00927
Ann-Marie Calonella 7243 South Ridge Blvd. Bakersfield, CA 96714	Ann-Marie Calonella 7243 South Ridge Blvd. Bakersfield, CA 96714
Pauline M. Thompson 872 Linden Ave. Houston, Texas 70321	Pauline M. Thomson 872 Linden Ave. Houston, Texas 70321

16.____

17.

Chester LeRoy Masterton 152 Lacy Rd. Kankakee, Ill. 54532	Chester LeRoy Masterson 152 Lacy Rd. Kankakee, Ill. 54532
William Maloney S. LaCrosse Pla. Wausau, Wisconsin 52146	William Maloney S. LaCross Pla. Wausau, Wisconsin 52146
Cynthia V. Barnes 16 Pines Rd. Greenpoint, Miss. 20376	Cynthia V. Barnes 16 Pines Rd. Greenpoint, Miss. 20376

17.____

18.   Marcel Jean Frontenac   Marcel Jean Frontenac   18.____
           8 Burton On The Water   6 Burton On The Water
           Calender, Me. 01471   Calender, Me. 01471

           J. Scott Marsden   J. Scott Marsden
           174 S. Tipton St.   174 Tipton St.
           Cleveland, Ohio   Cleveland, Ohio

           Lawrence T. Haney   Lawrence T. Haney
           171 McDonough St.   171 McDonough St.
           Decatur, Ga. 31304   Decatur, Ga. 31304

Questions 19-26.

DIRECTIONS: Each of Questions 19 through 26 has two lists of numbers. Each list contains three sets of numbers. Check each of the three sets in the list on the right to see if they are the same as the corresponding set in the list on the left. Mark your answers:

      A.   if none of the sets in the right list are the same as those in the left list
      B.   if only one of the sets in the right list is the same as those in the left list
      C.   if only two of the sets in the right list are the same as those in the left list
      D.   if all three sets in the right list are the same as those in the left list

19.   7354183476   7354983476   19.____
      4474747744   4474747774
      57914302311   57914302311

20.   7143592185   7143892185   20.____
      8344517699   8344518699
      9178531263   9178531263

21.   2572114731   257214731   21.____
      8806835476   8806835476
      8255831246   8255831246

22.   331476853821   331476858621   22.____
      6976658532996   6976655832996
      3766042113715   3766042113745

23.   8806663315   8806663315   23.____
      74477138449   74477138449
      211756663666   211756663666

24.   990006966996   99000696996   24.____
      53022219743   53022219843
      4171171117717   4171171177717

25.   24400222433004   24400222433004   25.____
      5300030055000355   5300030055500355
      20000075532002022   20000075532002022

26. 6111666406600011116
    71113001170011100733
    26666446664476518

    61116664066001116
    71113001170011100733
    26666446664476518

    26.____

Questions 27-30.

DIRECTIONS: Questions 27 through 30 are to be answered by picking the answer which is in the correct numerical order, from the lowest number to the highest number, in each question.

27. A. 44533, 44518, 44516, 44547
    B. 44516, 44518, 44533, 44547
    C. 44547, 44533, 44518, 44516
    D. 44518, 44516, 44547, 44533

    27.____

28. A. 95587, 95593, 95601, 95620
    B. 95601, 95620, 95587, 95593
    C. 95593, 95587, 95601, 95620
    D. 95620, 95601, 95593, 95587

    28.____

29. A. 232212, 232208, 232232, 232223
    B. 232208, 232223, 232212, 232232
    C. 232208, 232212, 232223, 232232
    D. 232223, 232232, 232208, 232212

    29.____

30. A. 113419, 113521, 113462, 113588
    B. 113588, 113462, 113521, 113419
    C. 113521, 113588, 113419, 113462
    D. 113419, 113462, 113521, 113588

    30.____

KEY (CORRECT ANSWERS)

1.	C	11.	A	21.	C
2.	B	12.	C	22.	A
3.	D	13.	A	23.	D
4.	A	14.	A	24.	A
5.	C	15.	C	25.	C
6.	B	16.	B	26.	C
7.	D	17.	B	27.	B
8.	A	18.	B	28.	A
9.	D	19.	B	29.	C
10.	C	20.	B	30.	D

PHILOSOPHY, PRINCIPLES, PRACTICES AND TECHNICS
OF
SUPERVISION, ADMINISTRATION, MANAGEMENT AND ORGANIZATION

TABLE OF CONTENTS

TABLE OF CONTENTS (CONTINUED)

PHILOSOPHY, PRINCIPLES, PRACTICES, AND TECHNICS
OF
SUPERVISION, ADMINISTRATION, MANAGEMENT AND ORGANIZATION

I. MEANING OF SUPERVISION

The extension of the democratic philosophy has been accompanied by an extension in the scope of supervision. Modern leaders and supervisors no longer think of supervision in the narrow sense of being confined chiefly to visiting employees, supplying materials, or rating the staff. They regard supervision as being intimately related to all the concerned agencies of society, they speak of the supervisor's function in terms of "growth", rather than the "improvement," of employees.

This modern concept of supervision may be defined as follows:

Supervision is leadership and the development of leadership within groups which are cooperatively engaged in inspection, research, training, guidance and evaluation.

II. THE OLD AND THE NEW SUPERVISION

TRADITIONAL
1. Inspection
2. Focused on the employee
3. Visitation
4. Random and haphazard
5. Imposed and authoritarian
6. One person usually

MODERN
1. Study and analysis
2. Focused on aims, materials, methods, supervisors, employees, environment
3. Demonstrations, intervisitation, workshops, directed reading, bulletins, etc.
4. Definitely organized and planned (scientific)
5. Cooperative and democratic
6. Many persons involved (creative)

III THE EIGHT (8) BASIC PRINCIPLES OF THE NEW SUPERVISION

1. *PRINCIPLE OF RESPONSIBILITY*
    Authority to act and responsibility for acting must be joined.
    a. If you give responsibility, give authority.
    b. Define employee duties clearly.
    c. Protect employees from criticism by others.
    d. Recognize the rights as well as obligations of employees.
    e. Achieve the aims of a democratic society insofar as it is possible within the area of your work.
    f. Establish a situation favorable to training and learning.
    g. Accept ultimate responsibility for everything done in your section, unit, office, division, department.
    h. Good administration and good supervision are inseparable.

2. *PRINCIPLE OF AUTHORITY*

The success of the supervisor is measured by the extent to which the power of authority is not used.

    a. Exercise simplicity and informality in supervision.
    b. Use the simplest machinery of supervision.
    c. If it is good for the organization as a whole, it is probably justified.
    d. Seldom be arbitrary or authoritative.
    e. Do not base your work on the power of position or of personality.
    f. Permit and encourage the free expression of opinions.

3. *PRINCIPLE OF SELF-GROWTH*

The success of the supervisor is measured by the extent to which, and the speed with which, he is no longer needed.

    a. Base criticism on principles, not on specifics.
    b. Point out higher activities to employees.
    c. Train for self-thinking by employees, to meet new situations.
    d. Stimulate initiative, self-reliance and individual responsibility.
    e. Concentrate on stimulating the growth of employees rather than on removing defects.

4. *PRINCIPLE OF INDIVIDUAL WORTH*

Respect for the individual is a paramount consideration in supervision.

    a. Be human and sympathetic in dealing with employees.
    b. Don't nag about things to be done.
    c. Recognize the individual differences among employees and seek opportunities to permit best expression of each personality.

5. *PRINCIPLE OF CREATIVE LEADERSHIP*

The best supervision is that which is not apparent to the employee.

    a. Stimulate, don't drive employees to creative action.
    b. Emphasize doing good things.
    c. Encourage employees to do what they do best.
    d. Do not be too greatly concerned with details of subject or method.
    e. Do not be concerned exclusively with immediate problems and activities.
    f. Reveal higher activities and make them both desired and maximally possible.
    g. Determine procedures in the light of each situation but see that these are derived from a sound basic philosophy.
    h. Aid, inspire and lead so as to liberate the creative spirit latent in all good employees.

6. *PRINCIPLE OF SUCCESS AND FAILURE*

There are no unsuccessful employees, only unsuccessful supervisors who have failed to give proper leadership.

    a. Adapt suggestions to the capacities, attitudes, and prejudices of employees.
    b. Be gradual, be progressive, be persistent.
    c. Help the employee find the general principle; have the employee apply his own problem to the general principle.
    d. Give adequate appreciation for good work and honest effort.
    e. Anticipate employee difficulties and help to prevent them.
    f. Encourage employees to do the desirable things they will do anyway.
    g. Judge your supervision by the results it secures.

7. *PRINCIPLE OF SCIENCE*

Successful supervision is scientific, objective, and experimental. It is based on facts, not on prejudices.

        a. Be cumulative in results.
        b. Never divorce your suggestions from the goals of training.
        c. Don't be impatient of results.
        d. Keep all matters on a professional, not a personal level.
        e. Do not be concerned exclusively with immediate problems and activities.
        f. Use objective means of determining achievement and rating where possible.

8. *PRINCIPLE OF COOPERATION*

Supervision is a cooperative enterprise between supervisor and employee.

        a. Begin with conditions as they are.
        b. Ask opinions of all involved when formulating policies.
        c. Organization is as good as its weakest link.
        d. Let employees help to determine policies and department programs.
        e. Be approachable and accessible - physically and mentally.
        f. Develop pleasant social relationships.

IV. WHAT IS ADMINISTRATION?

Administration is concerned with providing the environment, the material facilities, and the operational procedures that will promote the maximum growth and development of supervisors and employees. (Organization is an aspect, and a concomitant, of administration.)

There is no sharp line of demarcation between supervision and administration; these functions are intimately interrelated and, often, overlapping. They are complementary activities.

1. *PRACTICES COMMONLY CLASSED AS "SUPERVISORY"*

        a. Conducting employees conferences
        b. Visiting sections, units, offices, divisions, departments
        c. Arranging for demonstrations
        d. Examining plans
        e. Suggesting professional reading
        f. Interpreting bulletins
        g. Recommending in-service training courses
        h. Encouraging experimentation
        i. Appraising employee morale
        j. Providing for intervisitation

2. *PRACTICES COMMONLY CLASSIFIED AS "ADMINISTRATIVE"*

        a. Management of the office
        b. Arrangement of schedules for extra duties
        c. Assignment of rooms or areas
        d. Distribution of supplies
        e. Keeping records and reports
        f. Care of audio-visual materials
        g. Keeping inventory records
        h. Checking record cards and books
        i. Programming special activities
        j. Checking on the attendance and punctuality of employees

3. *PRACTICES COMMONLY CLASSIFIED AS BOTH "SUPERVISORY" AND "ADMINISTRATIVE"*
    a. Program construction
    b. Testing or evaluating outcomes
    c. Personnel accounting
    d. Ordering instructional materials

V. RESPONSIBILITIES OF THE SUPERVISOR

A person employed in a supervisory capacity must constantly be able to improve his own efficiency and ability. He represents the employer to the employees and only continuous self-examination can make him a capable supervisor.

Leadership and training are the supervisor's responsibility. An efficient working unit is one in which the employees work with the supervisor. It is his job to bring out the best in his employees. He must always be relaxed, courteous and calm in his association with his employees. Their feelings are important, and a harsh attitude does not develop the most efficient employees.

VI. COMPETENCIES OF THE SUPERVISOR

1. Complete knowledge of the duties and responsibilities of his position.
2. To be able to organize a job, plan ahead and carry through.
3. To have self-confidence and initiative.
4. To be able to handle the unexpected situation and make quick decisions.
5. To be able to properly train subordinates in the positions they are best suited for.
6. To be able to keep good human relations among his subordinates.
7. To be able to keep good human relations between his subordinates and himself and to earn their respect and trust.

VII. THE PROFESSIONAL SUPERVISOR-EMPLOYEE RELATIONSHIP

There are two kinds of efficiency: one kind is only apparent and is produced in organizations through the exercise of mere discipline; this is but a simulation of the second, or true, efficiency which springs from spontaneous cooperation. If you are a manager, no matter how great or small your responsibility, it is your job, in the final analysis, to create and develop this involuntary cooperation among the people whom you supervise. For, no matter how powerful a combination of money, machines, and materials a company may have, this is a dead and sterile thing without a team of willing, thinking and articulate people to guide it.

The following 21 points are presented as indicative of the exemplary basic relationship that should exist between supervisor and employee:

1. Each person wants to be liked and respected by his fellow employee and wants to be treated with consideration and respect by his superior.
2. The most competent employee will make an error. However, in a unit where good relations exist between the supervisor and his employees, tenseness and fear do not exist. Thus, errors are not hidden or covered up and the efficiency of a unit is not impaired.
3. Subordinates resent rules, regulations, or orders that are unreasonable or unexplained.
4. Subordinates are quick to resent unfairness, harshness, injustices and favoritism.
5. An employee will accept responsibility if he knows that he will be complimented for a job well done, and not too harshly chastised for failure; that his supervisor will check the cause of the failure, and, if it was the supervisor's fault, he will assume the blame therefore. If it was the employee's fault, his supervisor will explain the correct method or means of handling the responsibility.

6. An employee wants to receive credit for a suggestion he has made, that is used. If a suggestion cannot be used, the employee is entitled to an explanation. The supervisor should not say "no" and close the subject.
7. Fear and worry slow up a worker's ability. Poor working environment can impair his physical and mental health. A good supervisor avoids forceful methods, threats and arguments to get a job done.
8. A forceful supervisor is able to train his employees individually and as a team, and is able to motivate them in the proper channels.
9. A mature supervisor is able to properly evaluate his subordinates and to keep them happy and satisfied.
10. A sensitive supervisor will never patronize his subordinates.
11. A worthy supervisor will respect his employees' confidences.
12. Definite and clear-cut responsibilities should be assigned to each executive.
13. Responsibility should always be coupled with corresponding authority.
14. No change should be made in the scope or responsibilities of a position without a definite understanding to that effect on the part of all persons concerned.
15. No executive or employee, occupying a single position in the organization, should be subject to definite orders from more than one source.
16. Orders should never be given to subordinates over the head of a responsible executive. Rather than do this, the officer in question should be supplanted.
17. Criticisms of subordinates should, whoever possible, be made privately, and in no case should a subordinate be criticized in the presence of executives or employees of equal or lower rank.
18. No dispute or difference between executives or employees as to authority or responsibilities should be considered too trivial for prompt and careful adjudication.
19. Promotions, wage changes, and disciplinary action should always be approved by the executive immediately superior to the one directly responsible.
20. No executive or employee should ever be required, or expected, to be at the same time an assistant to, and critic of, another.
21. Any executive whose work is subject to regular inspection should, whever practicable, be given the assistance and facilities necessary to enable him to maintain an independent check of the quality of his work.

VIII. MINI-TEXT IN SUPERVISION, ADMINISTRATION, MANAGEMENT, AND ORGANIZATION

A. BRIEF HIGHLIGHTS

Listed concisely and sequentially are major headings and important data in the field for quick recall and review.

1. *LEVELS OF MANAGEMENT*
   Any organization of some size has several levels of management. In terms of a ladder the levels are:

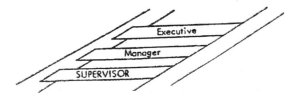

The first level is very important because it is the beginning point of management leadership.

2. *WHAT THE SUPERVISOR MUST LEARN*

A supervisor must learn to:
(1) Deal with people and their differences
(2) Get the job done through people
(3) Recognize the problems when they exist
(4) Overcome obstacles to good performance
(5) Evaluate the performance of people
(6) Check his own performance in terms of accomplishment

3. *A DEFINITION OF SUPERVISOR*

The term supervisor means any individual having authority, in the interests of the employer, to hire, transfer, suspend, lay-off, recall, promote, discharge, assign, reward, or discipline other employees or responsibility to direct them, or to adjust their grievances, or effectively to recommend such action, if, in connection with the foregoing, exercise of such authority is not of a merely routine or clerical nature but requires the use of independent judgment.

4. *ELEMENTS OF THE TEAM CONCEPT*

What is involved in teamwork? The component parts are:

(1) Members	(3) Goals	(5) Cooperation
(2) A leader	(4) Plans	(6) Spirit

5. *PRINCIPLES OF ORGANIZATION*

(1) A team member must know what his job is.
(2) Be sure that the nature and scope of a job are understood.
(3) Authority and responsibility should be carefully spelled out.
(4) A supervisor should be permitted to make the maximum number of decisions affecting his employees.
(5) Employees should report to only one supervisor.
(6) A supervisor should direct only as many employees as he can handle effectively.
(7) An organization plan should be flexible.
(8) Inspection and performance of work should be separate.
(9) Organizational problems should receive immediate attention.
(10) Assign work in line with ability and experience.

6. *THE FOUR IMPORTANT PARTS OF EVERY JOB*

(1) Inherent in every job is the *accountability* for results.
(2) A second set of factors in every job is *responsibilities*.
(3) Along with duties and responsibilities one must have the *authority* to act within certain limits without obtaining permission to proceed.
(4) No job exists in a vacuum. The supervisor is surrounded by key *relationships*.

7. *PRINCIPLES OF DELEGATION*

Where work is delegated for the first time, the supervisor should think in terms of these questions:
(1) Who is best qualified to do this?
(2) Can an employee improve his abilities by doing this?
(3) How long should an employee spend on this?
(4) Are there any special problems for which he will need guidance?
(5) How broad a delegation can I make?

8. PRINCIPLES OF EFFECTIVE COMMUNICATIONS
    (1) Determine the media
    (2) To whom directed?
    (3) Identification and source authority
    (4) Is communication understood?

9. PRINCIPLES OF WORK IMPROVEMENT
    (1) Most people usually do only the work which is assigned to them
    (2) Workers are likely to fit assigned work into the time available to perform it
    (3) A good workload usually stimulates output
    (4) People usually do their best work when they know that results will be reviewed or inspected
    (5) Employees usually feel that someone else is responsible for conditions of work, workplace layout, job methods, type of tools/equipment, and other such factors
    (6) Employees are usually defensive about their job security
    (7) Employees have natural resistance to change
    (8) Employees can support or destroy a supervisor
    (9) A supervisor usually earns the respect of his people through his personal example of diligence and efficiency

10. AREAS OF JOB IMPROVEMENT
The areas of job improvement are quite numerous, but the most common ones which a supervisor can identify and utilize are:

(1) Departmental layout	(5) Work methods
(2) Flow of work	(6) Materials handling
(3) Workplace layout	(7) Utilization
(4) Utilization of manpower	(8) Motion economy

11. SEVEN KEY POINTS IN MAKING IMPROVEMENTS
    (1) Select the job to be improved
    (2) Study how it is being done now
    (3) Question the present method
    (4) Determine actions to be taken
    (5) Chart proposed method
    (6) Get approval and apply
    (7) Solicit worker participation

12. CORRECTIVE TECHNIQUES OF JOB IMPROVEMENT

Specific Problems	General Improvement	Corrective Techniques
(1) Size of workload	(1) Departmental layout	(1) Study with scale model
(2) Inability to meet schedules	(2) Flow of work	(2) Flow chart study
(3) Strain and fatigue	(3) Work plan layout	(3) Motion analysis
(4) Improper use of men and skills	(4) Utilization of manpower	(4) Comparison of units produced to standard allowance
(5) Waste, poor quality, unsafe conditions	(5) Work methods	(5) Methods analysis
(6) Bottleneck conditions that hinder output	(6) Materials handling	(6) Flow chart & equipment study
(7) Poor utilization of equipment and machine	(7) Utilization of equipment	(7) Down time vs. running time
(8) Efficiency and productivity of labor	(8) Motion economy	(8) Motion analysis

13. A *PLANNING CHECKLIST*

(1) Objectives	(6) Resources	(11) Safety
(2) Controls	(7) Manpower	(12) Money
(3) Delegations	(8) Equipment	(13) Work
(4) Communications	(9) Supplies and materials	(14) Timing of improvements
(5) Resources	(10) Utilization of time	

14. *FIVE CHARACTERISTICS OF GOOD DIRECTIONS*

In order to get results, directions must be:

(1) Possible of accomplishment	(3) Related to mission	(5) Unmistakably clear
(2) Agreeable with worker interests	(4) Planned and complete	

15. *TYPES OF DIRECTIONS*

(1) Demands or direct orders	(3) Suggestion or implication
(2) Requests	(4) Volunteering

16. *CONTROLS*

A typical listing of the overall areas in which the supervisor should establish controls might be:

(1) Manpower	(3) Quality of work	(5) Time	(7) Money
(2) Materials	(4) Quantity of work	(6) Space	(8) Methods

17. *ORIENTING THE NEW EMPLOYEE*

(1) Prepare for him	(3) Orientation for the job
(2) Welcome the new employee	(4) Follow-up

18. *CHECKLIST FOR ORIENTING NEW EMPLOYEES*   Yes   No

(1) Do your appreciate the feelings of new employees when they first report for work? ____ ____

(2) Are you aware of the fact that the new employee must make a big adjustment to his job? ____ ____

(3) Have you given him good reasons for liking the job and the organization? ____ ____

(4) Have you prepared for his first day on the job?

(5) Did you welcome him cordially and make him feel needed?

(6) Did you establish rapport with him so that he feels free to talk and discuss matters with you? ____ ____

(7) Did you explain his job to him and his relationship to you? ____ ____

(8) Does he know that his work will be evaluated periodically on a basis that is fair and objective? ____ ____

(9) Did you introduce him to his fellow workers in such a way that they are likely to accept him? ____ ____

(10) Does he know what employee benefits he will receive?

(11) Does he understand the importance of being on the job and what to do if he must leave his duty station? ____ ____

(12) Has he been impressed with the importance of accident prevention and safe practice? ____ ____

(13) Does he generally know his way around the department? ____ ____

(14) Is he under the guidance of a sponsor who will teach the right ways of doing things? ____ ____

(15) Do you plan to follow-up so that he will continue to adjust successfully to his job? ____ ____

19. *PRINCIPLES OF LEARNING*
      (1) Motivation   (2) Demonstration or explanation   (3) Practice

20. *CAUSES OF POOR PERFORMANCE*
      (1) Improper training for job
      (2) Wrong tools
      (3) Inadequate directions
      (4) Lack of supervisory follow-up
      (5) Poor communications
      (6) Lack of standards of performance
      (7) Wrong work habits
      (8) Low morale
      (9) Other

21. *FOUR MAJOR STEPS IN ON-THE-JOB INSTRUCTION*
      (1) Prepare the worker
      (2) Present the operation
      (3) Tryout performance
      (4) Follow-up

22. *EMPLOYEES WANT FIVE THINGS*
      (1) Security (2) Opportunity (3) Recognition (4) Inclusion (5) Expression

23. *SOME DON'TS IN REGARD TO PRAISE*
      (1) Don't praise a person for something he hasn't done
      (2) Don't praise a person unless you can be sincere
      (3) Don't be sparing in praise just because your superior withholds it from you
      (4) Don't let too much time elapse between good performance and recognition of it

24. *HOW TO GAIN YOUR WORKERS' CONFIDENCE*
Methods of developing confidence include such things as:
      (1) Knowing the interests, habits, hobbies of employees
      (2) Admitting your own inadequacies
      (3) Sharing and telling of confidence in others
      (4) Supporting people when they are in trouble
      (5) Delegating matters that can be well handled
      (6) Being frank and straightforward about problems and working conditions
      (7) Encouraging others to bring their problems to you
      (8) Taking action on problems which impede worker progress

25. *SOURCES OF EMPLOYEE PROBLEMS*
On-the-job causes might be such things as:
      (1) A feeling that favoritism is exercised in assignments
      (2) Assignment of overtime
      (3) An undue amount of supervision
      (4) Changing methods or systems
      (5) Stealing of ideas or trade secrets
      (6) Lack of interest in job
      (7) Threat of reduction in force
      (8) Ignorance or lack of communications
      (9) Poor equipment
     (10) Lack of knowing how supervisor feels toward employee
     (11) Shift assignments

Off-the-job problems might have to do with:
      (1) Health   (2) Finances   (3) Housing   (4) Family

26. *THE SUPERVISOR'S KEY TO DISCIPLINE*
    There are several key points about discipline which the supervisor should keep in mind:
    (1) Job discipline is one of the disciplines of life and is directed by the supervisor.
    (2) It is more important to correct an employee fault than to fix blame for it.
    (3) Employee performance is affected by problems both on the job and off.
    (4) Sudden or abrupt changes in behavior can be indications of important employee problems.
    (5) Problems should be dealt with as soon as possible after they are identified.
    (6) The attitude of the supervisor may have more to do with solving problems than the techniques of problem solving.
    (7) Correction of employee behavior should be resorted to only after the supervisor is sure that training or counseling will not be helpful.
    (8) Be sure to document your disciplinary actions.
    (9) Make sure that you are disciplining on the basis of facts rather than personal feelings.
    (10) Take each disciplinary step in order, being careful not to make snap judgments, or decisions based on impatience.

27. *FIVE IMPORTANT PROCESSES OF MANAGEMENT*
    (1) Planning   (2) Organizing   (3) Scheduling
    (4) Controlling   (5) Motivating

28. *WHEN THE SUPERVISOR FAILS TO PLAN*
    (1) Supervisor creates impression of not knowing his job
    (2) May lead to excessive overtime
    (3) Job runs itself -- supervisor lacks control
    (4) Deadlines and appointments missed
    (5) Parts of the work go undone
    (6) Work interrupted by emergencies
    (7) Sets a bad example
    (8) Uneven workload creates peaks and valleys
    (9) Too much time on minor details at expense of more important tasks

29. *FOURTEEN GENERAL PRINCIPLES OF MANAGEMENT*
    (1) Division of work
    (2) Authority and responsibility
    (3) Discipline
    (4) Unity of command
    (5) Unity of direction
    (6) Subordination of individual interest to general interest
    (7) Remuneration of personnel
    (8) Centralization
    (9) Scalar chain
    (10) Order
    (11) Equity
    (12) Stability of tenure of personnel
    (13) Initiative
    (14) Esprit de corps

30. *CHANGE*
    Bringing about change is perhaps attempted more often, and yet less well understood, than anything else the supervisor does. How do people generally react to change? (People tend to resist change that is imposed upon them by other individuals or circumstances.

    Change is characteristic of every situation. It is a part of every real endeavor where the efforts of people are concerned.

A. Why do people resist change?
   People may resist change because of:
   (1) Fear of the unknown
   (2) Implied criticism
   (3) Unpleasant experiences in the past
   (4) Fear of loss of status
   (5) Threat to the ego
   (6) Fear of loss of economic stability

B. How can we best overcome the resistance to change?
   In initiating change, take these steps:
   (1) Get ready to sell
   (2) Identify sources of help
   (3) Anticipate objections
   (4) Sell benefits
   (5) Listen in depth
   (6) Follow up

B. BRIEF TOPICAL SUMMARIES

I. WHO/WHAT IS THE SUPERVISOR?
1. The supervisor is often called the "highest level employee and the lowest level manager."
2. A supervisor is a member of both management and the work group. He acts as a bridge between the two.
3. Most problems in supervision are in the area of human relations, or people problems.
4. Employees expect: Respect, opportunity to learn and to advance, and a sense of belonging, and so forth.
5. Supervisors are responsible for directing people and organizing work. Planning is of paramount importance.
6. A position description is a set of duties and responsibilities inherent to a given position.
7. It is important to keep the position description up-to-date and to provide each employee with his own copy.

II. THE SOCIOLOGY OF WORK
1. People are alike in many ways; however, each individual is unique.
2. The supervisor is challenged in getting to know employee differences. Acquiring skills in evaluating individuals is an asset.
3. Maintaining meaningful working relationships in the organization is of great importance.
4. The supervisor has an obligation to help individuals to develop to their fullest potential.
5. Job rotation on a planned basis helps to build versatility and to maintain interest and enthusiasm in work groups.
6. Cross training (job rotation) provides backup skills.
7. The supervisor can help reduce tension by maintaining a sense of humor, providing guidance to employees, and by making reasonable and timely decisions. Employees respond favorably to working under reasonably predictable circumstances.
8. Change is characteristic of all managerial behavior. The supervisor must adjust to changes in procedures, new methods, technological changes, and to a number of new and sometimes challenging situations.
9. To overcome the natural tendency for people to resist change, the supervisor should become more skillful in initiating change.

III. PRINCIPLES AND PRACTICES OF SUPERVISION

1. Employees should be required to answer to only one superior.
2. A supervisor can effectively direct only a limited number of employees, depending upon the complexity, variety, and proximity of the jobs involved.
3. The organizational chart presents the organization in graphic form. It reflects lines of authority and responsibility as well as interrelationships of units within the organization.
4. Distribution of work can be improved through an analysis using the "Work Distribution Chart."
5. The "Work Distribution Chart" reflects the division of work within a unit in understandable form.
6. When related tasks are given to an employee, he has a better chance of increasing his skills through training.
7. The individual who is given the responsibility for tasks must also be given the appropriate authority to insure adequate results.
8. The supervisor should delegate repetitive, routine work. Preparation of recurring reports, maintaining leave and attendance records are some examples.
9. Good discipline is essential to good task performance. Discipline is reflected in the actions of employees on the job in the absence of supervision.
10. Disciplinary action may have to be taken when the positive aspects of discipline have failed. Reprimand, warning, and suspension are examples of disciplinary action.
11. If a situation calls for a reprimand, be sure it is deserved and remember it is to be done in private.

IV. DYNAMIC LEADERSHIP

1. A style is a personal method or manner of exerting influence.
2. Authoritarian leaders often see themselves as the source of power and authority.
3. The democratic leader often perceives the group as the source of authority and power.
4. Supervisors tend to do better when using the pattern of leadership that is most natural for them.
5. Social scientists suggest that the effective supervisor use the leadership style that best fits the problem or circumstances involved.
6. All four styles -- telling, selling, consulting, joining -- have their place. Using one does not preclude using the other at another time.
7. The theory X point of view assumes that the average person dislikes work, will avoid it whenever possible, and must be coerced to achieve organizational objectives.
8. The theory Y point of view assumes that the average person considers work to be as natural as play, and, when the individual is committed, he requires little supervision or direction to accomplish desired objectives.
9. The leader's basic assumptions concerning human behavior and human nature affect his actions, decisions, and other managerial practices.
10. Dissatisfaction among employees is often present, but difficult to isolate. The supervisor should seek to weaken dissatisfaction by keeping promises, being sincere and considerate, keeping employees informed, and so forth.
11. Constructive suggestions should be encouraged during the natural progress of the work.

V. PROCESSES FOR SOLVING PROBLEMS

1. People find their daily tasks more meaningful and satisfying when they can improve them.
2. The causes of problems, or the key factors, are often hidden in the background. Ability to solve problems often involves the ability to isolate them from their backgrounds. There is some substance to the cliché that some persons "can't see the forest for the trees."
3. New procedures are often developed from old ones. Problems should be broken down into manageable parts. New ideas can be adapted from old ones.

4. People think differently in problem-solving situations. Using a logical, patterned approach is often useful. One approach found to be useful includes these steps:

    (a) Define the problem   (d) Weigh and decide
    (b) Establish objectives   (e) Take action
    (c) Get the facts   (f) Evaluate action

VI. TRAINING FOR RESULTS

1. Participants respond best when they feel training is important to them.
2. The supervisor has responsibility for the training and development of those who report to him.
3. When training is delegated to others, great care must be exercised to insure the trainer has knowledge, aptitude, and interest for his work as a trainer.
4. Training (learning) of some type goes on continually. The most successful supervisor makes certain the learning contributes in a productive manner to operational goals.
5. New employees are particularly susceptible to training. Older employees facing new job situations require specific training, as well as having need for development and growth opportunities.
6. Training needs require continuous monitoring.
7. The training officer of an agency is a professional with a responsibility to assist supervisors in solving training problems.
8. Many of the self-development steps important to the supervisor's own growth are equally important to the development of peers and subordinates. Knowledge of these is important when the supervisor consults with others on development and growth opportunities.

VII. HEALTH, SAFETY, AND ACCIDENT PREVENTION

1. Management-minded supervisors take appropriate measures to assist employees in maintaining health and in assuring safe practices in the work environment.
2. Effective safety training and practices help to avoid injury and accidents.
3. Safety should be a management goal. All infractions of safety which are observed should be corrected without exception.
4. Employees' safety attitude, training and instruction, provision of safe tools and equipment, supervision, and leadership are considered highly important factors which contribute to safety and which can be influenced directly by supervisors.
5. When accidents do occur they should be investigated promptly for very important reasons, including the fact that information which is gained can be used to prevent accidents in the future.

VIII. EQUAL EMPLOYMENT OPPORTUNITY

1. The supervisor should endeavor to treat all employees fairly, without regard to religion, race, sex, or national origin.
2. Groups tend to reflect the attitude of the leader. Prejudice can be detected even in very subtle form. Supervisors must strive to create a feeling of mutual respect and confidence in every employee.
3. Complete utilization of all human resources is a national goal. Equitable consideration should be accorded women in the work force, minority-group members, the physically and mentally handicapped, and the older employee. The important question is: "Who can do the job?"
4. Training opportunities, recognition for performance, overtime assignments, promotional opportunities, and all other personnel actions are to be handled on an equitable basis.

IX. IMPROVING COMMUNICATIONS

1. Communications is achieving understanding between the sender and the receiver of a message. It also means sharing information -- the creation of understanding.
2. Communication is basic to all human activity. Words are means of conveying meanings; however, real meanings are in people.
3. There are very practical differences in the effectiveness of one-way, impersonal, and two-way communications. Words spoken face-to-face are better understood. Telephone conversations are effective, but lack the rapport of person-to-person exchanges. The whole person communicates.
4. Cooperation and communication in an organization go hand in hand. When there is a mutual respect between people, spelling out rules and procedures for communicating is unnecessary.
5. There are several barriers to effective communications. These include failure to listen with respect and understanding, lack of skill in feedback, and misinterpreting the meanings of words used by the speaker. It is also common practice to listen to what we want to hear, and tune out things we do not want to hear.
6. Communication is management's chief problem. The supervisor should accept the challenge to communicate more effectively and to improve interagency and intra-agency communications.
7. The supervisor may often plan for and conduct meetings. The planning phase is critical and may determine the success or the failure of a meeting.
8. Speaking before groups usually requires extra effort. Stage fright may never disappear completely, but it can be controlled.

X. SELF-DEVELOPMENT

1. Every employee is responsible for his own self-development.
2. Toastmaster and toastmistress clubs offer opportunities to improve skills in oral communications.
3. Planning for one's own self-development is of vital importance. Supervisors know their own strengths and limitations better than anyone else.
4. Many opportunities are open to aid the supervisor in his developmental efforts, including job assignments; training opportunities, both governmental and non-governmental -- to include universities and professional conferences and seminars.
5. Programmed instruction offers a means of studying at one's own rate.
6. Where difficulties may arise from a supervisor's being away from his work for training, he may participate in televised home study or correspondence courses to meet his self-develop- ment needs.

XI. TEACHING AND TRAINING

A. The Teaching Process

Teaching is encouraging and guiding the learning activities of students toward established goals. In most cases this process consists in five steps: preparation, presentation, summarization, evaluation, and application.

1. Preparation

Preparation is twofold in nature; that of the supervisor and the employee.

Preparation by the supervisor is absolutely essential to success. He must know what, when, where, how, and whom he will teach. Some of the factors that should be considered are:

(1) The objectives	(5) Employee interest
(2) The materials needed	(6) Training aids
(3) The methods to be used	(7) Evaluation
(4) Employee participation	(8) Summarization

Employee preparation consists in preparing the employee to receive the material. Probably the most important single factor in the preparation of the employee is arousing and maintaining his interest. He must know the objectives of the training, why he is there, how the material can be used, and its importance to him.

2. Presentation

In presentation, have a carefully designed plan and follow it.
The plan should be accurate and complete, yet flexible enough to meet situations as they arise. The method of presentation will be determined by the particular situation and objectives.

3. Summary

A summary should be made at the end of every training unit and program. In addition, there may be internal summaries depending on the nature of the material being taught. The important thing is that the trainee must always be able to understand how each part of the new material relates to the whole.

4. Application

The supervisor must arrange work so the employee will be given a chance to apply new knowledge or skills while the material is still clear in his mind and interest is high. The trainee does not really know whether he has learned the material until he has been given a chance to apply it. If the material is not applied, it loses most of its value.

5. Evaluation

The purpose of all training is to promote learning. To determine whether the training has been a success or failure, the supervisor must evaluate this learning.

In the broadest sense evaluation includes all the devices, methods, skills, and techniques used by the supervisor to keep him self and the employees informed as to their progress toward the objectives they are pursuing. The extent to which the employee has mastered the knowledge, skills, and abilities, or changed his attitudes, as determined by the program objectives, is the extent to which instruction has succeeded or failed.

Evaluation should not be confined to the end of the lesson, day, or program but should be used continuously. We shall note later the way this relates to the rest of the teaching process.

B. Teaching Methods

A teaching method is a pattern of identifiable student and instructor activity used in presenting training material.

All supervisors are faced with the problem of deciding which method should be used at a given time.

As with all methods, there are certain advantages and disadvantages to each method.

1. Lecture

The lecture is direct oral presentation of material by the supervisor. The present trend is to place less emphasis on the trainer's activity and more on that of the trainee.

2. Discussion

Teaching by discussion or conference involves using questions and other techniques to arouse interest and focus attention upon certain areas, and by doing so creating a learning situation. This can be one of the most valuable methods because it gives the employees 'an opportunity to express their ideas and pool their knowledge.

3. Demonstration

The demonstration is used to teach how something works or how to do something. It can be used to show a principle or what the results of a series of actions will be. A well-staged demonstration is particularly effective because it shows proper methods of performance in a realistic manner.

4. Performance

Performance is one of the most fundamental of all learning techniques or teaching methods. The trainee may be able to tell how a specific operation should be performed but he cannot be sure he knows how to perform the operation until he has done so.

5. Which Method to Use

Moreover, there are other methods and techniques of teaching. It is difficult to use any method without other methods entering into it. In any learning situation a combination of methods is usually more effective than anyone method alone.

Finally, evaluation must be integrated into the other aspects of the teaching-learning process. It must be used in the motivation of the trainees; it must be used to assist in developing understanding during the training; and it must be related to employee application of the results of training.

This is distinctly the role of the supervisor.

ANSWER SHEET

TEST NO. ________ PART ______ TITLE OF POSITION ______________________________
(AS GIVEN IN EXAMINATION ANNOUNCEMENT - INCLUDE OPTION, IF ANY)

PLACE OF EXAMINATION ______________________ (CITY OR TOWN) ______________ (STATE) DATE ________

RATING

USE THE SPECIAL PENCIL. MAKE GLOSSY BLACK MARKS.

1 A B C D E	26 A B C D E	51 A B C D E	76 A B C D E	101 A B C D E
2 A B C D E	27 A B C D E	52 A B C D E	77 A B C D E	102 A B C D E
3 A B C D E	28 A B C D E	53 A B C D E	78 A B C D E	103 A B C D E
4 A B C D E	29 A B C D E	54 A B C D E	79 A B C D E	104 A B C D E
5 A B C D E	30 A B C D E	55 A B C D E	80 A B C D E	105 A B C D E
6 A B C D E	31 A B C D E	56 A B C D E	81 A B C D E	106 A B C D E
7 A B C D E	32 A B C D E	57 A B C D E	82 A B C D E	107 A B C D E
8 A B C D E	33 A B C D E	58 A B C D E	83 A B C D E	108 A B C D E
9 A B C D E	34 A B C D E	59 A B C D E	84 A B C D E	109 A B C D E
10 A B C D E	35 A B C D E	60 A B C D E	85 A B C D E	110 A B C D E

Make only ONE mark for each answer. Additional and stray marks may be counted as mistakes. In making corrections, erase errors COMPLETELY.

11 A B C D E	36 A B C D E	61 A B C D E	86 A B C D E	111 A B C D E
12 A B C D E	37 A B C D E	62 A B C D E	87 A B C D E	112 A B C D E
13 A B C D E	38 A B C D E	63 A B C D E	88 A B C D E	113 A B C D E
14 A B C D E	39 A B C D E	64 A B C D E	89 A B C D E	114 A B C D E
15 A B C D E	40 A B C D E	65 A B C D E	90 A B C D E	115 A B C D E
16 A B C D E	41 A B C D E	66 A B C D E	91 A B C D E	116 A B C D E
17 A B C D E	42 A B C D E	67 A B C D E	92 A B C D E	117 A B C D E
18 A B C D E	43 A B C D E	68 A B C D E	93 A B C D E	118 A B C D E
19 A B C D E	44 A B C D E	69 A B C D E	94 A B C D E	119 A B C D E
20 A B C D E	45 A B C D E	70 A B C D E	95 A B C D E	120 A B C D E
21 A B C D E	46 A B C D E	71 A B C D E	96 A B C D E	121 A B C D E
22 A B C D E	47 A B C D E	72 A B C D E	97 A B C D E	122 A B C D E
23 A B C D E	48 A B C D E	73 A B C D E	98 A B C D E	123 A B C D E
24 A B C D E	49 A B C D E	74 A B C D E	99 A B C D E	124 A B C D E
25 A B C D E	50 A B C D E	75 A B C D E	100 A B C D E	125 A B C D E

ANSWER SHEET

TEST NO. _____ PART _____ TITLE OF POSITION _____

(AS GIVEN IN EXAMINATION ANNOUNCEMENT - INCLUDE OPTION. IF ANY)

PLACE OF EXAMINATION _____

(CITY OR TOWN)   (STATE)   DATE _____

RATING

USE THE SPECIAL PENCIL. MAKE GLOSSY BLACK MARKS.

1   26   51   76   101

2   27   52   77   102

3   28   53   78   103

4   29   54   79   104

5   30   55   80   105

6   31   56   81   106

7   32   57   82   107

8   33   58   83   108

9   34   59   84   109

10   35   60   85   110

Make only ONE mark for each answer. Additional and stray marks may be counted as mistakes. In making corrections, erase errors COMPLETELY.

11   36   61   86   111

12   37   62   87   112

13   38   63   88   113

14   39   64   89   114

15   40   65   90   115

16   41   66   91   116

17   42   67   92   117

18   43   68   93   118

19   44   69   94   119

20   45   70   95   120

21   46   71   96   121

22   47   72   97   122

23   48   73   98   123

24   49   74   99   124

25   50   75   100   125